AF478616

Morpho-Lexical Alternation in Noun Formation

Morpho-Lexical Alternation in Noun Formation

Zeki Hamawand
University of Hamburg

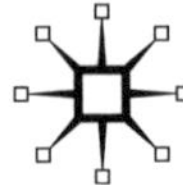

First published 2008 by
PALGRAVE MACMILLAN
Houndmills, Basingstoke, Hampshire RG21 6XS and
175 Fifth Avenue, New York, N.Y. 10010
Companies and representatives throughout the world

PALGRAVE MACMILLAN is the global academic imprint of the Palgrave Macmillan division of St. Martin's Press, LLC and of Palgrave Macmillan Ltd. Macmillan® is a registered trademark in the United States, United Kingdom and other countries. Palgrave is a registered trademark in the European Union and other countries.

ISBN-13: 978-0-230-53738-5   hardback
ISBN-10: 0-230-53738-3   hardback

This book is printed on paper suitable for recycling and made from fully managed and sustained forest sources. Logging, pulping and manufacturing processes are expected to conform to the environmental regulations of the country of origin.

A catalogue record for this book is available from the British Library.

Library of Congress Cataloging-in-Publication Data

Hamawand, Zeki.
    Morpho-lexical alternation in noun formation / Zeki Hamawand.
            p. cm.
    Includes bibliographical references and index.
    ISBN 0–230–53738–3 (alk. paper)
    1. English language—Noun. I. Title.

    PE1205.H35 2008
    425'.54—dc22   2007050061

10   9   8   7   6   5   4   3   2   1
17   16   15   14   13   12   11   10   09   08

Printed and bound in Great Britain by
CPI Antony Rowe, Chippenham and Eastbourne

*To my mother
a fountain of love,
a paragon of generosity,
and the epitome of kindness.*

Contents

Figures

Tables

Preface

Aims

This book describes the semantic relationship between morpho-lexical items in forming nouns in English. The main focus is on noun pairs that share a single root but end in different suffixes. To do so, two approaches are adopted. Theoretically, the book is cognitive-oriented. It is geared towards substantiating some tenets of Cognitive Semantics. One tenet is that linguistic items are polysemous in nature. In view of this, the book seeks to show that noun-forming suffixes have a wide range of senses that gather around a centre. Another tenet is that the meaning of a linguistic item is defined in terms of the domain in which it is embedded. In relation to this, the book strives to show that noun-forming suffixes form sets which highlight their similarities as well as differences. A further tenet is that no two expressions are synonymous even if they look similar. In connection with this, the book attempts to show that although the noun pairs evoke the same content they differ in terms of the alternative ways the speaker construes that content. Empirically, the book is usage-based. It is oriented towards substantiating some axioms of Corpus Linguistics. One axiom places emphasis on authentic data. In this regard, the book relies upon the British National Corpus and the Web for the occurrences of a word with its surroundings. Another axiom lays emphasis on meaning distinction. In this respect, the book relies upon collocations associated with the noun pair for sense discrimination.

Chapters

The book falls into six chapters. Chapter 1 provides an overview of the issue of nominalisation in English. It proposes a novel approach to tackle it, hinging on the three cognitive tenets of *category*, *domain*, and *construal*. Chapter 2 explores the tenets in the investigation of de-verbal nominalisers. First, it reviews the role of category in describing their internal structures. Next, it discusses the role of domain in diagnosing the minimal differences between them. Finally, it demonstrates the impact of construal on the interpretation of the derivatives they form. Chapter 3 implements the tenets in the description of de-adjectival nominalisers. In the beginning, it shows how category highlights their multiple senses. In the middle, it explains how domain discloses their specific meanings. In the end, it elucidates how construal disengages the nominal pairs they derive. Chapter 4 examines the tenets with references to de-nominal nominalisers. Initially, it considers their semantic structure. Midway, it addresses their specific meanings. Ultimately, it defines the semantic constraints which separate the noun pairs they form. Chapter 5 applies the tenets to agent-forming suffixes. First, it portrays their semantic networks. Second, it underlines their specificity. Third, it focuses on the meaning determinants which guide the choice of the nouns they derive. Chapter 6 sums up in tabular form the main findings of the analysis.

Audiences

This book is a synchronic analysis of noun-forming suffixes in English. It integrates the principles of both Cognitive Semantics and Usage-based Semantics. The main issue the book involves is the roles of suffixes in bringing about differences in meaning between pairs of nouns sharing the same roots. To achieve that, the book gives information about preferences speakers or writers have for one choice over another. As such, the book will attract a diverse audience. One strand of audience will be scholars of morpho-lexicology who will find a detailed treatment of an area which is neglected in the central texts in the discipline. Of central significance for them will be the cognitive tools employed to account for morphological data. A second strand of audience will be language teachers and text-book writers who will find solutions to the usage complications. The focal point for them will be the meaning differences between noun pairs that are in current use, shedding light on the conditions under which lexical choices are made. A third strand of audience will be advanced students and general learners of English who will find a thorough discussion of an area of the language that is likely to pose problems for them. At the core of their interest will be the mechanisms used in noun formation, particularly how the suffixes are associated with communicative needs.

Acknowledgements

There are several people I would like to thank for helping me in different ways, direct or indirect, to carry out the research reported on in this book. First, I record my indebtedness to Wendy Anderson, of the University of Glasgow, for devoting her time to reading and commenting on an earlier draft of the work, giving perspicacious remarks, keen insights, and invaluable feedback on the whole manuscript. Second, I am grateful to John Newman, of the University of Alberta, for making various suggestions which helped to sharpen the issues and tighten the discussion. Third, I am indebted to Geoffrey Williams, of Université de Bretagne Sud, for providing bright ideas concerning corpus issues. Fourth, I would like to thank Geoff Thompson, of the University of Liverpool, and Olga Fischer, of the University of Amsterdam, for answering my queries about other language theories. Fifth, a special debt of gratitude goes to Jill Lake, the Linguistics Editor at Palgrave Macmillan, for her indispensable advice and prudent guidance, which helped to make this a better book than it would otherwise have been. Likewise, thanks are due to Smitha Manoj and the staff of Macmillan India Ltd for the attentiveness and professionalism which they showed in the production process of the work. Responsibility for any errors is entirely my own. Last, but far from least, my sincere thanks go to my mother for her unswerving love and ceaseless support over the years. I am so grateful to her for all that she has done. This book is dedicated to her as a token of my gratitude.

1
Nominalisation

In this chapter, I introduce the descriptive system needed to address the semantics of noun formation in general and morpho-lexical alternation in particular. To sketch the system, I divide the chapter into five sections. In section 1.1, I look at the area of suffixation and specify the questions that require investigation. In section 1.2, I provide an overview of the stances of the theoretical paradigms on the issue of morpho-lexical alternation. This section is subdivided into two parts: the first part displays the *formalist* paradigm and the hypotheses it embraces, while the second part exhibits the *functionalist* paradigm and the hypotheses it subsumes. In section 1.3, I propose a new approach to the topic, outlining its skeleton, goals, and procedures. In section 1.4, I elaborate on the models of analysis within which my treatment of nominal suffixation is conducted. The first part of section 1.4 focuses on the fundamental tenets of the theoretical approach, namely, Cognitive Semantics. The second part of section 1.4 singles out the techniques of the empirical approach, namely, Corpus Linguistics. In section 1.5, I sum up the chapter.

1.1   Introduction

To communicate thoughts and express emotions, the speakers of a language use the lexical knowledge stored in their minds. The basic unit of lexical knowledge is a *lexeme*, a word with a specific form and a specific meaning. A lexeme can be simple, consisting of one morpheme, as in *friend*, or complex, consisting of two or more morphemes, as in *friendship*. In using a complex lexeme, the speaker activates its morphemic parts in parallel. In this way, a complex lexeme emerges as a result of a mental operation which connects its component parts. The study of the lexemes, i.e. words, of a language comes under the rubric of *lexicology*, a branch of linguistics which studies the use of a word as a whole. The study of the combination of morphemes to form lexemes, i.e. words, comes under the rubric of *morphology*, a subdiscipline of linguistics, which studies the internal structure of a word. Lexeme or word formation is concerned with the ways in which speakers derive new lexemes from the existing ones. *Morpho-lexicology* then is the study of the morphological and lexical properties in the formation of words in a language.

The majority of word-formational patterns can be placed under two processes. One is *compounding*, the process of forming a lexeme by combining two or more roots, as in *blackboard*. The other is *derivation*, the process of forming a lexeme by adding an affix to a root, as in *skilful*.[1] Affixes are bound morphemes which never occur on their own; they must be joined to other morphemes. Derivation of complex words comprises three modes. The first mode is *prefixation*, a morphological process whereby a bound morpheme is attached to the front of a root, as in *defrost*. The second mode is *infixation*, a morphological process whereby a bound morpheme is inserted into a root, as in *speedometer*. The third mode is *suffixation*, a morphological process whereby a bound morpheme is attached to the end of a root, as in *classic*. In each example, the affix functions as a bound morpheme, whereas the root functions as a free morpheme. Of the three modes of derivation, I confine myself to the semantic description of suffixes.

Suffixes attach to roots which are identifiable with members of the major word classes: verbs, adjectives, and nouns. Verbs can be derived from nouns, as in *personify* from *person*, and from adjectives, as in *modernise* from *modern*. Sometimes, only one verb is derived from a root, as in *hyphenate* from *hyphen*. Sometimes, two or more verbs are derived from a root, as in *syllabise/syllabify* from *syllable*. Adjectives can be derived from nouns, as in *postal* from *post*, and from verbs, as in *defiant* from *defy*. Sometimes, only one adjective is derived from a root, as in *smoky* from *smoke*. Sometimes, two or more adjectives are derived from a root, as in *joyful/joyous* from *joy*. Nouns can be derived from verbs, as in *inspection* from *inspect*, and from adjectives, as in *diligence* from *diligent*. Sometimes, only one noun is derived from a root, as in *advancement* from *advance*. Sometimes, two or more nouns are derived from a root, as in *domination/dominance* from *dominate*. Of the three types of suffixation, I concern myself with the semantic characterisation of nominalisation.

The derivation of a single noun from a root has been covered by many morphological studies. Yet, the derivation of a noun pair from a root, a process known as *alternation*, has been left unaccounted for. By *alternation*, I mean rivalry between two, or more, suffixes in deriving new forms from the same root, exhibiting both phonological distinctness and semantic dissimilarity. In the present analysis, I delimit the scope to cases where pairs of nouns share a single root but end in different suffixes. To tackle this phenomenon, some questions are posed. The first question is: do suffixes display multiple meanings, and if yes, how are the meanings related? The second question is: can suffixes stand for the same concept, and if yes, what provides the basis for the contrast? The third question is: are the resulting derivatives distinct, and if yes, what accounts for the distinction? My task in the present analysis is to develop a new framework that is capable of answering these questions and justifying the discussions. Before embarking on the task, let me first show how such questions are treated in different theoretical paradigms.

1.2 Theoretical paradigms

Language is a systematic means of communicating ideas or feelings by the use of conventional symbols. Two mainstream paradigms undertake language description. The first paradigm is labelled *formalist* because it focuses on the formal aspects of language. It considers language as a system that should be studied in isolation from both meaning and cognitive processes. It is concerned with the formal relationships between linguistic elements, independently of the meanings they hold. This paradigm is associated with the theory of Generative Grammar (Chomsky: 1957, 1965), which describes language only with reference to formal rules. The second paradigm is labelled *functionalist* because it underlines the functional aspects of language. It considers language as a tool of communication, where language structure reflects what people use language for. It focuses on the form–meaning relationships between linguistic elements. This paradigm is associated with the theory of Cognitive Grammar (Langacker: 1987, 1991), which is symbolic in nature. It takes form plus meaning as being fundamental.

On English morphology, there is a rich amount of literature. A large number of works such as Hockett (1954), Adams (1973), Matthews (1974), Aronoff (1976), Dressler (1985), Bauer (1988), Jensen (1990), Spencer (1991), Katamba (1993), Beard (1995), Haspelmath (2002), Booij (2005), and Aronoff & Fudeman (2005) serve as introductions to the basic notions used in morphology. A considerable number of studies such as Aronoff (1980), Cutler (1980), Fabb (1988), Baayan & Lieber (1991), Plag (1999), and Bauer (2001) deal with the productivity of

English affixes conducting corpus-based analyses. Within word formation, some handbooks such as Marchand (1969), Urdang (1982), Bauer (1983), Szymanek (1998), Adams (2001), Plag (2003), and Lieber (2005) shed light on aspects of derivation and offer detailed surveys of English affixes. A few sources such as Beard & Szymanek (1988), Carstairs-McCarthy (1992), and Stekauer (2000) survey the history of research done so far in morphology. Because the topics of lexicalisation, productivity, and semantic drift are extensively covered in the literature, they will be outside the scope of my current project.

Within morphology, one area that has not received enough attention pertains to the synchronic description of alternation, or the case where the speaker has an alternative: the choice between two mutually exclusive items, in which the occurrence of one excludes the occurrence of the other. The research which has been done in the area, to date, can be described as bitty and undersized. In what follows, I will briefly review the literature with two objectives. First, I will classify the literature into the two mainstream paradigms to show how the subject of morpho-lexical alternation has been treated. Second, within each paradigm, I will classify the literature into discrete hypotheses, on the basis of the different ways used to solve the problem; elaborate on them under separate headings; and touch upon some representative samples of research done so far. Meanwhile, I will assess the hypotheses in terms of their relevance or irrelevance to the present work. In doing so, my intention is not to criticise any of these hypotheses, but to extract from them some general principles that motivate suffix selection. These hypotheses can be described as useful because they have, in one way or another, made contributions to the overall study of morphology.

1.2.1   Formalist paradigm

Linguists involved in the generative paradigm, specifically Chomsky (1995: 4), believe that there is no relationship between the form of a linguistic element and the meaning it expresses. The relationship between form and meaning is arbitrary. Given such a core assumption, the dominant tendency deems a suffix as a meaningless linguistic element which is summoned simply to derive a new word. A suffix turns up in the final position of the derived word, plays no role in its semantic make-up, and acts as a mere category classifier. Unlike a lexeme, which has an identifiable meaning, a morpheme, as Beard (1981: 196) claims, has no meaning apart from signalling that a derivation has taken place. The difference between derivatives does not belong to the affix but to the lexeme. Spencer (2001: 227) clarifies this by saying, 'Thus, the derivational morphology which creates the adjectives changes the syntactic category of the word but does not add any element of meaning and thus, strictly speaking, is a kind of cranberry suffix'. Rival forms are lexical exceptions which should, as Aronoff (1976) proposes, be left to the area of lexicology.

Within the context of the formalist paradigm, two trends in morphology can be recorded. Adherents of the first trend, which is referred to as Item-and-Process (IP),[2] trace back morphological derivations to the same deep structure and attribute the surface differences to transformational rules. Since transformations do not change meaning, the resulting variations are similar. This trend has been brought to the attention of linguists by, among others, Lees (1960), Beard (1995), and Anderson (1992), who consider morphological constructions as the output of phrase structure rules operating on lexical items. The meaning of a given construction is determined by its deep structure; so transformationally-related constructions, i.e. those sharing the same deep structure, are semantically equivalent. Relating this to suffixation, the members of a nominal pair are supposed to have one deep structure, and hence be semantically alike. The surface differences are the result of different transformational operations. Rival suffixes are treated as interchangeable, and the choice between them is the result of different syntactic transformations. The presence of rival suffixes is a matter of idiosyncrasy and an instance of synonymy.

Adherents of the second trend, which is referred to as Item-and-Arrangement (IA),[3] exclude transformational rules and deep structures from derivational morphology. Morphological constructions are not related by transformational rules. Word formation cannot be governed by purely syntactic transformations; rather it should be governed by specific considerations which mediate the relationship between the base and the affix. This trend has been advocated by linguists such as, among others, Williams (1981), Selkirk (1982), and Lieber (2004), who reckon morphological constructions as the outcome of morphological, phonological, or semantic considerations. Each consideration has a different impact with respect to the status of the affix or the value of the resultant derivative. Relating this to suffixation, the members of a nominal pair are hypothesised to be more or less different. Rival suffixes are treated as substitutable, and the choice between them is explained in terms of three types of selectional hypotheses: the morphological shape of the base, the phonological property of the suffix, and the semantic category of the base. To make the picture clear, I now introduce the hypotheses and touch upon the few works done so far.[4]

1.2.1.1   The form-of-the-base hypothesis

In the light of this hypothesis, the selection of a rival suffix is seen as a matter of the base form. In the sphere of nominal suffixation, rival suffixes that have been studied by morphologists are *-ness* and *-ity*. On the one hand, Aronoff (1976) and Anshen & Aronoff (1984) suggest that the choice between the rival suffixes is based on the morphological form of the base. For example, *-ity* is said to be more productive with bases ending in *-ible*, whereas *-ness* is more productive with bases ending in *-ive*. As for stress, Aronoff (1976: 40) argues that *-ness* follows a word boundary and *-ity* a morpheme boundary. On the other hand, Cutler (1980) suggests that the choice between the rival suffixes is regulated by their effect on the morphological transparency of the base. For example, *-ity* changes the stress pattern of the base as in *sensible/sensibility*, while *-ness* preserves it as in *sensible/sensibleness*. In addition, *-ity* may cause velar softening as in *toxic/toxicity*, and trisyllabic laxing as in *grave/gravity*. The difference in stress behaviour may cause some Latinate bases to prefer *-ness* to *-ity*. Each work discusses the difference between the rival suffixes at the formal level, and so is agnostic about the meaning difference.

1.2.1.2   The phonology-of-the-suffix hypothesis

In view of this hypothesis, phonology is regarded as the main factor in the selection of a rival suffix. In the area of verbal suffixation, Plag (1999) argues that the choice between the rival suffixes *-ise/-ize*, *-ify*, and *-ate* is governed by the phonological property of each suffix. Plag considers the suffixes as allomorphs of a single morpheme. They are phonologically different but semantically synonymous. So, true rivalry does not exist. For example, both *-ise/-ize* and *-ify* express the same range of meanings, and so are synonymous. The meanings of *-ate* are a subset of those of *-ize* and *-ify* derivatives. These suffixes are complementarily distributed with regard to two restrictions. According to syllable pattern, the suffix *-ise/-ize* attaches to disyllabic stems as in *technicise*, whereas the suffix *-ify* attaches to monosyllabic stems as in *technify*. According to stress pattern, formations in *-ise* are stressed on the antepenultimate syllable as in *flúoridise*, while formations in *-ate* are stressed on the penultimate syllable as in *fluorídate*. Plag's work attributes the difference between the rival suffixes to phonology, and so disregards the meaning difference.

1.2.1.3   The category-of-the-base hypothesis

According to this hypothesis, the choice of a rival suffix is predictable from the meaning of the host predicate. Aronoff & Cho (2001: 167–73) explore the distinction between stage- and individual-level bases, whereby the selection of a given suffix is determined by the semantics of the base. A stage-level base expresses a temporary property. Such bases select the suffix *-ship*. For example, *friendship* denotes a property that holds at a given time. In contrast, an individual-level base expresses a stable property. Such bases select the suffix *-hood*. For example, *sisterhood* denotes a property that holds all the time. Some bases, however, have both properties, and so accept both suffixes. The word *father* serves as a base for both *-ship* and *-hood*. Yet, the derived nouns do not have the same meaning. *Fathership* means 'the state or condition of being the oldest member of a community', a property that is transient in nature. By contrast, *fatherhood* means 'the state or condition of being a father', a property that is permanent in nature. Aronoff & Cho's work does not give the rival suffixes any explicit meaning, and so ignores their functions altogether. Besides, it is not hard to find counter-examples. Words like *cousinship, sonship* or *twinship*, seem to be based on individual-level nouns, yet they take *-ship*.

Let me now touch upon the conclusions that emerge from the preceding discussion. What the hypotheses show is that there are indeed different sorts of restrictions that tackle the issue of morpheme combination. Researchers of the first two hypotheses overlook meaning as a possible factor in the choice between rival suffixes. They prefer to interpret rival suffixes mainly in terms of formal constraints or phonological rules. Clearly, the solutions they offer are irrelevant for the present analysis. Researchers of the third hypothesis include meaning in their work but their solution is half-baked, as they shrug off the role of the suffix in the choice. Accordingly, none of the hypotheses is entirely suitable to tackle the issue of morpho-lexical alternation. For one, they have described individual affixes. As such, they are insufficient for a full discussion of derivational suffixation. For another, the factors they suggest seem to work in some cases, but they fail to work in many others. The verb *deviate* accepts both *-ion* and *-ance*, as in *deviation* and *deviance*. In both, it is neither the morphological form of the base nor the phonological property of the suffix that motivates the choice; it is something that belongs, I argue, to the factor of meaning.

1.2.2   Functionalist paradigm

Linguists working in the cognitive paradigm, most notably Lakoff (1987: 228), argue that the primary purpose of language is to frame thoughts and convey them in communication. Language knowledge and language use appear to interact. The link between form and meaning is not arbitrary but motivated. Langacker (1987: 82) contends that syntactic structure is determined by a set of cognitive principles, and there is a direct mapping from a cognitive structure to a syntactic structure. The usual practice of morphologists working within the functionalist paradigm is to brand any suffix a reflection of a conceptual structure, and so associate it with a variety of meanings. The potential context in which a suffix appears is a response to the communicative needs of the discourse. In Bybee's (1985: 19) analysis, each distinct sense of a word is associated with a distinction in form, and the form of a word is shaped in part by conceptual principles. Morphological rivalry is described in terms of features present on the surface, which includes reference to all kinds of knowledge, be it linguistic or non-linguistic.

Proponents of this paradigm consider meaning as the most important factor in the choice between rival suffixes. The surface structure of an expression is directly linked to its meaning. There are no rules akin to transformations. A morpheme is conceived as a unit of form and meaning. Just as a plus sign has a meaning (addition) and a form (+) to express it, a morpheme also has a meaning that is expressed by sound waves in speech or by letters in writing. According to this paradigm, the suffixes are not considered as being in complementary distribution. Nor are the derivational pairs they give rise to in free variation. Suffixes are considered the locus of the difference in meaning. For example, both *continuation* and *continuance* are derived from the verb *continue*, but they are different in use. In *The advertising campaign served to develop the continuation of the trend*, the noun *continuation* means 'the act of continuing', referring to the prolongation or resumption of an action. In *The management ensured his continuance in office*, the noun *continuance* means 'the state of continuing', referring to the duration of a condition.

The issue of morpho-lexical alternation has been scarcely tackled by functional morphologists. A review of the literature indicates that some suffixes have been studied and that discrete solutions about the choice between them have been offered. Broadly, the purpose of the review is to establish the criteria that govern the choice between rival suffixes for any root. Specifically, the purpose of the review is to find out if functional morphologists consider rival suffixes as synonymous in meaning and if they treat the resulting derivatives as interchangeable. In this regard, two hypotheses can be recognised. The first hypothesis considers the semantics of the suffix as a crucial yardstick in the choice between rival suffixes. The second hypothesis considers the semantics of the derivative as an essential dimension in the choice between rival suffixes. To elaborate the issue, I shall now present the hypotheses and discuss the few works carried out so far. I will see if they have any beneficial effect on my analysis or see if my argument can build on any of them.

1.2.2.1   The semantics-of-the-suffix hypothesis

With reference to this hypothesis, the primary factor that determines the choice between rival suffixes lies in the semantic property of each suffix. In Riddle's (1985: 435–61) view, the suffix *-ness* tends to denote an embodied attribute, whereas the suffix *-ity* tends to denote an abstract or concrete entity. To clarify the distinction, Riddle provides examples. In *The brutalness/brutality of Jill's remarks shocked us*, either noun is possible, but the resulting sentences have different meanings. The nominal form ending in *-ness* focuses on the brutal nature of the remarks themselves, while the nominal form ending in *-ity* focuses on their utterance as being brutal. To support her claim, Riddle provides some evidence. Colour words, which describe inherent traits, only take *-ness*, as in *redness*. Ethnic names, which describe inherent traits, almost always take *-ness*, as in *Slavicness*. In addition, count nouns, which denote abstract or concrete entities, mostly take *-ity*, as in *oddities*, although the bases of some count nouns can take *-ness* to denote an attribute. Riddle's work regards the rival suffixes non-synonymous; each has a meaning of its own. Yet, her data are not particularly naturalistic – note, for example, that the nouns *senileness* and *suaveness* are not found in the British National Corpus.

1.2.2.2   The semantics-of-the-derivative hypothesis

As regards this hypothesis, the choice of a rival suffix is ascribed to the overall meaning of the derivative. In the realm of adjectival suffixation, Malkiel (1977: 341–64) examines the rival suffixes *-ish* and *-y*, when used to derive adjectives from animal names. Malkiel expatiates on their general usages, with a view to finding out their semantic cores. Both suffixes seem to be productive, which can be demonstrated by the large number of resulting coinages. In the process of the investigation, Malkiel comes across some doublets that end in the two suffixes as in *rammish/rammy*. Such derivatives are not free from a certain overlap since they exhibit only partial differentiation of meaning. The adjective *rammish* means 'like a ram in having a disagreeable taste or smell', while the adjective *rammy* means 'resembling a ram'. In fact, there are on record a very few triplets, as in *doggish/doggy/dogged*. The adjective *doggish* means 'like a dog in temper', the adjective *doggy* means 'resembling a dog in smell', and the adjective *dogged* means 'obstinate'. Malkiel's work establishes the difference in semantics, but it rates the derivatives only partially different. Moreover, the data are based on intuition, rather than being established by corpus-based methods.

In two of her articles, Górska (1994: 413–35, 2001: 189–202) analyses privative adjectives ending in *-less* and *-free*. Even though the two suffixes mean 'without the thing named by the nominal base', the derivatives differ in meaning. The difference is generalised in terms of control and intention. With derivatives in *-less*, the speaker has neither control over the course of events nor the intention to change it, as in *moonless night*. That is why it is not possible to say *moon-free night*. With derivatives in *-free*, the speaker has both control over the course of events and the intention to change it to fulfil a desire, as in *smoke-free city*. That is why it is not possible to say *smokeless city*. In some cases, two derivatives exist as in *sugarless/sugar-free tea*, but they are used in different contexts. *Sugarless tea* is tea without sugar although we want sugar in it, while *sugar-free tea* is tea without sugar because we do not want sugar in it. Górska's work does not attach any specific meaning to the rival suffixes. Instead, it lays emphasis on the meaning of the derivatives. Besides, the distinction is ineffective for it does not work in such examples as *a stainless watch, a cordless telephone, a collarless shirt, spiceless salad, a flawless performance*, and many others, where the speaker has both control over and the intention to control the course of action.

Let me now draw the conclusions from the preceding discussion. In theory, the solutions offered by the hypotheses are relevant for the present analysis. For one, they downplay the role of form and focus on the meaning of lexical items. For another, they perceive linguistic forms as closely corresponding to characteristics of the entities which they denote. In practice, however, they are inadequate. One reason is that they provide only a superficial account of the mechanism underpinning morpho-lexical alternation. That is, they fail to provide any detailed distinctions between the occurrences of alternatives. This is so because their characterisation is based on individual cases, and so the evidence they present is insufficient. Another reason is that they don't try to specify the paradigmatic sets of morphological rivals and define the (dis)similarity existing among them. Consequently, they neglect to look at rival suffixes as a coherent class in morphology, a class whose members may represent the same concept but have contrastive behaviour. This calls for a new approach which provides for a fuller description.

1.3 New approach

In order to resolve the questions raised at the beginning of the study, I propose a new approach which concentrates on the semantics of word formation, namely, on the meanings of morphemes and how they combine to form complex words. The discussion is largely about noun derivation, the process by means of which a dependent morpheme (suffix) is integrated, due to phonological and semantic correspondences, with an autonomous morpheme (root) to form a composite structure (new lexeme). The discussion is specifically about morpho-lexical alternation, the cases where noun alternatives are derived from the same root but end in two suffixes. My discussion aims at exploring the nuances of such alternatives and how these nuances differ. To achieve this, I propose two apparatuses of semantic description: Cognitive Semantics and Corpus Linguistics. The apparatuses prove vital for two reasons. For one, they justify the existence of a noun pair formed on one root. Although the suffix variants are permissible, each gives the host root a different meaning. For another, they demonstrate a clear-cut differentiation in the usage of the derived nouns. Although the noun pair shares a single root, their meanings are distinctive. In section 1.4, I offer a detailed coverage of the apparatuses I adopt here.

1.3.1 Keystones

Building upon my earlier work on adjectives (see Hamawand, 2007), the prime objective of this work is to show the direct relevance of meaning to the phenomenon of morpho-lexical alternation. The choice of an alternative, I argue, is a matter of two keystones. One keystone resides in *conceptual content.* The content of the root is multi-faceted, whereas the suffix has its own content – which it imposes on the root, and so gives the resulting alternative a different meaning in the derivational process. That is, when two rival suffixes attach to a root, each serves to highlight a different facet of the root's content. Each of the resulting alternatives encodes, therefore, a distinct meaning. Another keystone resides in *construal.* The meaning of a derived alternative involves the particular construal the speaker employs to describe a situation. Linguistically, the construal is encoded by means of a suffix. That is, when two alternatives have the same conceptual content, they differ semantically by virtue of the construals they represent and the suffixes they host. The suffixes, therefore, are responsible for disengaging the alternatives. Alternation in morpho-lexicology is semantically motivated, and differences in behaviour reflect differences in meaning.

Before I go on to analyse an example, it is necessary to elaborate on the descriptive steps I take to unveil the semantic distinctions between noun alternatives. Obviously, the aim is to elucidate differences in meaning between near-synonymous pairs of nouns or more specifically pairs of nominal suffixes. In the first step, I check the uses of rival suffixes by studying their occurrences in numerous nouns in the corpus, with a view to arriving at their definitions. In the second step, which considers the rival suffixes that occur in the same environment or perform the same function, I diagnose their subtle nuances by contrasting their occurrences in examples of nouns which host the rival forms. In the third step, to demonstrate the subtle nuances, I cite pairs of sentences which are concise but clear in reflecting the meanings diagnosed. In the fourth step, I analyse the pairs of sentences in precise details by giving the meanings of the root and the derived alternatives, and highlighting the function of the suffix in the derivation. In the final step, I provide evidence to support the analysis, which comes in the form of different sorts of collocations. To avoid inconsistencies and confusion, I concentrate only on the discriminating collocates that form general patterns of usage and help to separate the alternatives. For easy reference, I group the collocations on the basis of the semantic fields to which they belong.

To exemplify all this, let me consider a noun pair like *deviation* and *deviance*. Although the two nouns are derived from word classes of the same root, they differ in terms of construal. The noun *deviation* is derived from the verbal root *deviate*, whose conceptual content means 'to differ from what is prescribed or expected'. When the speaker construes a situation as an act, s/he uses the suffix *-ion*, whose conceptual content means 'the act of doing the process referred to in the verbal root'. In *They gauged the cow's deviation in the milk yield*, the noun *deviation* means 'the act of deviating', i.e. doing something that is different from the usual way of behaving. This meaning is borne out by certain collocates of the noun, which are verbs such as *calculate, figure, gauge, measure, reckon*; adjectives such as *absolute, gross, obvious, slight, standard*; or nouns such as *frequency, output, price, product, yield*, etc. The noun *deviation* is used mainly in the context of physical sciences, referring to violations of arithmetical, mathematical, or statistical norms. As an evidence, none of the collocates of *deviation* is compatible with *deviance*. For example, it would not be possible to say *deviance in yield*, because *yield* is a scientific, not social, term.

The noun *deviance* is derived from the adjectival root *deviant*, whose conceptual content means 'different from what is prescribed or expected'. When the speaker construes a situation as a state, s/he uses the suffix *-ce*, whose conceptual content means 'the state indicated by the adjectival root'. In *Crime and delinquency are one form of deviance*, the noun *deviance* means 'the state of being deviant', i.e. behaviour that is generally counted as unacceptable. This meaning is borne out by certain collocates of the noun, which are verbs such as *classify, diagnose, identify, reveal, understand*; adjectives such as *human, original, primary, secondary, sexual*; or nouns such as *culture, politics, psychology, religion, sociology*, etc. The noun *deviance* is used mainly in the context of social sciences, referring to violations of cultural, legal, or societal norms. As an evidence, none of the collocates of *deviance* is compatible with *deviation*. For example, it would not be possible to say *deviation in culture*, because *culture* is a social, not scientific, term. In each derivation, the suffix is the most important part because it lends its character to the whole outcome. It stands for the particular construal which the speaker imposes on the content of the root.

1.3.2 Goals

The general goal of the present study is to show that morpho-lexical phenomena are not only amenable to formal restrictions, but also describable with reference to semantic considerations. The study strives to fulfil this goal by exploring the sorts of meaning distinctions which guide the speaker in the choice between lexemes. The specific goals which the study seeks to attain are

1. Illustrating that the senses of a suffix can be understood in terms of the category to which it belongs. A *category* is a network made up of multiple senses exhibiting minimal differences. To achieve this goal, the study draws a categorial characterisation for each suffix. The present analysis adopts the *prototype* approach, which assumes that not all senses of a category are equal. Some senses are typical, while others are atypical. Using the *prototype* approach, the study posits for each suffix a prototypical sense, from which the peripheral senses are derived. The category of a suffix cannot be defined in terms of attributes applicable to all its senses. Rather, it is marked by vague boundaries between the peripheral zones that gather around a centre. That is, it may have marginal instantiations that do not conform rigidly to the central sense. In Cognitive Semantics, the meaning of a lexical item is not fixed. Through the creativity of the language user, it can be extended into new realms of experience, thus resulting in new senses.

2. Demonstrating that the meaning of a suffix can be identified through comparison with the meanings of other suffixes in the same domain. A *domain* is an integrated conceptualisation into which our mental experiences are registered. To reach this goal, the study furnishes complete descriptions of the cognitive domains which the suffixes presuppose as a basis for their characterisation. The present analysis adopts the *domain* approach, which assumes that lexical structures are characterised relative to the cognitive domains in which they are embedded. Each domain consists of a number of members, but their membership is based on perceived similarity rather than identity. The members converge at some general points, but diverge with regard to some minute details. Employing the domain approach, the study groups the suffixes into semantic sets relative to the common features they display. In Cognitive Semantics, the meaning of an expression is describable in terms of a cognitive domain, and not in terms of a bundle of semantic primitives.

3. Elucidating that the difference between a noun pair can be explained by the different construals of their common content. A *construal* is a way of conceiving and expressing a situation. To attain this goal, the study compiles a list of noun pairs that share the same content. The present analysis adopts the construal approach, which assumes that the specific form of an expression reflects the particular way in which the speaker chooses to describe its scene. Utilising the *construal* approach, the study seeks to show that seemingly similar nouns are neither synonymous nor free variants. Therefore, they should not be turned about in their usages. The distinction between them, though subtle, is quite significant. The distinction is not based on the operation of formal rules; it is exclusively a property of construal, which gives the speaker the flexibility to construe the same conceptual content in alternate ways. In Cognitive Semantics, the form of an expression is characterised by the particular construal it presents of the scene it describes.

1.3.3   Procedures

In the preceding sections, I introduced the goals of this study. Now, it is time to turn to the steps for achieving the goals. These are

1. Retrieving data. As a first step, I compiled a list of 22 suffixes by relying on major dictionaries and reference books. Relative to the part of speech of the combining root, I then classified the suffixes into four categories. De-verbal bound suffixes comprise *-al, -ce, -ion,*

-ment, and *-ure.* De-adjectival bound suffixes consist of *-ce, -cy, -ity,* and *-ness.* De-nominal bound suffixes include *-age, -dom, -hood, -ism, -ship, -(e)ry,* and *-eer.* Agent-forming de-verbal suffixes include: *-ant, -ee,* and *-er.* Agent-forming de-nominal suffixes include: *-(i)an, -ist,* and *-ster.* Then, I used the WordSmith Tools concordancer to retrieve from the British National Corpus all the occurrences of these suffixes, together with the nouns they form. The occurrences allow the researcher to reveal the different meanings of the suffixes and of the resulting nouns hosting them.

2. Defining suffixes. As a second step, I defined the multiple senses of each suffix. In the course of the characterisation, I examined the occurrences of the nouns containing each suffix. The occurrences were numerous enough to meet the requirements of the characterisation. Based on the analyses of the occurrences of nouns, I diagnosed the different senses of each suffix. To corroborate the definitions, I utilised major reference works on word formation such as Marchand (1969), *Collins COBUILD: Word Formation* (1993) and Urdang (1982). To verify the senses diagnosed, I provided multiple examples. For each sense, I gave three examples of nouns with their paraphrases. These examples confirm the polysemy of each suffix and the application of each sense to a distinct context. These and similar examples provide sufficient data for the researcher to make meaningful generalisations.

3. Establishing pairs. As a third step, I collected the nominal pairs. Given the lack of appropriate software tools, I conducted a manual search of noun pairs by putting the lists of nouns containing the suffixes side by side with a view to picking out the pairs. Meanwhile, I checked major manuals on English usage, e.g. Partridge (1961) and Greenbaum & Whitcut (1988), Fowler (1996), Peters (2004), and a few others cited in the references, to see if they contain any examples of a nominal pair. The use of a pair has double import. Theoretically, it achieves emphasis by placing focus on a particular segment within a word, and provides evidence that the segments compared have different meanings. Empirically, it helps, by relying on a corpus, to determine the contextual preferences of the pair members, and to stress the role of the rival suffixes in signalling the meaning differences between them.

4. Providing examples. As a fourth step, I provided examples of sentences to demonstrate the uses of the nominal pairs. For each of the semantic distinctions, I provided 3-5 pairs of sentences. For the definitions of the common roots of the pairs, I relied on major

online English dictionaries such as *Cambridge Advanced Learner's Dictionary, Merriam-Webster Dictionary, Oxford English Dictionary,* and a few others cited in the references. For the exemplification of the meanings diagnosed, I provided sentences based on the British National Corpus. To make the sentences reader friendly but still rigorous in effect, I shortened them by deleting all the non-essential elements. Through these examples, it becomes easy to see how rival suffixes serve as a locus of meaning difference, how related nouns are used in different ways, and how they are appropriate in different contexts, whether they are formal or informal, technical or non-technical.

5. Discriminating senses. As a final step, I discussed distinguishing the noun pairs and identifying their individual behaviour. To achieve that, I made use of the technique of *collocation*, the tendency of certain words to occur together in a text. The information provided by the collocation analysis can be used as a major source of evidence for the allocation of a specific meaning to an occurrence of a word within a stretch of text, thus removing the ambiguity surrounding its use. In this respect, I build on the works done by Kennedy (1991), Clear (1994), Biber et al. (1998), Kilgarriff & Tugwell (2001), and Williams (2002). However, my work departs from theirs in two ways. First, they look at the different senses of individual or separate words, whereas I look at noun pairs that relate to the same root but end in different suffixes. Second, they use statistics to measure the frequency of occurrence of a given collocate, whereas I consider both common and rare collocates as long as they play a role in sense disambiguation.

1.4 Models of analysis

To come to grips with the issue of morpho-lexical alternation, I apply two approaches to the study of nominal suffixation. One is theoretical; the other is empirical. It is assumed that the two approaches can work together and provide a cogent description of the way language is used. The theoretical approach, represented by Cognitive Linguistics, makes the necessary assumptions. It is chosen because it explains linguistic structure with reference to cognitive processing and concentrates on the link between linguistic and non-linguistic worlds. The empirical approach, represented by Usage-based Linguistics, provides the useful tools to verify the assumptions. It is chosen because the data used are objective, the evidence presented is reliable, and the findings attained are valid. Significantly, it is the linguist who interprets the data, which are represented by the collocations; discovers the semantic distinctions between the nominal pairs; and draws the conclusions at the end.

1.4.1 Cognitive Linguistics

In broad terms, the theoretical framework within which the analysis of adjectival suffixation is conducted is Cognitive Linguistics. Being a relatively new theory of language, Cognitive Linguistics is built upon the idea that language reflects fundamental properties and cognitive abilities of the human mind. It focuses on language as an instrument for organising, processing, and conveying information. Cognitive Linguistics seeks, therefore, to hinge descriptions of linguistic phenomena on the mental operations of the human brain. It explains language creation, learning, and usage by reference to concepts formed in the mind. It also attaches central importance to meaning, the role of cognition, and the embodiment of experience. Linguistic phenomena are motivated by conceptual knowledge, which is grounded in experience. Cognitive Linguistics aims, therefore, to characterise how the human mind understands the world and encodes that understanding in language. For overviews of the scope of Cognitive Linguistics, see Rudzka-Ostyn (1988), Dirven & Verspoor (1998), Ungerer & Schmid (1996), Lee (2001), and Croft & Cruse (2004).

In specific terms, the theoretical framework within which the analysis of nominal suffixation is carried out is Cognitive Semantics, which is exemplified by linguists such as Fillmore (1977, 1982), Talmy (1983, 1985), Fauconnier (1985, 1997), Lakoff (1987, 1990), and Langacker (1988, 1997b), among others. Cognitive Semantics is a novel theory that links meaning with conceptualisation. The meaning of a linguistic expression does not refer to the entity in the real world, but to a concept in the mind. The prime slogan for Cognitive Semantics is that meaning is embodied; i.e. it is perceptually grounded and experientially based. Cognitive Semantics describes meaning representation as being encyclopaedic, rejecting thus the boundary between linguistic and non-linguistic worlds. Everything that is known about an entity is allowed to contribute to its meaning. The guiding principle behind Cognitive Semantics is that meaning is not fixed, but a matter of construal. Cognitive Semantics lays emphasis on the capacity of the human to construe a given situation in alternate ways. Cognitive Semantics, therefore, takes into account the role of the human being in providing the basic meanings coded in language.

The viability of Cognitive Semantics rests on several fundamental tenets. Such tenets are not specific to language, but are a part of our general system of cognition. They are, at the same time, considered mental capacities on which the creation of linguistic units rests. One tenet is that all linguistic items have semantic values. In this regard, I argue that suffixes have meanings of their own, give substance to the host roots, and shape the final meanings of the derivatives. A suffix forms a category subsuming all of its meanings which gather around a central sense. Another tenet is that linguistic items gather in domains. In this respect, I argue that suffixes form sets which reveal their specific uses. When two rival suffixes compete for one concept, they are not in complementary distribution. A close investigation of their behaviour makes it clear that they have individual meanings. A further tenet is that linguistic items are not synonymous even if they look alike. On this basis, I argue that if two rival derivatives exist, they reflect a clear distinction in use. Despite sharing the same root, they differ in terms of the alternate ways the speaker construes their common content, represented by the root, when describing a situation.

In what follows, I give a detailed presentation of the central tenets of Cognitive Semantics as they apply to nominal suffixation.

1.4.1.1   Category

Most dictionaries of language describe the senses of a lexical item as homonyms: items that are the same in spelling and pronunciation but different in meaning. In this way, dictionaries ignore how such senses are related to one another, or how such senses are motivated. As a result, they miss the point that the meaning a lexical item has is vital in explaining the peculiarity associated with its behaviour. To remedy this problem, Cognitive Semantics, as demonstrated by Lakoff (1987) and Taylor (1989), builds linguistic descriptions on the *category* theory, which was developed first by Rosch (1977, 1978). According to this theory, most lexical items are polysemous in nature, in the sense of having numerous senses. A lexical item constitutes a complex network of inter-related senses. One sense, described as prototypical, serves as a standard from which other senses, described as peripheral, are derived via semantic extensions. The senses are related to each other like the members of a family, where they share some general properties but differ in specific details. For instance, a *kitchen chair* is regarded as the prototype of the *chair* category because it possesses almost all of its features, whereas *rocking chair, swivel chair, armchair, wheelchair,* or *highchair* are regarded as the periphery because they possess only some of those features.

The *category* theory is relevant in many areas of language.[5] In Hamawand (2003a), I applied it to the description of complementisers in English. In the present analysis, I extend its relevance to morphology, where it is used to describe the semantic structure of a nominal suffix. In this respect, I argue that a nominal suffix forms a category of distinct but related senses. The distinct senses, which are related in a semantic network, are the result of a dynamic process of meaning extension. A suffix category is characterised by an intersection of properties that make up its members. The member that has all of the properties of the category and best represents it is described as prototypical. The other members that contain some, but not all, of the properties are described as peripheral. That is, the category is specified in general terms; the different members flesh out the category in contrasting ways. A member inherits the specifications of the category, but fleshes out the category in more detail. *Category* is then a powerful tool which reveals the general properties of structures of a given kind via their relationships with one another.

For establishing the prototype and periphery of a suffix, I follow the criteria proposed by Evans (2004) and Tyler & Evans (2001). A likely candidate for the prototype should satisfy three criteria: (i) It should be the sense that comes to mind first. It is the sense that is first learned and the easiest to recall. (ii) It should be the sense whose meaning components are most frequent in the other senses. It is the sense that is most predominant in the semantic network. (iii) It should be the sense that gives rise to additional senses through extension. It is the sense from which the other senses would most naturally be derived. The reason for positing a prototype is that language users intuitively categorise senses in terms of a semantic network. For a particular instance to count as a distinct sense, it should satisfy three criteria: (i) It should have an additional meaning that is not apparent in the other senses. (ii) It should not be derived from context or inferred from another sense. (iii) It should have structural properties and display collocational restrictions. Some senses are related to the prototype. Others are related to other derived senses. This is so because different interpretations reflect different uses.

The interpretation of a derived noun can be either strictly or partially compositional(Taylor, 2002). In strict compositionality, which is a key principle in Formal Semantics, the meaning of a derivative is merely a function of the meanings of its constituent parts. For example, the meaning of *kindness* is a combination of the meanings of the root and the suffix: the trait of being kind. Although this analysis works for a number of derivatives, it is inconsistent in the majority of cases. The reason is that the meaning of any expression is not fixed, but tends to vary according to contextual use, or is based on conceptual knowledge that goes beyond what is actually symbolised. In partial compositionality, which is a key principle in Cognitive Semantics, the meaning of a derivative resides in both the meanings of its constituent parts and the pragmatic interpretation of the whole. For example, the meaning of *kindness* is not only a function of the meanings of the root and the suffix, the trait of being kind, but may also be an act that is helpful or considerate.

Let me demonstrate this by taking an example. Prototypically, the suffix *-ure* is tacked on to verbs to form nouns. Based on the nature of the root, the suffix has the following interpretations:

a. 'the act of performing the thing described in the verbal root'. In such formations, the verbal root is transitive. For example, *closure* is the act of closing a road or bridge, *erasure* is the act of removing something, and *seizure* is the act of taking control of a country or town. In some formations, the verbal root is both transitive and intransitive. For example, *departure* is the act of leaving a place, *mixture* is the act of mixing different substances together, and *pressure* is the act of forcing somebody to do something.

b. 'the result of the action described in the verbal root'. In such formations, the verbal root is transitive. For example, *composure* is the state of being calm and in control of your feelings or behaviour, and *sculpture* is the work of art made by carving or shaping wood, stone, clay, or metal. In some formations, the verbal root is both transitive and intransitive. For example, *failure* is somebody or something that is not successful, and *pleasure* is the state of feeling or being happy or satisfied.

c. 'a group of people who perform the thing described in the verbal root'. In this case, the verbal root is intransitive. For example, *legislature* is a group of people who have the power to make and change laws.

Peripherally, the suffix *-ure* is tacked on to nouns to form nouns. Based on the nature of the root, the suffix has the following interpretations:

a. 'the state of being the thing described in the nominal root'. In such derivations, the nominal root refers to common nouns denoting persons. For example, *candidature* is the state of being a candidate.

b. 'the office held by the thing described in the nominal root'. In such derivations, the nominal root refers to common nouns denoting persons. For example, *prefecture* is the office, territory or residence of a prefect.[6]

Before going any further, let me draw some conclusions from the preceding discussion about the suffix *-ure*. One conclusion is that a suffix forms a category of its own, which includes its multiple senses. Another conclusion is that the senses of a suffix gather around one representative sense, referred to as the *prototype*. A further conclusion is that the category of a suffix is a powerful conceptual framework which allows us to see how the different senses are related to one another. A look at the categorial descriptions of the suffixes will show where the senses converge and where they diverge. On the basis of the converging senses, i.e. when the senses mean more or less the same, the suffixes can be grouped into sets, referred to as *domains*. It is within these domains that the suffixes can stand against each other as rivals. So, a domain is concerned with a knowledge configuration in which suffixes gather, showing similarity on the surface but dissimilarity below the surface. Two suffixes may stand for one concept but differ in the specifics. The elaboration of this cognitive tenet will be the task of the next section.

1.4.1.2   Domain

Most dictionaries of language describe the lexicon by allotting the lexical items of any language separate entries, with information about meaning, usage, or register. In this way, dictionaries fail to show that many of these items have something in common as well as an element of difference. As a result, dictionaries stop short of showing how they are related to one another. To solve this problem, Cognitive Semantics, as suggested by Langacker (1987, 1991), builds linguistic descriptions on the *domain* theory. The theory centres around the idea that the meaning of a lexical item can best be described with reference to the domain to which it belongs. A *domain* is a knowledge structure with respect to which the meaning of a lexical item can be characterised. It comprises a set of lexical items related in such a way that to understand the meaning of any one item, it is necessary to understand the conceptual knowledge that it evokes. The meaning of any lexical item can be defined in terms of the background knowledge that underlies its usage. For example, in describing the meaning of the word *father*, the speaker needs to activate the domain of *kinship* as the background knowledge for his description.

The *domain* theory is significant to all areas of language.[7] In Hamawand (2003b), I applied it to the description of verbs taking *for-to* complement clauses in English. In the present analysis, I utilise it in morphology. The meaning of a morpheme, I argue, depends on the domain to which it belongs, knowledge of which is necessary for its appropriate use. A *domain* is used as a cognitive device which allows one to describe the distribution of different suffixes and provide the motivation for their use in discourse. In this regard, I argue that suffixes form sets so that to understand the semantic structure of any suffix, it is necessary to understand the properties of the set in which it occurs as well as the properties of the other members of the set. The interpretation of a suffix can then be defined against the domain that it invokes. A *domain* captures semantic information about suffixes. It includes information about the specific meanings or the distinctive uses of the suffixes. A *domain* is then a powerful mechanism which reveals specification and guides usage.

Let me demonstrate this by taking an example. The suffixes *-ette*, *-kin*, *-let*, and *-ling* evoke, I argue, the domain of *diminution*, an area of knowledge in which somebody or something is made small in size, young in age, or little in value. Diminutives combine with nominal roots to form new nouns mainly implying a derogatory shade of meaning. The suffixes *-ette*, *-kin*, and *-let* are used mostly to form *inanimate* derivatives, whereas the suffix *-ling* forms *animate* derivatives. They, however, differ in that each has a particular nuance. The suffix *-ette* is used chiefly to describe places or works of literature. For example, *kitchenette* is a small kitchen and *novelette* is a short novel. The suffix *-kin* is used chiefly to describe fabric. For example, *napkin* is a piece of fabric used for cleaning. The suffix *-let* is used chiefly to describe things. For example, *droplet* is a small drop of a liquid and *bracelet* is a piece of jewellery worn around the wrist or arm. The suffix *-ling* is used chiefly to describe persons, animals, or plants. For example, *princeling* is a prince who rules a small or unimportant country, *duckling* is a young duck, and *seedling* is a young plant that has grown from a seed.

In the foregoing discussion, I showed how the *domain* theory applies to the description of suffixes in English. The description comprised four steps. In the first step, I placed all the suffixes under one domain, which I named *diminution*. In the second step, I grouped the suffixes into two subdomains, which I name *inanimate* and *animate*. This is done relative to the type of derivation they form and the behaviour they have in context. In the third step, I identified the suffixes that represent each subdomain. In the fourth step, I explained the rivalry between the suffixes by pinpointing the peculiarity of each suffix which makes it different from its counterpart. When and how to use a suffix is a matter decided by the speaker. The choice of the speaker comes under the rubric of *construal*. *Construal* is concerned with the ways the speaker conceives a situation and the right expressions s/he chooses to realise them. Two suffixes that stand as rivals construe a situation in different ways. The elaboration of this cognitive tenet will be the task of the following section.

1.4.1.3   Construal

Most dictionaries of language describe lexical pairs sharing common roots as synonymous. Formalist paradigms regard them as an idiosyncrasy of the lexicon and often present them as semantic alternatives. In this way, formalist paradigms disregard the fact that every lexical item has a certain mission to achieve in discourse. According to the present analysis, it is an axiomatic fact that lexical items are in no way interchangeable, even if they look similar or share the same source. To prove this, I build the analysis on Langacker's (1987, 1991) theory of *construal*. *Construal* is a language strategy which allows the speaker to conceptualise a situation and choose the linguistic structure to represent it in discourse. In cognitive semantics, the meaning of a linguistic expression, as Langacker (1997a: 4–5) states, does not reside in its conceptual content alone, but includes the particular way of construing that content. The constructions *He sent a letter to Susan* and *He sent Susan a letter* share similar wording, but they involve different ways of construing the same content. In the prepositional construction, it is the issue of movement that is foregrounded, whereas in the ditransitive construction it is the result of the action that is foregrounded. Therefore, only the second construction implies that *Susan* has received the letter.

The *construal* theory is present in almost every area of a language.[8] In Hamawand (2002), I applied it to the description of complement clauses in English. In the present analysis, I extend its impact to morphology. In this connection, I argue that the choice of a derived noun correlates with the particular construal imposed on its root. At first sight, any nominal pairs may appear to be synonymous. A closer look, however, reveals that they are neither identical in meaning nor interchangeable in use. There is a clear-cut distinction in their definitions. There are two keys to using these nouns correctly. One key is to know that the two nouns constitute different conceptualisations of the same situation. The different conceptualisations reflect different mental experiences of the speaker. The other key is to know that, as a result, the two nouns are realised morphologically differently. In each derivational case, it is the nominal suffix that encodes the intended conceptualisation. The different suffixes, therefore, single out different aspects of the meaning of the root.

Such pairs, if ever mentioned in dictionaries, are listed without clear distinction. Dictionaries confirm that they are interchangeable. Usage books often present such pairs as reciprocal nouns. However, database evidence shows that they are different in use. It is true they share a common root, but they are far from being equal. The derived nouns relate to the slightly different aspects of the root. The difference is a matter of the alternate ways the root is construed, which is morphologically mirrored by different suffixes. Two construals are at work here (Langacker: 1988). One is *profiling*, the act of conferring prominence on a particular substructure within an expression. The other is *perspective*, the viewpoint imposed on a scene which changes relative to one's intention or the context. Two expressions differ in meaning depending on which aspects within the situation they designate. In addition, speakers have the ability to construe the same situation in many ways and choose the appropriate structures to represent them. Consequently, the perspective embodied by a linguistic expression constitutes a crucial facet of its meaning.

Let me demonstrate this by taking an example. The suffixes *-ion* and *-ce* are attached to verbal roots to form nouns. They evoke the domain of *process*, but each profiles a specific aspect of it. The suffix *-ion* means 'the overall act named by the verbal root', whereas the suffix *-ce* means 'the specific result labelled in the verbal root'. The difference in meaning can be borne out by an example of a nominal pair. The two nouns *acceptation* and *acceptance* are derived from the verbal root *accept*, which means 'to take something that someone offers, or to agree to do something that someone asks'. Despite the similarity in derivation, the two nouns differ in terms of the perspective imposed on their common root or the prominence given to their particular aspects. In *The expression has won people's acceptation*, the noun *acceptation* means 'the overall act of accepting'. *Acceptation* is a generally favourable approval of something. In *He had acceptance from three universities*, the noun *acceptance* means 'the specific result of accepting'. *Acceptance* is a formal agreement allowing a student to study at a university.

1.4.2 Usage-based Linguistics

In broad terms, the empirical framework within which the analysis of nominal suffixation is conducted is Usage-based Linguistics. In this approach, grammar is seen as a dynamic system which is shaped by cognitive and psychological processes involved in language use. Three key notions underlie this approach. First, Usage-based Linguistics focuses on language use. To gain insight into the language system, one must analyse the usage events that instantiate it. The usage events constitute the empirical source from which the grammatical patterns can be abstracted. Second, Usage-based Linguistics treats competence and performance alike. There is an interplay between knowledge of the language system and the processes of language use. Third, Usage-based Linguistics rejects rule-list fallacy. The division between the lexicon as a list of irregularities and the grammar as a list of regularities is blurred. Instead, a network model for language is presented, which includes both abstract grammatical patterns and their lexical instantiations. For overviews of the key notions of Usage-based Linguistics, see Langacker (1990), Bybee & Hopper (2001), Kemmer & Barlow (2000), Tomasello (2000) and Croft & Cruse (2004), among others.

In gathering relevant data and describing language units, Usage-based Linguistics involves three methodologies: surveys, experiments, and corpora. A *survey* is a way of getting information through a questionnaire from a sample of informants, in order to verify a research question. An *experiment* is a way of collecting information through a test on a sample of respondents, so as to validate a research question. Because the informants are aware of the procedure and the information is elicited, there is a danger that the results of surveys and experiments only partially reflect actuality. A *corpus* is a collection of actual, non-elicited, and spontaneous language products realised by native speakers who are unaware of the procedure. It is a large collection of examples, recorded utterances or written texts, of the usage of a language which serves as an empirical basis for linguistic description. Owing to all this, a corpus occupies a central position in a usage-based study of a linguistic phenomenon. For a comprehensive coverage of methodologies proposed in Usage-based Linguistics, see Tummers et al. (2005).

In specific terms, the empirical framework within which the analysis of nominal suffixation is carried out is Corpus Linguistics, which is exemplified by linguists such as Sinclair (1991), Stubbs (2001), McEnery & Wilson (2001), Tognini-Bonelli (2001), and Meyer (2002), among others. Corpus Linguistics considers language a social phenomenon and an applied science with practical implications. Corpus Linguistics gives priority to usage data as the empirical foundation of language research, which are presented in a corpus. Corpus Linguistics assigns the linguist the task of investigating performance rather than competence, i.e. analysing language observationally rather than introspectively. Corpus Linguistics provides a methodology to describe language, which involves a given set of computational procedures to retrieve data from a corpus, sort them and process them for analysis. Corpus Linguistics focuses on the interaction between language use and language system. The usage data do not only instantiate the language system but also modify it in a dynamic way. Corpus Linguistics aims to identify the significant features of language use. To do so, the analysis requires the use of such parameters as frequency or collocation.

As a source of data, I have chosen the *British National Corpus*. This is a 100-million-word corpus of modern British English of the late twentieth century. It includes different styles and varieties, and comprises 90 per cent written texts and 10 per cent spoken texts. The use of different text types has the advantage that the examples studied represent a high diversity of speakers and situational contexts. Therefore, it serves to minimise the impact of idiolects or dialects on the results of the research. In some cases, the corpus fails to provide examples for a certain keyword. In fact, such a situation backs up Chomsky's (1957: 15) argument that corpora are 'finite and somewhat accidental', while the set of grammatical utterances is 'presumably infinite'. To cope with the problem, the linguist should, as Biber et al. (1998: 41) suggest, seek feedback of different kinds to complement the corpus-based analysis. In this regard, I have solicited help from Internet pages and native speakers. For the former, I examine the total number of hits returned by the search engine Google. Integrating data from different sources can be a powerful way for arguing for a claim or documenting the actual use of the words in language.

In what follows, I give a detailed presentation of the central axioms of Corpus Linguistics as they apply to nominal suffixation.

1.4.2.1 Authenticity

Corpus Linguistics deals with real language data. Because the data are real, not invented, the results are indubitable. As a social phenomenon, language is realised in texts or text segments. By *text*, it is meant a spoken or written instance of language which has occurred naturally, without intervention on the part of the linguist. This tenet runs counter to the generative practice, where the focus is on sentences composed by the researcher and advanced as credible data. In illustrating a point in a linguistic argument, the linguist relies on data, usually of his or her own or an informant, and passes judgement on the basis of intuition. This is against the scientific norm for two reasons. For one, it reveals only narrow aspects of the human competence. For another, the invention of the data precedes the development of the theory, which should be the other way round. In Corpus Linguistics, the linguist relies on attested data, which helps to make generalisations about the overall tendencies of usage and show how the properties of utterances in communication determine the representation of grammatical units in the speaker's mind.

To retrieve texts, Corpus Linguistics provides a powerful tool called a *concordancer*. In this work, WordSmith Tools has been used. A *concordancer* is a software programme that searches for and displays the occurrences of a chosen word, referred to as *Key Word in Context* (KWIC), with the words surrounding it. To provide sufficient context for the task of disambiguation, each word selected will be accompanied by a maximum of 70 characters to the left and to the right. The occurrences of a word help to identify the main senses of a word and produce definitions for each of the senses identified. Recall that one advantage of a corpus is that it can be used to show all the contexts in which a word occurs. From these contexts, the investigator can reveal the semantic and syntactic patterning of a word. In the present study, the aim is not to consider the frequency of any of the suffixes nor of their host words, as this sort of quantification is covered in Ljung (1974). Rather, the aim is to consider the range of different but related meanings which nominal suffixes have and the roles they play in distinguishing between words.

1.4.2.2   Semanticity

Corpus Linguistics focuses on meaning. Meaning is what is being communicated between the members of the language community. Since the main function of language is to mean, the core task of linguistics is to explain how language means. Meaning does not exist in the world outside the discourse. It exists in a text which is an integral part of a context and a reflection of discourse-internal reality. Any unit of meaning is provisional in the sense that everyone can paraphrase it in the way they like. In Corpus Linguistics, any text can be described under two aspects: meaning and form. There is no form without meaning. Consequently, meaning and form are interdependent. This tenet contrasts with the generative premise which stipulates that grammar is autonomous and independent of meaning. Corpus Linguistics rejects the view that the meaning of a text exists independently of its form. The meaning of a text can only be derived from the context in which it occurs. When a sensory verb refers to a physical sense, it is preceded by a modal, as in *I can see him*. Otherwise, it refers to a non-physical sense, as in *I see his viewpoint*.

Corpus Linguistics establishes two parameters in analysing meaning. One parameter is qualitative and represented by *collocation*. It refers to the occurrence of two or more words next to each other in a text. All lines of concordances will be examined for the sake of compiling the collocates associated with a noun. All grammatical relations holding between the noun and the collocates surrounding it will be considered in the compilation. The collocates will then be classified into semantic areas, for which around five examples will be given as evidence. To avoid possibility of confusion, the focus will be placed only on those discriminating collocates that help to distinguish the noun pairs, which have gone unnoticed in many, if not all, previous analyses. From such collocates, it becomes fairly clear what the meaning of a noun is. The other parameter is quantitative and represented by *frequency*. It refers to a rate of occurrence of a word within a given text. It helps to detect the number of times a given word occurs in a text, and so is an essential feature for making general claims about the discourse.

Of the two parameters, the present study opts for the qualitative one. One reason, as McEnery & Wilson (2001: 76) stress, is that in a qualitative analysis both rare and frequent linguistic phenomena receive equal attention. This is so because it aims to provide a detailed description of usage aspects. Accordingly, it enables delicate distinctions to be drawn, since it is not necessary to fit the data into a finite number of classifications. Another reason, as Bartsch (2004: 112) contends, is that although the quantitative analysis is efficient, its results only partially reveal the linguistic reality. A quantitative analysis does not inherently supply information which aids the interpretation of the results. This can be done only by the application of a qualitative analysis whose ultimate goal is a meaningful description of the linguistic data. A further reason, as Teubert (2005: 5) writes, is that statistics are significant but their significance is never enough. When linguistic items occur next to each other, they should be semantically relevant. A grammatically correct sentence will stand out as weird if it violates collocational conditions.

1.5 Summary

In this chapter, the aim has been to give an introduction to the field of word formation, in general, and nominal suffixation, in particular. What I tried to do is suggest a new approach that is capable of resolving the inconsistencies found in the dictionaries and the literature concerning the semantic differences between pairs of nouns that share the same root but end in different suffixes. In section 1.1, I defined the phenomenon of alternation and highlighted its prevalence in morpho-lexicology. In section 1.2, I reviewed the literature and showed that the explanations hypothesised by the different paradigms are overwhelmingly non-semantic in nature. In section 1.3, I posited my novel approach, which underlines the role of meaning in deriving nouns, predicts the distribution of nominal suffixes and guides the choice between nominal alternatives. In section 1.4, I did two things. First, I discussed the basic tenets of Cognitive Semantics which provide the theoretical basis for the analysis. Second, I presented the basic axioms of Corpus Linguistics, which provide empirical support for the analysis. In the coming chapters, I will apply the new approach to the description of suffixes deriving nouns in English. In each chapter, I will look in depth and detail at a particular area within nominal suffixation.

Notes

1. A *root* is a word portion that cannot be analysed further into meaningful elements, as in *touch*. A *base* is analysable. It consists of a root and a derivational affix to which a further derivational affix can be added. The word *touchable* functions as a base for a prefix like *un-*, to give *untouchable*. A *stem* is reserved for inflection. It consists of a root and a derivational affix, to which an inflectional affix can be added. The word *untouchable* functions as a stem for an inflectional affix like *-s*, to give *untouchables*.

2. In IP approach , which is alternatively called Lexeme-based morphology, the underlying form of a word is the basic element of morphological description. A word is formed by deriving its surface form from an underlying base by means of certain rules. Each rule changes the form of the base and concomitantly has some characteristic semantic or morpho-syntactic effect. The form–meaning correspondence is presumed to be one-to-one. The form of a word is analysed as being the result of applying rules to its deep structure to transform it into its surface structure. A derivational rule takes a stem, makes some changes to it, and outputs a new form. For example, *careful* is the result of the basic form *care* undergoing a transformation that changes it into the surface form *careful*. This approach does not have any difficulty when faced with irregular forms. While the plural of *dog* is formed by adding an *-s* to the end, the plural *geese* is formed by changing the vowel in the stem. This approach was dominant in the generative tradition. Works that fall into this IP camp include, among others, Aronoff (1976), Anderson (1992), and Beard (1995). For a thorough treatment of this approach, see Hockett (1954) and Spencer (1991), among others.

3. In IA approach, which is alternatively called Morpheme-based morphology, the morpheme is the basic element of morphological description. A word is built up by inserting morphemes into appropriate positions within it. Each morpheme contributes a distinct meaning to the complex word. The form–meaning correspondence is presumed to be one-to-one. The form of a word is analysed as consisting of a set of morphemes arranged in sequence by rules. A word like *carefulness* is made up of the morphemes *care*, *-ful*, and *-ness*, which are put after each other like beads on a string. *Care* is the root and the other two morphemes are derivational suffixes. Although this sort of analysis applies to regular cases like *dogs*, it fails to account for irregular cases like *geese*, for example. Adherents of this type of morphology defend their approach by

saying that *geese* is *goose* followed by a *null* morpheme, a morpheme that has no phonological structure. This approach was pursued in American Structuralism. Works that fall into this IA camp include, among others, Lieber (1992), Selkirk (1982), and Williams (1981). For a thorough treatment of this approach, see Hockett (1954) and Spencer (1991), among others.

4. In Word-and-Paradigm (WP) approach, which is alternatively called Word-based morphology, the form of a word is analysed as a whole, as the basic element of morphological description. A word is formed by defining a root within a paradigm, which is neutral with respect to the variant forms of the paradigm, and deriving the variant forms of the word from this root by using rules. The form-meaning correspondence is presumed to be many-to-one. Whereas the Morpheme-based approach treats the inflectional *-s* plural and the inflectional *-s* third person singular as belonging to one morpheme having two categories, the Lexeme-based approach assumes two separate rules for them, and the Word-based approach considers them as whole words related to each other by analogical rules. Words can be categorised based on the pattern that they fit into. Application of a new pattern can give rise to a new word such as *older* replacing *elder*, which fits the pattern of adjectival comparatives. This approach was fundamental in Traditional Grammar. Works that fall into this WP camp include, among others, Matthews (1972) and Stump (2001). For a thorough treatment of this approach, see Hockett (1954) and Spencer (1991), among others.

5. The tenet of *category* has been explored in some detail in other areas of language by linguists such as Brugman (1988), Dewell (1994), Vandeloise (1994), Sandra & Rice (1995), Kreitzer (1997), Tyler & Evans (2001), and Hamawand (2002, 2003a, 2003b, 2005, 2007), among others.

6. The other approach to the analysis of suffixes traces their development over time. This approach is called *grammaticalisation*, defined by Hopper & Traugott (1993: XV) as 'the process whereby lexical items and constructions come in certain linguistic contexts to serve grammatical functions, and, once grammaticalised, continue to develop new grammatical functions'. *Grammaticalisation* is viewed as a historical process of obtaining a grammatical element or a new meaning from lexical items. Concerning derivational suffixes, the major source is full words or free morphemes, which have gradually evolved into bound morphemes. For example, in tracing the source of the suffix *-ful*, we find that it originates from the adjective *full*. As a suffix, it has gradually acquired the more abstract meaning of possessing some value to a high degree. This explains why derivatives ending in *-ful* tend to be restricted to abstract stems, as in *beautiful*.

7. The tenet of *domain* has been explored in some detail in other areas of language by linguists such as Fillmore (1982), Croft (1993), Clausner & Croft (1999), Taylor (2002), and Hamawand (2002, 2003a, 2003b, 2005, 2007), among others.

8. The tenet of *construal* has been explored in some detail in other areas of language by linguists such as Haiman (1985), Johnson (1987), Wierzbicka (1988), Dixon (1991), Deane (1992), Casad (1995), Heine (1997) and Hamawand (2002, 2003a, 2003b, 2005, 2007), among others.

2
De-Verbal Nominalisers

In this chapter, I describe the semantics of de-verbal nominalisers. More precisely, I deal with the meanings of morphemes and how they combine to derive nouns. In the course of the investigation, I apply three tenets of Cognitive Semantics to de-verbal nominalisations. To that end, I organise the chapter as follows. In section 2.1, I define a de-verbal suffix and touch on the factors that underlie its integration with a root to form a noun. In section 2.2, I argue that a de-verbal suffix has a wide range of meanings that gather around a central sense. In section 2.3, I argue that the best way to understand nominal suffixes is to group them into domains exhibiting both similarities and differences. In section 2.4, I argue that the difference between a noun pair results from the different ways the speaker describes their common content. To show that the noun pair is not synonymous, I identify the distinctive collocates associated with each member of the pair. To substantiate all the above-mentioned arguments, I rely on actual data offered in the corpus. In section 2.5, I present the key points of the chapter.

2.1 Introduction

A de-verbal suffix is a word-final element that is added to a verb to form a noun. It is a bound morpheme because it never occurs by itself, but is integrated with a free morpheme. When the two morphemes integrate, they show what Langacker (1987: 277–327) calls *valence* relations.[1] First, the two morphemes are integrated because they have certain elements in common at both semantic and phonological poles. Second, of the two morphemes, the free morpheme qualifies as autonomous, while the bound morpheme qualifies as dependent. Third, the bound morpheme is primarily responsible for the character of the composite structure.

It acts as a profile determinant and has twofold import in the derivation process. As a categorial marker, it changes a lexical item from one class into another. As a meaning marker, it causes a shift of a kind in the semantic structure of the root, and so adds a special meaning to the derived formation. Fourth, the two morphemes form a head-complement structure, with the bound morpheme being the head and the free morpheme being the complement.[2] In some derivational cases, the root undergoes a phonetic change, as in *decision* from *decide*, whereas in others it preserves its phonetic shape, as in *enrolment* from *enrol*.

2.2   Semantic networks

In this section, I address the question of the *category* theory in morpho-lexicology,[3] where it is used to describe the semantic structure of a de-verbal suffix. A de-verbal suffix, I argue, forms a category of distinct but related senses. The distinct senses, which are related by virtue of a semantic network, are the result of dynamic processes of meaning-extensions. The category is characterised by an intersection of properties that make up its members. The member that has the key properties of the category is described as prototypical. It is the sense that comes to mind first or is the easiest to recall. The other members that contain some, but not all, of the properties are described as peripheral. The peripheral senses inherit the specifications of the category, but flesh out the category in contrasting ways. The senses of a category are related to each other like the members of a family, where they share some general properties but differ in specific details. *Category* is a cognitive ability which reveals the general properties of structures of a given kind via their relationships with one another.

To show how the polysemy of a de-verbal suffix is accounted for in a principled manner, I need to consider the cognitive model of *transitivity*. The model is scalar in dimension in that it subsumes other components. Let me demonstrate the model by giving an example of the suffix *-ion*. Prototypically, the suffix *-ion* combines with a root to mean action. The action can vary in terms of transitivity. In the prototypical sense, the suffix is attached to transitive roots to form nouns, as in *inspection*. One step removed from the prototype is the case where the suffix is attached to (in)transitive roots, as in *reduction*. A further step removed from the prototype is the case where the suffix is attached to intransitive roots, as in *eruption*. Peripherally, the suffix *-ion* combines with a root to mean result. The result can vary relative to the type of entity affected. In some cases, the entity affected by the action is human, as in *emigration*. In other cases, the entity affected by the action is either human or non-human, as in *separation*. In further cases, the entity affected by the action is non-human, as in *stagnation*.

In what follows, I present synchronic descriptions of the de-verbal nominalisers in English.

2.2.1   *-al*

Prototypically, the suffix *-al* combines with nouns denoting entities to form adjectives. In terms of animacy, the nominal root can vary:

1. In some combinations, the nominal root is inanimate. In this case, the suffix has the following senses:

   a. 'relating closely to the thing named by the nominal root'. This meaning comes to attention when the suffix is added to roots referring to inanimate entities. In such formations, the suffix specifies the type of entity that the noun modified is related to. For example, *an environmental issue* is an issue that is related to the environment, *a medicinal product* is a product that is related to medicine, and *a postal delivery* is a delivery that is related to a mail service.
   b. 'showing the proportion of the thing named by the nominal root'. This meaning comes to attention when the suffix is added to roots referring to dimensionality. The suffix modifies the noun as having the number, size, or degree of the thing named by the root. For example, *an occasional vacation* is a vacation that occurs at infrequent intervals, *a colossal statue* is a statue that is of gigantic size, and *a proportional punishment* is a punishment that corresponds with the degree of seriousness of a crime.
   c. 'showing the location of the thing named by the nominal root'. This meaning comes to attention when the suffix is added to roots referring to names of places. The suffix modifies the noun as being situated in or near the thing named by the root. For example, *a coastal town* is a town that is located near the coast, *marginal land* is land that is located on the edge of a cultivated area, and *a central hole* is a hole that is located in, at, or near the centre of something.

2. In other combinations, the nominal root is animate. In such combinations, the suffix means 'showing the character of the thing named by the nominal root'. This meaning comes to attention when the suffix is added to roots referring to humans. For example, *a brutal dictator* is

a dictator who shows his people cruelty and inhuman feelings, *a maternal nurse*, from *mater*, is a nurse who shows his/her patients the compassionate feelings of a mother, and *a cynical reviewer* is a reviewer who is unwilling to believe that people have good, honest, or sincere reasons for doing things.

Peripherally, the suffix *-al* combines with verbs to form nouns. In this case, the suffix means 'the act of doing the process named by the verbal root'. In terms of transitivity, the verbal root can vary:

a. In some combinations, the verbal root is transitive. For example, *approval* is the act of approving something, *denial* is the act of denying something, and *removal* is the act of taking away something.
b. In other combinations, the verbal root is both transitive and intransitive. For example, *rehearsal* is the act of practising a play or piece of music, *survival* is the act of continuing to live or exist, and *withdrawal* is the act of taking or moving out or back.
c. In further, but rare, combinations, the verbal root is intransitive. For example, *arrival* is the act of arriving at a place.

A graphical representation of the multiple senses of the de-verbal suffix *-al* is offered in Figure 2.1. Note that the solid arrow represents the prototypical sense, whereas the dashed arrows represent the semantic extensions.

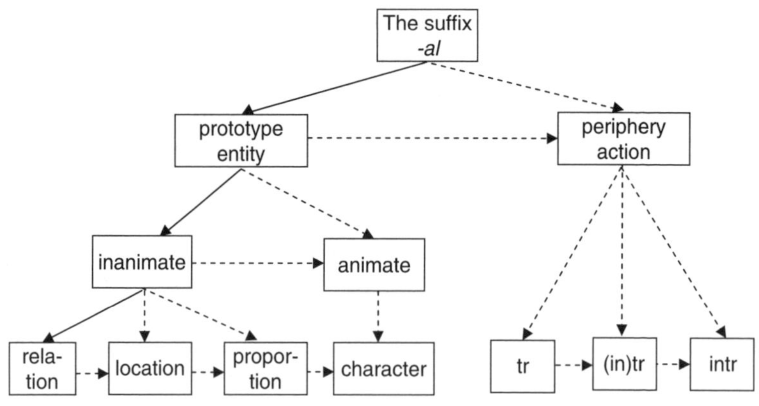

Figure 2.1 The semantic network of the de-verbal suffix *-al*

2.2.2 *-ce*

The suffix *-ce* attaches productively to roots ending in *-ant* or *-ent*. Prototypically, the suffix *-ce* is added to adjectives originally ending in *-ant* or *-ent* to form nouns. Relative to the nature of the combining root, the suffix expresses the following senses:

a. 'the state indicated by the adjectival root'. This sense emerges when the suffix is attached to qualitative adjectives to form abstract nouns. Some adjectival roots apply to humans. For example, *brilliance* is the state of being brilliant, *ignorance* is the state of being ignorant, and *vigilance* is the state of being vigilant. Other adjectival roots apply to non-humans. For example, *fragrance* is the state of being fragrant, *repugnance* is the state of being repugnant, and *significance* is the state of being significant. Examples of nouns in *-ce* attached to adjectives ending in *-ent* are *absence, confidence, diligence, eloquence, negligence, obedience, presence, violence*, etc.

b. 'the amount indicated by the adjectival root'. This sense develops when the suffix is attached to quantitative adjectives to form abstract nouns. For example, *abundance* is an amount of something that is large in size, *affluence* is an amount of something that is great in quantity, *exuberance* is an amount of something that is excessive in degree, and *luxuriance* is an amount of something that is rich in extent.

c. 'the thing indicated by the adjectival root'. This sense comes out when the suffix is attached to qualitative adjectives to form concrete nouns. For example, *protuberance* is a rounded part that sticks out from the surface of something.

Peripherally, the suffix *-ce* is added to verbs to form nouns, whose adjectives end in *-ant* or *-ent*. In this sense, the suffix expresses 'the act of doing the process indicated by the verbal root'. The verbal root can vary in terms of transitivity.

a. In some formations, the root is transitive. For example, *defiance* is the act of defying a ban, *observance* is the act of observing something, and *resistance* is the act of resisting a plan. Examples of nouns in *-ce* attached to adjectives ending in *-ent* include *preference, transcendence, transference*, etc. For example, *transference* is the act of moving someone or something from one place to another.

b. In other formations, the root is both transitive and intransitive. For example, *assistance* is the act of giving help, *insurance* is the act of protecting oneself against risks, and *resistance* is the act of opposing something. Examples of nouns in -*ce* attached to adjectives ending in -*ent* include *defence, indulgence,* etc. For example, *indulgence* is the act of allowing oneself or someone else to have something enjoyable.

c. In further formations, the root is intransitive. For example, *appearance* is the act of appearing in public; *compliance* is the act of obeying an order, rule, or request; and *forbearance* is the act of showing self-control in a difficult situation. Examples of nouns in -*ce* attached to adjectives ending in -*ent* include *adherence, convergence, divergence, dependence, emergence, insistence, persistence, residence,* etc. For example, *divergence* is the act of following a different direction.

A graphical representation of the multiple senses of the de-verbal suffix -*ce* is offered in Figure 2.2. Note that the solid arrow represents the prototypical sense, whereas the dashed arrows represent the semantic extensions.

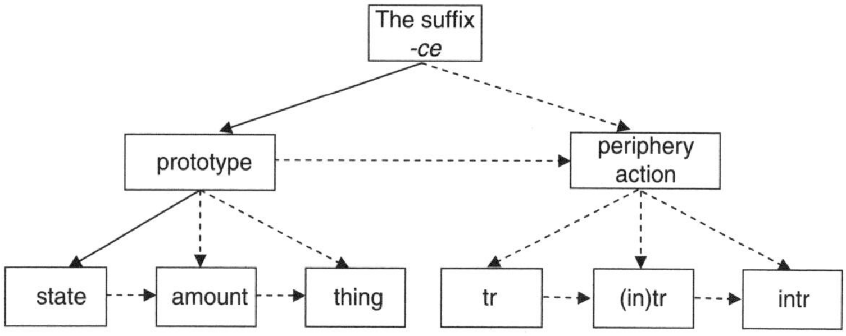

Figure 2.2   The semantic network of the de-verbal suffix -*ce*

2.2.3   -*ion*

This suffix takes a number of forms. The form -*ion* is by far the most frequent and has become a living formative. Other rare forms are -*ation*, -*sion*, and -*xion*.

Prototypically, the suffix -*ion* is added to verbs to derive nouns. In this case, the suffix means 'the act of doing the process referred to in the verbal root'. The verbal root can vary in terms of transitivity.

a. In some derivations, the verbal root is transitive. For example, *construction* is the act of making something, *restoration* is the act of returning something to its earlier condition or position, and *validation* is the act of making something officially acceptable. Other derivations are *affirmation, completion, detention, inspection, narration, organisation, production, transformation,* etc.

b. In other derivations, the root is transitive and intransitive. For example, *celebration* is the act of celebrating a special event, *explanation* is the act of giving details to make something clear or easy to understand, and *protection* is the act of protecting something or state of being protected. Other derivations are *alteration, combination, decision, explanation, navigation, operation, protection, reduction,* etc.

c. In further derivations, the root is intransitive. For example, *eruption* is the act of exploding suddenly, *option* is the act of making a choice, and *rebellion* is the act against people in authority or against the rules or against accepted ways of behaving.

Peripherally, the suffix *-ion* is added to verbs to derive nouns. In this case, the suffix means 'the result of the process referred to by the verbal root'. The result can vary relative to the types of entities affected:

a. In some derivations, the entity affected is human. For example, *alienation* is the result when one has no connection with the people around him/her, *expulsion* is the result when one is forced to leave somewhere, and *nomination* is the result when one is officially chosen for a job or position. Other derivatives are *abdication, emigration, hesitation, immigration, obligation,* etc.

b. In other derivations, the entity affected is either human or non-human. For example, *citation* is the result when someone or something is officially named in a court of law, *consultation* is the result when one gets information or advice from a knowledgeable person or book, and *demotion* is the result when someone or something is lowered in rank or position. Other derivatives are *combination, consolidation, deviation, modulation, separation, vibration,* etc.

c. In further derivations, the entity affected is non-human. For example, *destruction* is the result when something is destroyed, *extension* is the result when something is added to something else, and *regulation* is the result when an official law is laid down by an authority. Other derivatives are *annexation, depreciation, manifestation, perspiration, revision, stagnation,* etc.

A graphical representation of the multiple senses of the de-verbal suffix *-ion* is offered in Figure 2.3. Note that the solid arrow represents the prototypical sense, whereas the dashed arrows represent the semantic extensions.

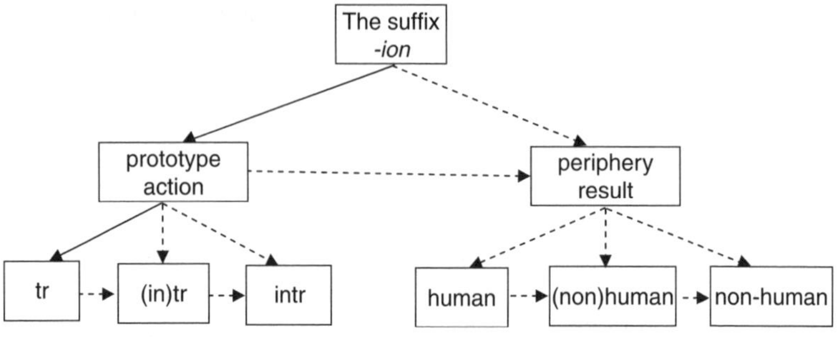

Figure 2.3   The semantic network of the de-verbal suffix *-ion*

2.2.4   *-ment*

Prototypically, the suffix *-ment* is attached to verbs to form nouns. In this case, the suffix means 'the result of the process referred to by the verbal root'. The result can vary relative to the types of entities affected.

a. In some formations, the entity affected is human. For example, *elope-ment* is the result when one leaves home secretly in order to get married without the permission of parents, *excitement* is the result when one has strong feelings of happiness and enthusiasm, and *retirement* is the result when one leaves a job and stops working because of old age or ill health. Similar coinages are *accomplishment, amusement, commitment, enrolment, punishment, resentment*, etc.

b. In other formations, the entity affected is either human or non-human. For example, *adjustment* is the result when one adjusts something to a particular need or adjusts the self to a situation, *development* is the result when someone or something grows or changes and becomes more advanced, and *employment* is the result when one is paid to work for a company or something is used for a particular purpose. Similar coinages are *advancement, assignment, involvement, deployment, replacement, requirement*, etc.

c. In further formations, the entity affected is non-human. For example, *investment* is the result when one puts money, effort, or time into something to make a profit or get an advantage, *payment* is the result when one pays an amount of money for something bought or for services provided, and *retrenchment* is the result when a government introduces a reduction in costs or expenditure. Similar coinages are *arrangement, assessment, embezzlement, entertainment, improvement, judgement*, etc.

Peripherally, the suffix *-ment* is attached to verbs to form nouns. Nouns formed in this way have different references:

1. 'the act of doing the process referred to in the verbal root'. The verbal root can vary in terms of transitivity.

    a. In some formations, the verbal root is transitive. For example, *enrichment* is the act of improving the quality of something by adding something else, *inducement* is the act of persuading someone or something, and *management* is the act of controlling an organisation. Similar coinages are *allotment, appeasement, banishment, bombardment, concealment, enforcement, enhancement, imprisonment,* etc.
    b. In other formations, the verbal root is both transitive and intransitive. For example, *adjournment* is the act of having a pause or rest during a formal meeting, *disappointment* is the act of failing to satisfy someone or their desires, *commencement* is the act of beginning something, and *rearmament* is the act of supplying people with new weapons to strengthen military capability.

2. 'the state referred to in the verbal root'. For example, *amazement* is the state of being amazed, *bewilderment* is the state of being confused, and *contentment* is the state of being satisfied. Other coinages are *astonishment, bereavement, enjoyment, enlightenment, merriment,* etc.
3. 'the means, instrument or agent referred to in the verbal root'. For example, *attachment* is an extra piece of equipment that can be added to a machine, *medicament* is a substance used for treating illness or injury, and *nourishment* is food one takes to keep healthy. Other coinages are *adornment, advertisement, entanglement, equipment, impediment, measurement, refreshment, reinforcement,* etc.
4. 'the location referred to in the verbal root'. For example, *embankment* is an artificial slope made of earth and/or stones, *emplacement* is a position specially prepared for large pieces of military equipment, *encampment* is a group of tents or temporary shelters put in one place, and *settlement* is a place where people live during a period in history.

A graphical representation of the multiple senses of the de-verbal suffix *-ment* is offered in Figure 2.4. Note that the solid arrow represents the prototypical sense, whereas the dashed arrows represent the semantic extensions.

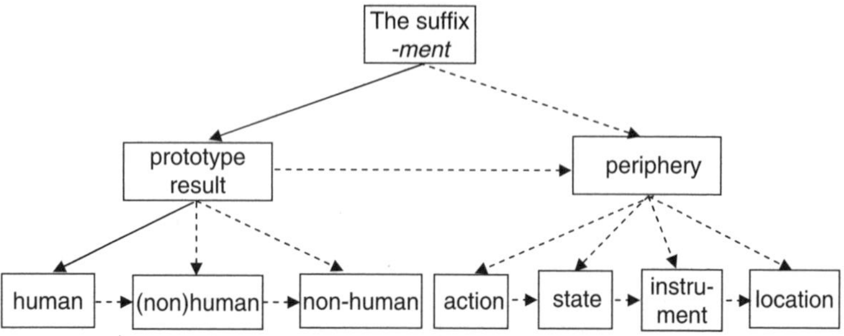

Figure 2.4   The semantic network of the de-verbal suffix *-ment*

Before going any further, let us draw some conclusions from the preceding discussion about the suffixes. One conclusion is that each suffix forms a category of its own, which includes its multiple senses. Another conclusion is that the senses of a suffix gather around one representative sense, referred to as the *prototype*. A further conclusion is that the category of a suffix is a powerful conceptual framework which allows us to see how the different senses are related to one another. A look at the categorial descriptions of the suffixes shows where the senses converge and where they diverge. On the basis of the converging senses, the suffixes can be grouped into sets, referred to as *domains*. It is within these domains that the suffixes can stand against each other as rivals. So, a domain is concerned with a knowledge configuration in which suffixes gather showing similarity on the surface but dissimilarity below the surface. Two suffixes may stand for one concept but differ in the specifics. The elaboration of this cognitive tenet will be the task of the next section.

2.3   Knowledge configurations

In this section, I address the question of the *domain* theory in morpho-lexicology, where it is used to characterise the meanings of de-verbal suffixes. The meaning of a de-verbal suffix, I argue, can best be described with reference to the domain to which it belongs. A *domain* is a knowledge structure in terms of which the exact role or the specialised status of a lexical item can be defined. De-verbal suffixes form sets so that to understand the meaning of any suffix it is necessary to understand the properties of the set in which it occurs, as well as the properties of the other members of the set. The meaning of a suffix can be demarcated by the web of semantic relations it has with its counterparts. A *domain* captures both semantic and morphological information about suffixes. Semantically, it reveals information about the specific meanings of the suffixes. Morphologically, it provides information about the relationships between the suffixes. A *domain* is a cognitive ability which reveals specification and guides usage of lexical items, via their relations with one another.

Applying the *domain* theory to the present topic, I argue that de-verbal nominalisers in English belong, relative to their definitional analyses, to the cognitive domain of *process*. *Process* is a coherent area of conceptualisation which includes an action that one takes to achieve a particular result. As the definition reveals, the domain of *process* incorporates two components: *action* and *result. Action* is anything that one does in order to deal with or achieve something. Morphologically, action is represented by the nominal suffixes *-al* and *-ion*. They differ, I argue, in that *-al* denotes the sequential act of achieving something, whereas *-ion* denotes the whole act of achieving something. By contrast, *result* is something that happens because of something else that has happened. Morphologically, result is represented by the nominal suffixes *-ce* and *-ment*. They differ, I argue, in that *-ce* indicates an instance of a result, whereas *-ment* indicates the type of a result.

For easy reference, I summarise in Table 2.1 the (sub)domains evoked by de-verbal suffixes in English.

Table 2.1 The (sub)domains evoked by de-verbal suffixes in English

Domain	Subdomains	Exponents	Meaning differences
	Action	*-al*	denotes a sequential act
		-ion	denotes a whole act
Process			
	Result	*-ce*	denotes an instance of a result
		-ment	denotes a type of a result

In Table 2.1, I show how the *domain* theory applies to the description of de-verbal nominal suffixes in English. The description comprises four steps. In the first step, I place all the de-verbal nominal suffixes under one domain, which I name *process*. In the second step, I group the suffixes into two subdomains, which I name *action* and *result*. This is done relative to the definitions provided in the previous section. In the third step, I identify the suffixes that represent each subdomain. In the fourth step, I explain the rivalry between the suffixes by pinpointing the peculiarity of each suffix which makes it different from its counterpart. When and how to use a suffix is a matter decided by the speaker. The choice of the speaker comes under the rubric of *construal*. *Construal* is concerned with the ways the speaker conceives a situation and the right expressions s/he chooses to realise them. Two suffixes that stand as rivals construe a situation in different ways. The elaboration of this cognitive tenet will be the task of the following section.

2.4 Conceptual distinctions

In this section, I address the question of the *construal* theory in morpho-lexicology, where it is used to describe the choice between alternatives. The choice of a derived noun, I argue, correlates with the particular construal imposed on its root. *Construal* is a cognitive ability which enables the speaker to conceptualise a situation in different ways and choose the appropriate linguistic structures to represent them in discourse. At first sight, a noun pair may appear to be synonymous. A closer look, however, reveals that they are neither identical in meaning nor interchangeable in use. There is a clear-cut distinction in their usages. There are two keys to using a noun pair correctly. One key is to know that the two nouns constitute different conceptualisations of the same situation. The different conceptualisations reflect different mental experiences of the speaker. The other key is to know that, as a result, the two nouns are morphologically realised differently. In each morphological realisation, it is the nominal suffix that encodes the intended conceptualisation.

The choice between members of a noun pair does not reside in their conceptual content alone, but includes the particular way of construing that content. The construal that is at the disposal of the speaker here is called *profiling*. According to Langacker (1990: 7), profiling refers to the act of conferring prominence on a particular substructure within an expression. A noun pair differs in meaning depending on which aspects within the situation they designate. It is true the two nouns share a common root, but they are far from being equal. The derived nouns relate to the slightly different aspects of the root. The difference is a matter of the alternative ways the root is construed, which is morphologically realised by different suffixes. The different suffixes, therefore, single out different aspects of the meaning of the root. In Cognitive Semantics, speakers have the ability to construe the same situation in many ways and choose the appropriate structures to represent them. Consequently, the construal employed by the speaker and embodied by the expression is a crucial facet of the expression's meaning.

Below are the different perspectives taken on the roots, which are responsible for the semantic distinctions.

2.4.1   The sequential–whole distinction: *-al* vs *-ion*

As explained earlier, the suffixes *-al* and *-ion* evoke the subdomain of action. Prototypically, both suffixes signify or describe the action denoted by the root, but they single out different aspects of it. Careful scrutiny of the concordances in the corpus shows that the difference pertains to the nature of the action. The suffix *-al* describes the action as sequential, i.e. in pieces, abridged and divided. A sequence is thought of as being concerned with dissection into parts or as having a series of movements. In the light of this, the suffix *-al* can be defined as 'the successive act named by the verbal root'. As evidence, nouns ending in *-al* are preceded by verbs denoting performance, modified by adjectives describing physical processes, and followed by nouns referring to people or things. Such nouns accept time expressions denoting continuation, as in *The dispersal of the crowd lasted two hours*.

By contrast, the suffix *-ion* describes the action as a whole, i.e. in one piece, unabridged and undivided. A whole is thought of as being concerned with one movement or as involving all of something. In the light of this, the suffix *-ion* can be defined as 'the overall act named by the verbal root'. As evidence, nouns ending in *-ion* are preceded by verbs denoting control, modified by adjectives describing vocal processes, and followed by nouns referring to substances or money. Such nouns, however, do not accept time expressions denoting continuation, as in **The dispersion of the odour lasted two hours*. A sample of examples will help to illustrate the distinction:

(1)   dispersal vs dispersion

    a. He protested against the dispersal of the crowd by force.
    b. She traced the dispersion of the odour all over the place.

The two nouns under (1) encompass the verbal root *disperse*, which means 'to diffuse over a large area, or to scatter abroad'. However, each noun imposes its own construal on the root, and so has its own meaning. In (1a), the noun *dispersal* means 'the successive act of dispersing'. *Dispersal* is the action of scattering people or spreading things over a wide area. It is preceded by verbs like *enforce, govern, lead to, protest, result in*; modified by adjectives like *explosive, gradual, quick, rapid, violent*; and followed by nouns referring to people, animals, flora, objects, etc. In (1b), the noun *dispersion* means 'the overall act of dispersing'. *Dispersion* is the action of spreading or the state of being scattered. It is preceded by verbs like *achieve, control, prevent, trace, reduce*; modified by adjectives like *atmospheric, digital, practical, spatial, wide*; and followed by nouns referring to substances – such as *air, gas, light, odour, pigment* – or money – such as *power, income, returns, material, installations*, etc.

(2) disposal vs disposition

    a. They resolved the disposal of the nuclear waste.
    b. They have a chart of the disposition of the fleet.

The two nouns under (2) are linked to the verbal root *dispose*, which means 'to put in place or arrange in readiness'. However, each noun imposes its own construal on the root, and so has its own meaning. In (2a), the noun *disposal* means 'the successive act of disposing'. *Disposal* is the action of getting rid of inconsequential items. It is preceded by verbs like *attend to, begin, complete, involve, resolve*; modified by adjectives like *illegal, improper, proper, routine, steady*; and followed by nouns referring to trash, such as *furniture, refuse, rubbish, sewage, waste*, etc. In (2b), the noun *disposition* means 'the overall act of disposing' *Disposition* is the position or arrangement of something in a place. It is preceded by verbs like *analyse, exhibit, find out, make, show*; modified by adjectives like *administrative, dynamic, final, regular, tactical*; and followed by nouns like *books, fleet, goods, records, troops*, etc.

(3) recital vs recitation

    a. The recital of the symphony revealed an entirely new talent.
    b. He got a prize for poetry recitation at school last September.

The two nouns under (3) represent the verbal root *recite*, which means 'to say a piece of writing aloud from memory, or to state in public a list of things'. However, each noun imposes its own construal on the root, and so has its own meaning. In (3a), the noun *recital* means 'the successive act of reciting'. *Recital* is the action of rehearsing or performing music using an instrument, usually given by one performer. It is preceded by verbs like *give, offer, play, present, stage*; modified by adjectives like *brief, long, poor, short, smooth*; and followed by nouns referring to musical instruments, such as *guitar, organ, piano, violin*, etc. In (3b), the noun *recitation* means 'the overall act of reciting'. *Recitation* is the action of narrating or reading poetry, or reporting from memory, of facts, quotes, summaries, or the like. It is preceded by verbs like *begin, chant, do, give, start*; adjectives like *beautiful, holy, live, popular, vocal*; and followed by nouns like *facts, narrative, poetry, prayers, story*, etc.[4]

2.4.2   The instance–type distinction: *-ce* vs *-ment*

As explained earlier, the suffixes *-ce* and *-ment* evoke the subdomain of result. Prototypically, both suffixes focus on the result of an action, which can be used as a means to a desired end. Yet, each suffix has a distinctly different type of focus. Close analysis of the concordances in the corpus and UK pages on the Internet shows that the difference has to be seen in terms of the nature of the result. The suffix *-ce* focuses on an instance of the result, used in a specific, definite or clear-cut context. In the light of this, the suffix *-ce* can be defined as 'the specific result labelled in the verbal root'. An instance is thought of as having a particular location in the domain of instantiation. As evidence, nouns ending in *-ce* are preceded by verbs denoting preservation or distribution and adjectives describing essence or effect, and are followed by nouns referring to physical objects.

By comparison, the suffix *-ment* focuses on a type of the result, used in a general, vague, or approximate context. A type specifies the basis for identifying various entities as being representatives of the same class, but is not tied to any particular instance of that class. In the light of this, the suffix *-ment* can be defined as 'the general result labelled in the verbal root'. As evidence, nouns ending in *-ment* are preceded by verbs denoting consideration or provision and adjectives describing quality or degree, and are followed by nouns referring to vocal objects. A collection of examples will help expound the distinction:

(4)   deterrence vs determent

    a. Heavy weapons maintain deterrence in the face of a threat.
    b. They consider tougher measures as a determent to truancy.

The two nouns under (4) involve the verbal root *deter*, which means 'to prevent from action by fear of consequences, or difficulty or risk'. Yet, each represents a particular construal, and so has a different use. In (4a), the noun *deterence* means 'the specific result of deterring'. Deterence is a means of preventing war by using weapons as a threat to people who might be enemies. It is used especially in criminal law and military contexts. It is preceded by verbs like *create, guarantee, maintain, require, select*; modified by adjectives like *absolute, dynamic, effective, massive, strategic*; and followed by nouns like *burglary, entry, nuclear, smoking, theft*, etc. In (4b), the noun *determent* means 'the general result of deterring'. Determent is a means of preventing something from happening. It is preceded by verbs like *consider, constitute, discuss, enhance, stimulate*; modified by adjectives like *basic, main, major, potential, primary*; and followed by nouns like *devices, methods, policy, steps, tactics*, etc.

(5) governance vs government

    a. Effective governance is essential for achieving objectives.
    b. What a state like this needs is really a stable government.

The two nouns under (5) involve the verbal root *govern*, which means 'to control something personal or public'. Yet, each represents a particular construal, and so has a different use. In (5a), the noun *governance* means 'the specific result of governing'. *Governance* is a means of having control or influence over affairs, e.g. business. It is preceded by verbs like *build, design, enhance, improve, implement*; adjectives like *democratic, effective, good, innovative, wise*; and followed by nouns like *codes, ethics, guidelines, issues, principles*, etc. In (b), the noun *government* means 'the general result of governing'. *Government* is a means of controlling or directing a country or city. It is preceded by verbs like *establish, form, influence, rock, lobby*, adjectives like *central, federal, interim, local, stable*, and followed by nouns like *grants, loans, offices, resources, services*, etc.

(6) sustenance vs sustainment

    a. Rice was the basis of their daily sustenance.
    b. Fishing was the villagers' main sustainment.

The two nouns under (6) link to the verbal root *sustain*, which means 'to cause or allow something to continue for a period of time'. Yet, each represents a particular construal, and so has a different use. In (6a), the noun *sustenance* means 'the specific result of sustaining'. *Sustenance* is a means of providing people physical support, i.e. food or liquid. It is preceded by verbs like *acquire, distribute, lack, procure, receive*; modified by adjectives like *daily, essential, poor, rich, scant*; and followed by nouns like *allowances, costs, expenses, productions, subscriptions*, etc. In (6b), the noun *sustainment* means 'the general result of sustaining'. *Sustainment* is a means of giving people mental or emotional support. It is preceded by verbs like *absorb, afford, consume, need, provide;* modified by adjectives like *basic, external, important, main, substantial;* and followed by nouns like *issues, plans, programmes, strategies, technologies,* etc.

2.4.3 The sequential–instance distinction: *-al* vs *-ce*

Both suffixes belong to the domain of *process*. The similarity ends there, for each represents a different aspect of it. The suffix *-al* means 'the successive act named by the verbal root'. Corpus concordances indicate that nouns ending in *-al* are preceded by verbs denoting obtainment or requirement, modified by adjectives describing phases or stages in a process, and followed by nouns referring to people or commodities. The suffix *-ce* means 'the specific result labelled in the verbal root'. Corpus concordances indicate that nouns ending in *-ce* are preceded by verbs denoting sending or issuing something, modified by adjectives describing quality or character, and followed by nouns referring to things or function. A set of examples will help to interpret the distinction:

(7) acquittal vs acquittance

    a. The acquittal of the presenter cheered all TV viewers.
    b. They sent him an acquittance upon paying their debts.

The two nouns under (7) contain the verbal root *acquit*, which means 'to discharge someone in a court of a crime or a debt'. Nevertheless, each noun symbolises a certain construal, and so has its individual sense. In (7a), the noun *acquittal* means 'the successive act of acquitting'. *Acquittal* is discharging someone of a debt or other liability after a trial. It is preceded by verbs like *obtain, gain, lead to, result in, secure;* modified by adjectives like *complete, formal, full, initial, official;* and followed by nouns referring to people, such as *defendant, journalist, officer, presenter, suspect,* etc. In (7b), the noun *acquittance* means 'the specific result of acquitting'. *Acquittance* is a legal document evidencing the discharge of a debt or obligation. This is reflected by the collocates of the noun. It is preceded by verbs like *give out an, send somebody an, sign;* modified by adjectives like *counterfeited, forged, genuine, sealed, true;* and followed by nouns referring to things discharged, such as *crime, debt, obligation, trespass, violation,* etc.

(8) referral vs reference

>   a. The practitioner gave the patient a referral to a specialist.
>   b. If the specialist refuses to act, the reference is at an end.

The two nouns under (8) involve the verbal root *refer*, which means 'to direct someone or something to a different place or person for information, help or action'. Nevertheless, each noun symbolises a certain construal, and so has its individual sense. In (8a), the noun *referral* means 'the successive act of referring'. *Referral* is sending an individual, especially a patient, to an expert for advice or a specialist for treatment. It is preceded by verbs like *make, provide, receive, require, warrant*; modified by adjectives like *initial, lengthy, proposed, urgent, voluntary*; and followed by nouns like *dietician, chiropodist, health professional, practitioner, specialist*, etc. In (8b), the noun *reference* means 'the specific result of referring'. *Reference* is an official document whereby something is submitted to some authority for consideration, decision, or settlement. It is preceded by verbs like *endorse, make, provide, quote, receive*; modified by adjectives like *easy, general, particular, scant, special*; and followed by nouns like *copy, guide, material, number, source*, etc.

(9) transferral vs transference

>   a. He inspects the transferral of the cargo onto the vessel.
>   b. The envoy observed the smooth transference of power.

The two nouns under (9) embrace the verbal root *transfer*, which means 'to move someone or something from one place to another'. Nevertheless, each noun symbolises a certain construal, and so has its individual sense. In (9a), the noun *transferral* means 'the successive act of transferring'. *Transferral* is transporting something from one location to another. It is preceded by verbs like *arrange, inspect, request, start, undergo*; modified by adjectives like *accurate, complete, direct, immediate, initial*; and followed by nouns referring to commodities dealt with in the stock market or stationery items. In (9b), the noun *transference* means 'the specific result of transferring'. *Transference* is a legal transmission of something from one person or place to another. It is preceded by verbs like *control, make, monitor, observe, oversee*; modified by adjectives like *annual, efficient, genuine, radical, simple*; and followed by nouns like *authority, energy, power, ownership, responsibility*, etc.

2.4.4 The sequential–type distinction: -al vs -ment

Both suffixes evoke the domain of *process*. Yet, each focuses on a different aspect of it. The suffix *-al* refers to 'the successive act named by the verbal root', picturing the action as a series of things following one another consecutively. Collocates of nouns ending in *-al* include verbs denoting performance or obtainment, adjectives describing process, and nouns referring to people or their actions. The suffix *-ment* refers to 'the general result labelled in the verbal root', picturing the result as something approximate. Collocates of nouns ending in *-ment* include verbs denoting demonstration or confirmation, adjectives describing type, and nouns referring to vocal objects. A batch of examples will help to clarify the distinction.

(10) appraisal vs appraisement

    a. The critic prepared a critical appraisal of the poet's literary works.
    b. The assessor conducted an appraisement of the company's assets.

The two nouns under (10) contain the verbal root *appraise*, which means 'to judge the quality, success, or needs of someone or something'. Nonetheless, a difference in construal gives each its own mission to carry out in the language. In (10a), the noun appraisal means 'the successive act of appraising'. *Appraisal* is judging or valuing something. It is preceded by verbs like *compose, draw up, formulate, prepare, write up*; modified by adjectives like *brief, critical, detailed, serious, thorough*; and followed by nouns like *performance, project, proposal, research, work*, etc. In (10b), the noun *appraisement* means 'the general result of appraising'. *Appraisement* is the judgement or valuation arrived at by an appraiser. It is preceded by verbs like *conduct, give, offer, make, propose*; modified by adjectives like *compulsory, independent, judicial, technical, unfair*; and followed by nouns like *assets, estates, liabilities, possessions, riches*, etc.

(11) committal vs commitment

    a. She articulates her strong committal to world peace.
    b. She reaffirmed her commitment to the new concern.

The two nouns under (11) involve the verbal root *commit*, which means 'to promise to give oneself, one's money, one's time, etc. to support something'. Nonetheless, a difference in construal gives each its own mission to carry out in the language. In (11a), the noun *committal* means 'the successive act of committing'. *Committal* is pledging oneself to a particular course of conduct, or a particular view or position. It is preceded by verbs like *articulate, discharge, draw up, seal, sign*; modified by adjectives like *brief, impeccable, strong, summary, suspended*; and followed by nouns like *application, hearing, order, proceedings, warrant,* etc. When it means sending someone to prison, it collocates with nouns such as *hearing, order, proceedings, report, warrant,* as in *The magistrate made a committal order in due time.* In (11b), the noun *commitment* means 'the general result of committing'. *Commitment* is the promise made by someone to do something, or to something one believes in. It is preceded by verbs like *demonstrate, display, make, reaffirm, show*; modified by adjectives like *complete, firm, great, long, real*; and followed by nouns like *economic recovery, environment, power sharing, soccer, social order,* etc.

(12) deferral vs deferment

> a. The deferral of a decision will have grave consequences.
> b. He received a three-year deferment from military service.

The two nouns under (12) embody the verbal root *defer*, which means 'to delay something until a later time'. Nonetheless, a difference in construal gives each its own mission to carry out in the language. In (12a), the noun *deferral* means 'the successive act of deferring'. *Deferral* is postponing or delaying or putting off something to a future time. It is preceded by verbs like *consider, extend, grant, issue, offer*; modified by adjectives like *constant, indefinite, long-term, perpetual, routine*; and followed by nouns like *decision, marriage, payment,* etc. In (12b), the noun *deferment* means 'the general result of deferring'. *Deferment* is the postponement of something which is supposed to happen later in time or date. It is preceded by verbs like *apply for, deliver, grant, issue, secure*; modified by adjectives like *appropriate, long-term, proposed, temporary, typical*; and followed by nouns like *aid, debt, fee, loan, service,* etc.

2.4.5 The whole–instance distinction: *-ion* vs *-ce*

Both suffixes embody the domain of *process*. All the same, each signifies a different aspect of it. The suffix *-ion* means 'the overall act named by the verbal root'. Concordance listings show that nouns ending in *-ion* most often collocate with verbs denoting establishment or obtainment, adjectives describing class, and nouns referring to a physical entity. The suffix -*ce* means 'the specific result labelled in the verbal root'. Concordance listings show that nouns ending in -*ce* most often collocate with verbs denoting practising or confirmation, adjectives describing degree or quality, and nouns referring to an abstract entity. A selection of examples will help to explain the distinction:

(13) domination vs dominance

    a. The team maintained its domination of the football league.
    b. They achieved dominance by skill, foresight and industry.

The two nouns under (13) relate to the verbal root *dominate*, which means 'to have control over a place or a person'. Even so, each noun has a construal that provides a solution to its individual use. In (13a), the noun *domination* means 'the overall act of dominating'. *Domination* is the action of controlling or ruling over something. It is preceded by verbs like *be free from/of, come under, establish, fall under, maintain, seek*; modified by adjectives like *class, colonial, economic, imperial, political*; and followed by nouns like *conference, league, party, relationship, world*, etc. In (13b), the noun *dominance* means 'the specific result of dominating'. *Dominance* is the control or power that one has over a person, place, or group. It is preceded by verbs such as *achieve, confirm, exercise, foster, retain*; modified by adjectives such as *clear, overwhelming, growing, increasing, total*; and followed by nouns such as *art, news media, painting, political interests, spoken language*, etc.[5]

(14) observation vs observance

    a. The doctors are keeping the patient under close observation.
    b. They took measures to secure strict observance of the laws.

The two nouns under (14) encompass the verbal root *observe*, which means 'to obey a law or rule, celebrate a holiday or religious event, or watch something or someone carefully'. Even so, each noun has a construal that provides a solution to its individual use. In (14a), the noun *observation* means 'the overall act of observing'. *Observation* is carefully watching somebody or something. It is preceded by verbs like *carry out, do, make, permit, trigger*; modified by adjectives like *clinical, close, direct, empirical, psychological* and nouns like *classroom, participant*; and followed by nouns such *carriage, cell, coaches, post*, etc. In (14b), the noun *observance* means 'the specific result of observing'. *Observance* is the compliance with a customs, rules, or laws; or the adherence to a practice, rite, or ceremony. It is preceded by verbs like *enforce, ensure, foster, practise, secure*; modified by adjectives like *austere, close, faithful, rigid, strict*; and followed by nouns like *custom, feast, law, Memorial Day, national holiday*, etc.

(15) toleration vs tolerance

    a. The toleration of the drug is beyond imagination.
    b. He preaches tolerance, compassion and patience.

The two nouns under (15) contain the verbal root *tolerate*, which means 'to accept behaviour and beliefs that are different from one's own, or to bear something unpleasant or annoying'. Even so, each noun has a construal that provides a solution to its individual use. (15a), the noun *toleration* means 'the overall act of tolerating'. *Toleration* is enduring pain or hardship. It is the key to modern empirical science. It is preceded by verbs like *contain, encourage, inhibit, oppose to, permit*; modified by adjectives like *dangerous, grudging, limited, popular, quiet*; and followed by nouns like *drug, means, noise, tourists, traveller*, etc. In (15b), the noun *tolerance* means 'the specific result of tolerating'. *Tolerance* is the acceptance of the different views, beliefs or practices of others. It expresses reverence for tradition. It is preceded by verbs such as *have, exercise, lack, practise, show*; modified by adjectives such as *mere, political, racial, religious, social*; and followed by nouns such as *aggressive behaviour, errors, opinion, practices, sexual behaviour*, etc.[6]

2.4.6   The whole–type distinction: *-ion* vs *-ment*

Both suffixes signal the domain of *process*. Each suffix, however, selects a different aspect of it. The suffix *-ion* focuses on the entirety of an action. It means 'the overall act named by the verbal root'. Concordance lines indicate that nouns ending in *-ion* commonly collocate with verbs denoting giving or stopping something, adjectives describing class, and nouns referring to technical terms. The suffix *-ment* focuses on the specificity of a result. It means 'the general result labelled in the verbal root'. Concordance lines indicate that nouns ending in *-ment* commonly collocate with verbs denoting communication or enjoyment, adjectives describing quality, and nouns referring to ordinary terms. A selection of examples will help to define the distinction:

(16) excitation vs excitement

> a. The excitation of the nerve is accomplished by tiny electrical charges.
> b. There was great excitement abroad when the riveting news came out.

The two nouns under (16) are derived from the verb *excite*, which means 'to make someone have strong feelings of happiness and enthusiasm'. Still, each noun is distinct in construal, and so has a distinct role to play in the language. In (16a), the noun *excitation* means 'the overall act of exciting'. *Excitation* refers to the act of rousing up or awakening, or putting in motion. It is preceded by verbs like *cause, discharge, produce, transmit, trigger*; modified by adjectives like *electrical, electronic, molecular, physical, sexual, wave*; and followed by nouns like *coil, filter, nerve, pulse, spectrum*, etc. In (16b), the noun *excitement* means 'the general result of exciting'. *Excitement* is a motive or an incentive that stirs or induces action. It is preceded by verbs like *communicate, discover, enjoy, experience, share*; modified by adjectives like *breathless, great, intense, new, pure*; and followed by nouns like *Christmas, development, event, media, rehearsal* and expressions like *a quiver of, an amount of, a sense of, a feeling of, a surge of, a bit of, a whoop of*, etc.

(17) medication vs medicament

> a. The patient is currently on medication for his heart.
> b. The doctor gave the patient a powerful medicament.

The two nouns under (17) subsume the verbal root *medicate*, which means 'to treat someone with a medicine', but they are not alike in use. Still, each noun is distinct in construal, and so has a distinct role to play in the language. In (17a), the noun *medication* means 'the overall act of medicating'. *Medication* is treating medically. It is preceded by verbs like *give, need, receive, stop, take*; modified by adjectives like *heavy, mild, prescribed, regular, safe*; and followed by nouns such as *abuse, information, practice, programme, regulation*, etc. In (17b), the noun *medicament* means 'the general result of medicating'. *Medicament* is a substance or a medicine used to heal ailment, or promote recovery from injury. Concordance lines show that it is preceded by verbs such as *check, drink, give, swallow, use*; modified by adjectives such as *effective, new, powerful, useful, vital*; and followed by nouns such as *consumption, distribution, preparation, prescription, technology*, etc.[7]

(18) reconciliation vs reconcilement

> a. There seemed little hope of reconciliation between the two parties.
> b. What happens if the warring parties fail to reach a reconcile-ment?

The two nouns under (18) embody the verbal root *reconcile*, which means 'to find a way in which two situations or beliefs that are opposed to each other can agree and exist together'. Still, each noun is distinct in construal, and so has a distinct role to play in the language. In (18a), the noun *reconciliation* means 'the overall act of reconciling'. *Reconciliation* is the ending of conflict or renewal of friendship between disputing people. It is preceded by verbs like *achieve, bring about, call for, hinder, promote*; modified by adjectives like *full, lasting, personal, political, royal*; and followed by nouns like *conference, forum, policy, process, talk*, etc. In (18b), the noun *reconcilement* means 'the general result of reconciling'. *Reconcilement* is an agreement or a deal reached between two parties. It is preceded by verbs like *establish, make, obtain, prepare, reach*; modified by adjectives like *easy, full, internal, national, partial*; and followed by nouns like *account, deposit, fund, interest, payment*, etc.[8]

2.5   Summary

In this chapter, the intention has been to provide semantic interpretations for complex nouns derived from verbal roots. To do so, I substantiated three arguments against data offered in the British National Corpus and Internet pages. In section 2.2, I argued that de-verbal nominal suffixes form a category, where their multiple senses are organised around a primary sense from which all the additional senses are derived via semantic extensions. In section 2.3, I argued that de-verbal nominal suffixes gather in a domain, in which they interact but differ in projecting different parts of it. In section 2.4, I argued that a suffix pair standing as rivals is by no means in complementary distribution, and the nouns they form are not in free variation. The distinction between the noun pair is not only governed by phonological and/or morphological constraints, but also ascribed to meaning. Precisely, the distinction resides in the alternative ways the noun pair is construed, which is realised by different suffixes. In each derivation, the suffix shifts the meaning of the root to a certain direction, and so reflects the intended construal. The semantic contrast is evidenced by the distinguishing collocates of each pair member, which corpus data show. In Cognitive Semantics, a morphological or lexical structure is to a significant degree a response to a conceptual structure.

Notes

1. The term *valence* is taken from chemistry, where it refers to the combining properties of atoms. In linguistics, it refers to the mechanism whereby two component units combine to form a composite unit.
2. The term *profile determinant* in the cognitive model is described as *head* in the formal model. In both models, the term lends its features to the phrase that contains it. The difference is that in the formal model the features are defined in grammatical terms like verb or noun, whereas in the cognitive model they are defined in semantic terms like process or thing. In both models, the relationship between the components of a phrase is described in terms of dependence. The difference is that in the formal model *dependence* relates to categorial selection, whereas in the cognitive model it relates to conceptual processing. A further difference relates to the term *constituency*. In the formal model, *constituency* emerges from 'words and rules', whereas in the cognitive model it emerges from properties of constructions.
3. The relevance of the *category* theory to morphology has in fact been pointed out by some cognitive morphoplogists like Bybee & Moder (1983), Bybee (1988), Ryder (1991, 1999), and Panther & Thornburg (2002), among others.
4. The same distinction applies to other pairs ending in *-al* vs *-ion*, such as *accusal/accusation, deprival/deprivation, proposal/proposition*, etc. Let us explain one pair. Both *deprival* and *deprivation* are derived from the verb *deprive*, which means 'to take something, especially something necessary or pleasant, away from someone'. Yet, they differ in their use. In *The sanctions shouldn't amount to the deprival of liberty*, the noun *deprival* means 'the successive act of depriving'. *Deprival* is the action of denying someone the freedom to live as you wish or go where you want. In *They used sleep deprivation as a form of torture*, the noun *deprivation* means 'the overall act of depriving'. *Deprivation* is the action of preventing someone from having things that are necessary for a pleasant life.
5. The same distinction applies to other pairs ending in *-ion* vs *-ce*, such as *acceptation/acceptance, adhesion/adherence, admission/admittance, affirmation/affirmance, cohesion/coherence, continuation/continuance, deviation/deviance, pretension/pretence, variation/variance*, etc. Let us explain one pair. Both *adhesion* and *adherence* are derived from the verb *adhere*, which means 'to stick firmly'. Yet, they differ in their use. In *This material has amazing adhesion to almost any surface*, the noun *adhesion* means 'the overall act of adhering'. *Adhesion* is the action of sticking. In *He was noted for his strict adherence to the*

rules, the noun *adherence* means 'the specific result of adhering'. *Adherence* is obeying a rule or maintaining a belief.

6. In this study, the noun pairs spark interaction between suffixes belonging to the same domain. Some noun pairs, however, spark interaction between suffixes belonging to different domains for their explanation. This is in line with the cognitive principle that the meanings of expressions can evoke different domains for their interpretation. For instance, the de-verbal suffix *-ion* evokes the domain of *process* (action), whereas the de-adjectival suffix *-cy* evokes the domain of *characterisation* (status). The two nouns *confederation* and *confederacy* pertain to *confederate*, but each picks up a different aspect of its meaning. In *The confederation of the six states took place in 1930*, the noun *confederation* means the act of forming a confederation. *Confederation* is the action of banding together a number of entities in a block or union. In *This confederacy consists of six states*, the noun *confederacy* means the status of being tied together. *Confederacy* is a union of entities which have combined together for a particular purpose, usually related to politics or trade.

7. The same distinction applies to other pairs ending in *-ion* vs *-ment* such as *abolition/abolishment, acquisition/acquirement, admonition/admonishment, assignation/assignment, incitation/incitement, pronunciation/pronouncement, requisition/requirement*, etc. Both *incitation* and *incitement* are derived from the verb *incite*, which means 'to encourage someone to do or feel something unpleasant or violent'. Yet, they differ in their use. In *He was charged with incitation of the students to riot*, the noun *incitation* means 'the overall act of inciting'. *Incitation* is stirring up feelings, or instigating action, especially military or violence. In *The claim could be an incitement to racial hatred*, the noun *incitement* means 'the general result of inciting'. *Incitement* is an impulse or a stimulus that provokes action or incites the mind.

8. In some noun pairs, the suffix *-ion* stands in contrast to the suffix *-ure*, as in *composition* vs *composure, creation* vs *creature, fixation* vs *fixture, exposition* vs *exposure, indention* vs *indenture, legislation* vs *legislature*, etc. For instance, the suffix *-ion* evokes the domain of *process* (action), whereas the suffix *-ure* evokes the domain of *entity* (abstract or concrete). The two nouns *legislation* and *legislature* pertain to *legislate*, but they manifest different meanings. In *Legislation will be difficult and will take time*, the noun *legislation* refers to the act of making and passing laws. *Legislation* is the act of law set up by one of the legislatures. In *It is a democratically elected legislature*, the noun *legislature* refers to a group of people who have the power to make and change laws. *Legislature* is the body which drafts and approves the laws of a country or state.

3
De-Adjectival Nominalisers

In this chapter, I turn to the semantics of de-adjectival nominalisers. More specifically, I deal with the meanings of morphemes and how they combine to form nouns. During the investigation, I explore three tenets of Cognitive Semantics on de-adjectival nominalisations. To that end, I structure the chapter as follows. In section 3.1, I say what a de-adjectival suffix is and enumerate the mechanisms that condition its integration with a root to form a noun. In section 3.2, I argue that a de-adjectival suffix is polysemous and its multiple senses gather around a prototype. In section 3.3, I argue that to reveal the subtle differences in meaning between nominal suffixes, it is necessary to organise them into domains in which they stand as rivals. In section 3.4, I argue that the members of a noun pair differ in terms of the different construals the speaker imposes on their common root. To show non-synonymy, I resort to the distinctive collocates associated with the members of the pair. This is done by examining actual data offered in the corpus. In section 3.5, I recapitulate the key points of the chapter.

3.1 Introduction

A de-adjectival suffix is a word-final element that is added to an adjective to form a noun. It is a bound morpheme because it does not occur alone; it needs to be integrated with a free morpheme. To form a composite structure, the two morphemes should exhibit what Langacker (1987: 277–327) calls valence relations. First, the two morphemes should exhibit correspondence in semantic and phonological specifications. Second, they should exhibit difference in dependence. The free morpheme qualifies as autonomous, whereas the bound morpheme qualifies as dependent. Third, they should exhibit difference in determinacy. The bound morpheme acts as a profile determinant and so lends its character to the entire structure. As a categorial marker, it changes a lexical item from one class into another. As a meaning marker, it causes a shift of a kind in the semantic structure of the root, and so adds a special meaning to the derived formation. Fourth, they should exhibit difference in function. The bound morpheme functions as the head, while the free morpheme functions as the complement in the structure. In some derivational cases, the root undergoes a phonetic change, as in *absence* from *absent*, whereas in others it preserves its phonetic shape, as in *captaincy* from *captain*.

3.2 Semantic networks

In this section, I turn to the question of the *category* theory in morpho-lexicology. The aim is to describe the semantic network of a de-adjectival suffix. A de-adjectival suffix, I argue, is associated with a range of distinct senses. Some senses are regarded as better examples of the category than others. The sense that is the best example of the category is the *prototype*, whereas the other senses are the *periphery*. The *prototype* is the sense that has the key properties of the category. It is the sense that comes to mind first or is the easiest to recall. The peripheral senses are linked to the prototype by a set of semantic principles. To put it differently, the *prototype* gives rise to a variety of peripheral senses. The peripheral senses have some, but not all, of the properties of the category. Like members of a family, the peripheral senses share the general properties of the category, but they differ in specific details. *Category* refers to a cognitive ability which organises the different senses of a given structure in the mind, and shows how they are related to one another.

To account for the multiple senses of a de-adjectival suffix and capture its semantic characteristics, I propose the two semantic features of quality and quantity. Let me demonstrate the model by giving an example of the suffix *-ce*. The suffix *-ce* combines with an adjectival root to form a noun. Prototypically, the suffix *-ce* is attached to adjectival roots denoting quality to form abstract nouns, as in *absence*. *Absence* is the state of being absent. One step removed from the prototype is the case where the suffix is attached to adjectival roots denoting quantity to form abstract nouns, as in *abundance*. *Abundance* is an amount of something that is large in size, Peripherally, the suffix *-ce* is attached to verbal roots denoting action to form abstract nouns, as in *preference*. *Preference* is the act of liking someone or something more than another, or the act of selecting someone or something over another.

In what follows, I give synchronic descriptions of the de-adjectival nominalisers in English.

3.2.1 *-ce*

The suffix *-ce* attaches productively to roots ending in *-ant* or *-ent*. Prototypically, the suffix *-ce* is added to adjectives originally ending in *-ant* or *-ent* to form nouns. Relative to the nature of the combining root, the suffix expresses the following senses:

a. 'the state indicated by the adjectival root'. This sense emerges when the suffix is attached to qualitative adjectives to form abstract nouns. Some adjectival roots apply to humans. For example, *brilliance* is the state of being brilliant, *ignorance* is the state of being ignorant, and *vigilance* is the state of being vigilant. Other adjectival roots apply to non-humans. For example, *fragrance* is the state of being fragrant, *repugnance* is the state of being repugnant, and *significance* is the state of being significant. Examples of nouns in *-ce* attached to adjectives ending in *-ent* are *absence, confidence, diligence, eloquence, negligence, obedience, presence, violence,* etc.
b. 'the amount indicated by the adjectival root'. This sense develops when the suffix is attached to quantitative adjectives to form abstract nouns. For example, *abundance* is an amount of something that is large in size, *affluence* is an amount of something that is great in quantity, *exuberance* is an amount of something that is excessive in degree, and *luxuriance* is an amount of something that is rich in extent.
c. 'the thing indicated by the adjectival root'. This sense comes out when the suffix is attached to qualitative adjectives to form concrete nouns. For example, *protuberance* is a rounded part that sticks out from the surface of something.

Peripherally, the suffix *-ce* is added to verbs to form nouns, whose adjectives end in *-ant* or *-ent*. In this sense, the suffix expresses 'the act of doing the process indicated by the verbal root'. The verbal root can vary in terms of transitivity.

a. In some formations, the root is transitive. For example, *defiance* is the act of defying a ban, and *observance* is the act of observing something. An example of a noun in *-ce* attached to an adjective ending in *-ent* is *transcendence*, which is the act of going beyond the limits. *Preference*, from *prefer*, is the act of selecting someone or something over another. *Transference*, from *transfer*, is the act of moving someone or something from one place to another.

b. In other formations, the root is both transitive and intransitive. For example, *assistance* is the act of giving help, *insurance* is the act of protecting oneself against risks, and *resistance* is the act of opposing something. An example of a noun in *-ce* attached to an adjective ending in *-ent* is *indulgence*, which is the act of allowing oneself or someone else to have something enjoyable. *Defence*, from *defend*, is the act of resisting attack.

c. In further formations, the root is intransitive. For example, *appearance* is the act of appearing in public, *compliance* is the act of obeying an order, rule or request, and *forbearance* is the act of showing self-control in a difficult situation. Examples of nouns in *-ce* attached to adjectives ending in *-ent* include *adherence, convergence, divergence, dependence, emergence, insistence, persistence, residence*, etc. For example, *divergence* is the act of following a different direction.

A graphical representation of the multiple senses of the de-adjectival suffix *-ce* is offered in Figure 3.1. Note that the solid arrow represents the prototypical sense, whereas the dashed arrows represent the semantic extensions.

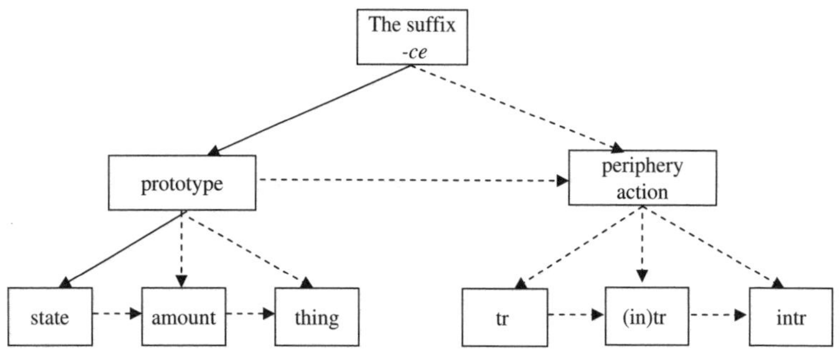

Figure 3.1 The semantic network of the de-adjectival suffix *-ce*

3.2.2 *-cy*

The suffix *-cy* attaches productively to roots ending in *-ant* or *-ent*. Prototypically, the suffix is attached to adjectives to form nouns. Relative to the nature of the joining root, the suffix signifies the following nuances:

a. 'the state indicated by the adjectival root'. This sense is present when the suffix is attached to qualitative adjectives to form mass nouns.

Some adjectival roots apply to humans. For example, *complacency* is the state of being complacent, *fluency* is the state of being fluent, and *hesitancy* is the state of being hesitant. Other adjectival roots apply to non-humans. For example, *frequency* is the state of being frequent, *poignancy* is the state of being poignant, and *potency* is the state of being potent.

b. 'an example of the state indicated by the adjectival root'. More precisely, the suffix refers to the status that an entity reaches. This sense is present when the suffix is attached to qualitative adjectives to form countable nouns. For example, *a dependency* is a country that is controlled by another country, *an emergency* is something dangerous that arises suddenly, and *a transparency* is a small piece of photographic film with a frame around it which can be projected onto a screen so that you can see the picture.

c. 'a period of time indicated by the adjectival root'. This sense holds when the suffix is attached to classifying adjectives. The resultant derivatives are either abstract or concrete. For example, *infancy* is the period of time when one is a very young child, and *pregnancy* is the period of time during which a woman is pregnant.

Peripherally, the suffix *-cy* is attached to other roots to form nouns. Relative to the nature of the root, the suffix displays the following nuances:

a. 'the practice, rank, job, or office indicated by the nominal root'. This sense arises when the suffix is attached to roots denoting common nouns. For example, *accountancy* is the practice of being an accountant; *captaincy*, from *captain*, is the rank of being captain; *a consultancy* is a company that give expert advice on a particular subject, and *presidency* is the job of being president.

b. 'the act of doing the process indicated by the verbal root'. This sense arises when the suffix is attached to verbal roots. For example, *advocacy*, from *advocate*, is the act of advocating; *prophecy*, from *prophesy*, is the act of foretelling the future; and *residency* is the act of living in a place.

A graphical representation of the multiple senses of the de-adjectival suffix *-cy* is offered in Figure 3.2. Note that the solid arrow represents the prototypical sense, whereas the dashed arrows represent the semantic extensions.

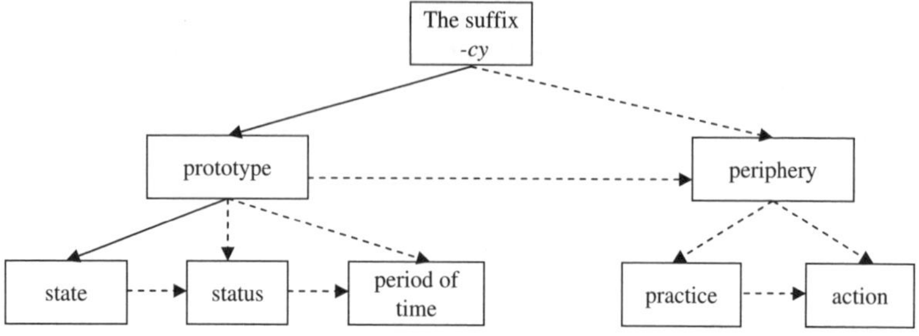

Figure 3.2 The semantic network of the de-adjectival suffix *-cy*

3.2.3 *-ity*

Prototypically, the suffix *-ity* is annexed to adjectives to form abstract nouns. Based on the nature of the combining root, the suffix expresses the following meanings:

a. 'the quality or property designated by the adjectival root'. This sense holds when the suffix is attached to qualitative adjectives to form abstract nouns. Some adjectival roots apply to humans. For example, *agility* is the quality of being agile, *creativity* is the quality of being creative, and *generosity* is the quality of being generous. Other adjectival roots apply to non-humans. For example, *diversity* is the property of being diverse, *intensity* is the property of being intense, and *simplicity* is the property of being simple.

b. 'the mode of dealing with the situation designated by the adjectival root'. This sense holds when the suffix is attached to qualitative adjectives to form abstract nouns. For example, *brutality* is the mode of being brutal, *hostility* is the mode of being hostile, and *sensitivity* is the mode of being sensitive.

c. 'the entity described by the adjectival root'. This sense holds when the suffix is attached to qualitative adjectives to form concrete nouns. Some linguists consider these nouns lexicalised forms. For example *oddity* is a person or thing that is unusual, *rarity* is a person or thing that is likely to be valuable, and *reality* is a thing that exists.

Peripherally, the suffix *-ity* is added to other roots to form nouns. In this sense, the suffix expresses 'the fact of being what the root describes'. Some roots are verbal. For example *prosperity* is the fact of being prosperous. Some roots are nominal. For example, *paternity* is the fact of being a father.

A graphical representation of the multiple senses of the de-adjectival suffix *-ity* is offered in Figure 3.3. Note that the solid arrow represents the prototypical sense, whereas the dashed arrows represent the semantic extensions.

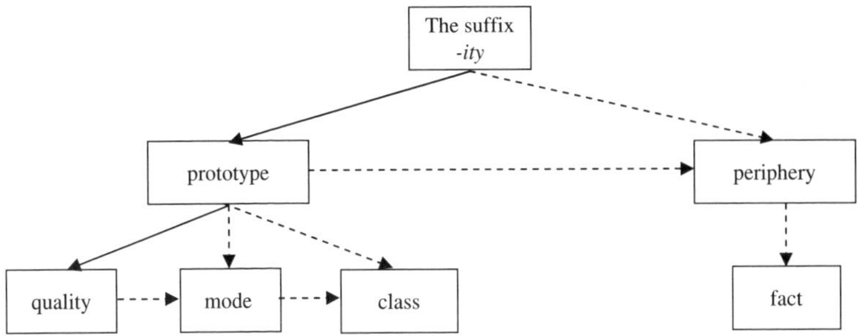

Figure 3.3 The semantic network of the de-adjectival suffix *-ity*

3.2.4 *-ness*

Prototypically, the suffix *-ness* is tacked on to adjectives to form abstract nouns. Based on the nature of the joining root, the suffix denotes the following senses:

a. 'the trait denoted by the adjectival root'. This sense arises when the suffix is attached to qualitative adjectives applying to humans. The resultant derivatives are abstract. For example, *awareness* is the trait of being aware, *boldness* is the trait of being bold, and *gentleness* is the trait of being gentle.
b. 'the property denoted by the adjectival root'. This sense arises when the suffix is attached to qualitative adjectives applying to non-humans. The resultant derivatives are abstract. For example, *awkwardness* is the property of being awkward, *brightness* is the property of being bright, and *emptiness* is the property of being empty. Some adjectival roots apply to both humans and non-humans. For example, *greatness* is the attribute of being great, *quietness* is the attribute of being quiet, and *toughness* is the attribute of being tough.
c. 'an instance or example of the quality denoted by the adjectival root'. The resultant derivatives are countable. For example, *an illness* is an instance of being ill, *a kindness* is an example of being kind, and *a sickness* is an instance of being sick.

Peripherally, the suffix *-ness* sheds light on 'the characteristic denoted by the adjectival root'. This sense arises when the suffix is attached to classifying adjectives applying to humans. The resultant derivatives are uncountable. For example, *blindness* is the inability to see, *dumbness* is the inability to speak, and *deafness* is the inability to hear.

A graphical representation of the multiple senses of the de-adjectival suffix *-ness* is offered in Figure 3.4. Note that the solid arrow represents the prototypical sense, whereas the dashed arrows represent the semantic extensions.

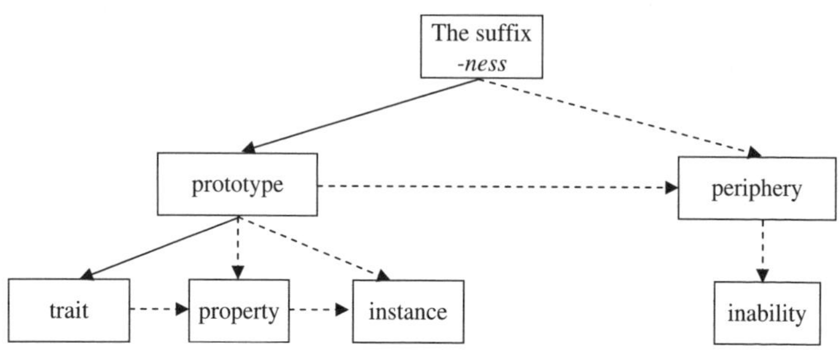

Figure 3.4　The semantic network of the de-adjectival suffix *-ness*

Before going any further, let us draw some conclusions from the preceding discussion about the suffixes. One conclusion is that each suffix forms a category of its own, which includes its multiple senses. Another conclusion is that the senses of a suffix gather around one representative sense, referred to as the *prototype*. A further conclusion is that the category of a suffix is a powerful conceptual framework which allows us to see how the different senses are related to one another. A look at the categorial descriptions of the suffixes shows where the senses converge and where they diverge. On the basis of the converging senses, the suffixes can be grouped into sets, referred to as *domains*. It is within these domains that the suffixes can stand against each other as rivals. So, a *domain* is concerned with a knowledge configuration in which suffixes gather showing similarity on the surface but dissimilarity below the surface. Two suffixes may stand for one concept but differ in the specifics. This cognitive tenet will be elaborated on in the next section.

3.3 Knowledge configurations

In this section, I turn to the question of the *domain* theory in morpho-lexicology. The aim is to characterise the meanings of de-adjectival suffixes. The meaning of a de-adjectival suffix, I argue, is best captured in terms of the domain in which it is positioned. A *domain* is a conceptual configuration which encodes knowledge about lexical items with special provision for the roles they play in language. De-adjectival suffixes are a collection of lexical items related in a way that to understand the meaning of one it is necessary to understand the domain in which it occurs as well as the meanings of the other participants. That is, the meaning of a suffix can be interpreted by setting it in contrast with the other participants of the domain. A *domain* is a context in which a number of lexical items are positioned, with each having a distinctive function. As an area of meaning, *domain* is important at two levels. At a general level, it groups together lexical items that are associated with one concept. At a specific level, it reveals the characteristic behaviour of each of the participating items.

Relating the *domain* theory to the present topic, I argue that de-adjectival nominalisers in English name, relative to their definitional analyses, things in the cognitive domain of *characterisation*. *Characterisation* is an area of knowledge in which the character of an entity, animate or inanimate, is described. Characterising an entity incorporates two features: apparent and inherent. An *apparent feature* is one that is exposed to sight or open to view, or one that is readily felt or clearly understood. Morphologically, an apparent feature is represented by the suffixes *-ce* and *-cy*. They differ, I argue, in that *-ce* denotes the state of being in which an entity is, whereas *-cy* denotes the status that the entity reaches. By contrast, an *inherent feature* is one that forms a permanent element of an entity, or one that exists as an essential constituent of it. Morphologically, an inherent feature is represented by the suffixes *-ness* and *-ity*. They differ, I argue, in that *-ness* denotes the trait that distinguishes an entity, whereas *-ity* denotes the mode in which the entity is carried out.

For easy reference, I summarise in Table 3.1, the (sub)domains evoked by de-adjectival suffixes in English.

Table 3.1 The (sub)domains evoked by de-adjectival suffixes in English

Domain	**Subdomains**	**Exponents**	**Meaning differences**
	Apparent features	*-ce*	denotes the state in which an entity is
		-cy	denotes the status which an entity reaches
Characterisation	Inherent features	*-ness*	denotes the trait distinguishing an entity
		-ity	denotes the mode distinguishing an entity

In Table 3.1, I show how the *domain* theory applies to the description of nominal suffixes in English. The description comprises four steps. In the first step, I place all the nominal suffixes under one domain, which I name *characterisation*. In the second step, I group the suffixes into two subdomains, which I name *apparent features* and *inherent features*. This is done relative to the definitions provided in the previous section. In the third step, I identify the suffixes that represent each subdomain. In the fourth step, I explain the rivalry between the suffixes by pinpointing the peculiarity of each suffix which makes it different from its counterpart. When and how to use a suffix is a matter decided by the speaker. The choice of the speaker comes under the rubric of *construal*. *Construal* is concerned with the ways the speaker conceives a situation and the right expressions he chooses to realise them. Two suffixes that stand as rivals construe a situation in different ways. The elaboration of this cognitive tenet will be the task of the following section.

3.4   Conceptual distinctions

In this section, I turn to the question of the *construal* theory in morpho-lexicology. The aim is to define the factors that determine the choice between morpho-lexical alternatives. The choice of a derived noun, I argue, correlates with the particular construal imposed on its root. *Construal* refers to the way in which a speaker perceives a situation, interprets its meaning, and codes it in language. One of the basic cognitive capacities of the speaker of language is the ability to conceive a situation in alternative ways and use different linguistic structures to express them. Language provides the speaker with bountiful resources to draw on for matching alternative morpho-lexical constructions with alternative conceptualisations of a scene. Two expressions that have identical truth values are nonetheless distinct semantically. Distinct nuances of meaning can be expressed quite precisely through the choice of particular constructions. Meaning does not reflect objective reality, but rather is subjective in nature. Meaning incorporates conventional imagery, which are experientially based.

The choice between members of a noun pair is not only a matter of conceptual content, but also of the way the speaker construes it. The construal that is at the disposal of the speaker here is called *perspective*. According to Langacker (1990: 7), *perspective* refers to the viewpoint imposed on a scene which changes relative to one's intention or the requirement of the discourse. Two nouns may designate the same thing in the objective scene, but they encode information in two different ways and are therefore not synonymous. The difference resides in the different perspectives the speaker takes on the scene, which are morphologically mirrored by different suffixes. Two nouns may share a common root and so look similar. Nevertheless, they are by no means identical in meaning. Each noun represents a different experience of the speaker, who frames its linguistic form by means of a distinct morpheme. Each morpheme, therefore, highlights a different aspect of the meaning of the root. Consequently, the *perspective* taken on a scene and the linguistic form it assumes is a crucial factor in the choice.

Below are the different perspectives taken on the roots, which are responsible for the semantic distinctions.

3.4.1   The state–status distinction: *-ce vs -cy*

As mentioned earlier, the nominal suffixes *-ce* and *-cy* highlight apparent features of an entity, but they differ in meaning. In contemporary English, the difference is seen in terms of *state* vs *status*. State is a condition of being that exists at a particular time, as with regard to circumstances. It is a condition that an entity is in at a given moment, which is subject to change. Morphologically, *state* is realised by the nominal suffix *-ce*, which means 'being in the state labelled by the adjectival root'. Specifically, the suffix refers to the experience that someone or something undergoes. By contrast, *status* is the relative position or standing of an entity. It is the stage of development that an entity reaches relative to the surroundings. Morphologically, *status* is realised by the nominal suffix *-cy*, which means 'being in the status labelled by the adjectival root'. Specifically, the suffix refers to the rank that someone or something arrives at a certain stage, or an instance of it. Concomitant with the state–status distinction, there are, I argue, distinctions at morphological and collocational levels.[1]

Let us now delve into the corpus to support the argument. Derivatives in *-ce* are treated as abstract nouns. Predominantly, they cannot be counted, as in *two dependences*; do not take determiners, as in *a dependence*; and cannot be introduced by existential *there*, as in *there is dependence*. Such derivatives can be used in an expression like *in a state of* .... By contrast, derivatives in *-cy* are treated as concrete nouns. Predominantly, they can be counted, as in *two dependencies*; can take determiners, as in *a dependency*; and can be introduced by existential *there*, as in *there is dependency*. Such derivatives can be used in an expression like *in a ... stage*. As for their collocates, *-ce* derivatives are modified by adjectives denoting quality as in *total dependence*, and verbs denoting endurance, indication or protection. By contrast, *-cy* derivatives are modified by adjectives denoting nationality as in *British dependency*, quantity as in *major/minor dependency*, and verbs denoting acquisition, management, or termination. A discussion of some pairs will clarify the distinction:

(1) belligerence vs belligerency

    a. She could not fathom or sustain his open belligerence.
    b. The constitution renounces the belligerency of a state.

The two nouns under (1) are derived from the adjectival root *belligerent*, which means 'wishing to fight or argue'. In each case, however, the speaker construes the root differently, and so uses the nouns discriminately. In (1a), the noun *belligerence* means 'the state of being belligerent', warlike attitude or hostile nature. *Belligerence* is preceded by verbs like *approve, bear, stand, sustain, tolerate*; adjectives like *childish, open, sinful, vicious, wicked*; and followed by *of* plus nouns like *message, remark, response, style*, etc. In (1b), the noun *belligerency* means 'the status of being belligerent'. A belligerency is a country that is legally at war. *Belligerency* is preceded by verbs like *abandon, end, oppose to, renounce, terminate*; adjectives like *audacious, foolhardy, illegal, reckless, unlawful*; and adjectives of nationality, such as *Cuban, Indian, Korean, Portuguese, Sudanese*, etc.

(2) dependence vs dependency

    a. The country displays a growing dependence on foreign aid.
    b. In 1918, the islands formally became a British dependency.

The two nouns under (2) are derived from the adjectival root *dependent*, which means 'needing support in order to continue operating'. In each case, however, the speaker construes the root differently, and so uses the nouns discriminately. In (2a), the noun *dependence* means 'the state of being dependent', reliant. *Dependence* is preceded by verbs like *display, exhibit, have, manifest, show*; adjectives like *absolute, complete, growing, necessary, total*; fields of knowledge like *economical, financial, institutional, physical, psychological*; and followed by *on* plus nouns denoting objects or people, such as *charity, foreign aid, fossil fuels, mechanical strength, oil, parents*, etc. In (2b), the noun *dependency* means 'the status of being dependent'. A dependency is a country that is supported and governed by another country. *Dependency* is preceded by the verb *to be* or by linking verbs like *become, remain*; adjectives like *colonial, overseas, regional, self-governed, separate*; adjectives of nationality, such as *British, Danish, French, Japanese, Norwegian*; and followed by nouns like *concept, culture, programme, territory, theory*, etc.

(3) emergence vs emergency

    a. The last decade saw the emergence of a dynamic economy.
    b. Call this number if any unforeseen emergency should arise.

The two nouns under (3) are derived from the adjectival root *emergent*, which means 'to appear by coming out of something'. In each case, however, the speaker construes the root differently, and so uses the nouns discriminately. In (3a), the noun *emergence* means 'the state of being emergent', rising into view. *Emergence* is preceded by verbs like *indicate, mark, see, signal, witness*; adjectives like *abrupt, gradual, rapid, swift, sudden*; and followed by *of* and phrases like *dynamic economy, free trade, high speed train, professional consultants, single market*, etc. In (3b), the noun *emergency* means 'the status of being emergent'. An emergency is a dangerous accident, which happens suddenly or unexpectedly and needs immediate action in order to avoid harmful results. *Emergency* is preceded by verbs like *cope with, deal with, handle, respond to, take care of*; adjectives like *major, minor, serious, unexpected, unforeseen*; and followed by nouns denoting help like *aid, assistance, funds, relief, supply*; steps, such as *laws, legislation, measures, procedures, regulations*; or objects, such as *kit, medicine, tool, treatment centres, vehicles*, etc.

(4) insurgence vs insurgency

    a. Last year saw an incredible insurgence of political parties.
    b. Troops were called in to suppress the ethnic insurgency.

The two nouns under (4) are derived from the adjectival root *insurgent*, which means 'rebelling against an authority'. In each case, however, the speaker construes the root differently, and so uses the nouns discriminately. In (4a), the noun *insurgence* means 'the state of being insurgent', being in revolt. *Insurgence* is preceded by verbs like *attest, betoken, bespeak, see, testify* and adjectives like *absurd, extreme, incredible, radical, unthinkable*, etc. In (4b), the noun *insurgency* means 'the status of being insurgent'. An insurgency is an organised rebellion aimed at overthrowing a constituted government, through the use of subversion and armed conflict. *Insurgency* is preceded by verbs like *crush, launch, plot, quell, suppress*; adjectives like *armed, civil, ethnic, military, popular*; and followed by nouns like *communist, guerrilla, Tamil*, etc.

(5) permanence vs permanency

> a. They aim to secure the permanence of the partnership.
> b. He seems to have become a permanency in her life.

The two nouns under (5) are derived from the adjectival root *permanent*, which means 'lasting for a long time'. In each case, however, the speaker construes the root differently, and so uses the nouns discriminately. In (5a), the noun *permanence* means 'the state of being permanent', durable. If something has permanence, it remains the same for a long time or for ever. *Permanence* is preceded by verbs like *assure, guarantee, guard, preserve, secure* and adjectives like *essential, inevitable, necessary, practical, virtual*, etc. It is used in phrases like *aspect of, element of, idea of, sense of*. In (5b), the noun *permanency* means 'the status of being permanent', durative. A permanency is someone who is always present or something that stays the same for an indefinite period. *Permanency* is preceded by verbs like *acquire, achieve, become, gain, obtain*; adjectives like *apparent, considerable, great, prominent, sizeable*; and followed by nouns like *framework, planning, policy, principles, programme*, etc.[2]

3.4.2   The trait–mode distinction: *-ness* vs *-ity*

As mentioned earlier, the nominal suffixes *-ness* and *-ity* highlight *inherent features* of an entity, but with a semantic difference. In contemporary English, the difference is seen in terms of *trait* vs *mode*. *Trait* is the feature that defines the nature of an entity. It is the peculiarity that distinguishes the nature of an entity. Morphologically, *trait* is realised by the nominal suffix *-ness*, which means 'describing the trait indicated by the adjectival root'. By contrast, *mode* is the feature that defines the manner of an entity. It is the peculiarity that characterises the behaviour of an entity. Morphologically, *mode* is realised by the nominal suffix *-ity*, which means 'describing the mode indicated by the adjectival root'. In examining the formations in the corpus, we find that the ones formed with *-ness* focus on the nature of the thing described, or its embodied trait, whereas the ones with *-ity* focus on the way the thing described is done or identify thegroup to which the thing described belongs. The trait–mode distinction entails, I argue, further distinctions at contextual or collocational levels.

Let us now turn to the corpus to uphold the argument. Derivatives in *-ness* accept, as shown by Riddle (1985: 439), the phrase *have got*, as in *Martin has got a brutalness the likes of which I have never seen*, or verbs of reinforcement, as in *The lanterns contributed to the ethnicness of the restaurant*. They seem to collocate with verbs denoting possession, as in *have falseness*; deprivation, as in *lack acuteness*; or disapproval, as in *criticise laxness*. As for the adjectival collocates, they seem to denote quality, as in *vivid falseness*, or type, as in *moral laxness*. By contrast, derivatives in *-ity* accept, as shown by Riddle (1985: 439), the phrase *come from*, as in *I can't stand any kind of brutality, whether it comes from rednecks or radicals*. They seem to collocate with verbs denoting reflection, as in *demonstrate falsity*; perception, as in *note acuity*; or experience, as in *suffer laxity*. As for the adjectival collocates, they seem to denote classification, as in *visual acuity*, or degree, as in *heightened sensitivity*. A survey of some pairs will illuminate the distinction:

(6) acuteness vs acuity

    a. Only acuteness of observation helps to affirm beauty.
    b. The doctor examines the visual acuity of the newborn.

The two nouns under (6) are derived from the adjectival root *acute*, which means 'keen in perception, or sharp in thought'. The nouns, nevertheless, represent different construals of the root, and so have individual meanings. In (6a), the noun *acuteness* means 'the trait of being acute'. It means the observation is very good, accurate and quick to notice things. *Acuteness* is preceded by verbs like *lack, need, own, possess, require*; adjectives like *connate, especial, innate, native, natural*; and followed by *of* plus nouns like *argument, conception, debate, inquiry, observation*, etc. In (6b), the noun *acuity* means 'the mode of being acute'. It means the doctor wants to check the ability of the baby to see accurately and clearly. *Acuity* is preceded by verbs like *cultivate, develop, increase, improve, raise*; adjectives like *auditory, hearing, psychological, rhythmic, visual*; and followed by *of* plus nouns like *eyesight, senses*, etc.[3]

(7) crudeness vs crudity

    a. They objected to the crudeness of her remarks.
    b. The parents noticed the crudity of the children.

The two nouns under (7) are derived from the adjectival root crude, which means 'vulgar or obscene'. The nouns, nevertheless, represent different construals of the root, and so have individual meanings. In (7a), the noun *crudeness* means 'the trait of being crude'. It means the remarks are tactless, rude, or offensive. *Crudeness* is preceded by verbs like *criticise, denounce, object, reject, spurn* and adjectives like *occasional, original, relative, startling, terrible*, etc. In (7b), the noun *crudity* means 'the mode of being crude'. It means the children behave in a way that is impolite, vulgar, or discourteous. *Crudity* is preceded by verbs like *detect, examine, note, notice, perceive*; adjectives like *adult, appalling, casual, childish, maximum*; and followed by *of* plus nouns like *comment, language, message, method, remark*, etc.

(8) falseness vs falsity

    a. She identified the falseness of his hopes.
    b. She revealed the falsity of his statements.

The two nouns under (8) are derived from the adjectival root *false*, which means 'not true'. The nouns, nevertheless, represent different construals of the root, and so have individual meanings. In (8a), the noun *falseness* means 'the trait of being false'. It means the hopes are delsuive. *Falseness* is preceded by verbs like *diagnose, identify, pinpoint, recognise, see* and adjectives like *apparent, awful, awkward, infinite, integral*, etc. In (8b), the noun *falsity* means 'the mode of being false'. It means the statements are invalid; it doesn't express real emotions. *Falsity* is preceded by verbs like *demonstrate, expose, indicate, manifest, reveal* and followed by *of* plus nouns like *assumptions, ideas, beliefs, claims, statements*, etc. By contrast, *falsehood* is a lie or untrue statement, as in *Many falsehoods were uttered during the campaign*.

(9) laxness vs laxity

    a. She was encouraged by the laxness of the conditions.
    b. The laxity of parents has become a problem nowadays.

The two nouns under (9) are derived from the adjectival root lax, which means 'lacking care, attention, or control'. The nouns, nevertheless, represent different construals of the root, and so have individual meanings. In (9a), the noun *laxness* means 'the trait of being lax'. It means the conditions are not severe or are not strong enough. *Laxness* is preceded by verbs like *criticise, decry, punish, report, reproach* and adjectives like *apparent, excessive, moral, shameful, unprecedented*, etc. In (9b), the noun *laxity* means 'the mode of being lax'. It means the behaviour of the parents lacks strictness or is deficient in firmness. *Laxity* is preceded by verbs like *endure, experience, face, know, sustain* and adjectives like *certain, mindless, relative, simple, soft*, etc.[4]

(10) sensitiveness vs sensitivity

    a. Quick sensitiveness is inseparable from a ready understanding.
    b. Few doctors show sensitivity when dealing with their patients.

The two nouns under (10) are derived from the adjectival root sensitive, which means 'having acute mental or emotional sensibility'. The nouns, nevertheless, represent different construals of the root, and so have individual meanings. In (10a), the noun *sensitiveness* means 'the trait of being sensitive'. It means the reaction is susceptible to the attitudes or feelings of others. It is a reaction to psychological forces. *Sensitiveness* is preceded by verbs like *analyse, define, expound, identify, specify* and adjectives like *abnormal, excessive, quick, unusual, vivid*, etc. In (10b), the noun *sensitivity* means 'the mode of being sensitive'. It means the doctors show a deep understanding and awareness of the feelings and needs of the patients. *Sensitivity* is preceded by verbs like *express, display, pose, reflect, show*; adjectives like *deep, extreme, great, heightened, optimum*; and followed by *to* plus nouns like *cold, danger, distress, trauma, values*, etc. In *The colours don't last because of their sensitivity to sunlight*, the noun *sensitivity* indicates a reaction to physical forces.[5]

3.4.3   The trait–existent distinction: *-ness vs -ity*

In the preceding section, the nominal suffix *-ness* has been shown to denote the trait that characterises an entity, whereas the nominal suffix *-ity* has been shown to denote the behaviour that is characteristic of an entity. In this section, the nominal suffix *-ness* keeps its meaning, but the nominal suffix *-ity* denotes the entity itself. More precisely, the suffix *-ity* refers to an existent, a living thing, especially one conceived of as real, not imaginary. Accordingly, it means 'naming the entity indicated by the adjectival root'. Evidence in support of the semantic distinction comes from the countability of nouns. (cf. Riddle,1985: 442). For the most part, *-ness* nouns are non-countable. Only a handful of such nouns pluralise. Many of them were established as count nouns before *-ity* was borrowed. Some examples are *illnesses, sicknesses, weaknesses*, etc.

By contrast, nouns in *-ity* frequently occur as count nouns, since they denote an entity. Such examples include *oddities, rarities, sensibilities,* etc. As shown by Riddle (1985: 440), only the *-ity* seems congruous with the use of words like *very* and *doubt*, which make it clear that existence is the question as in *Its very tangibility/*tangibleness is in doubt.* A survey of the concordance lines in the corpus shows that *-ness* derivatives follow verbs of assessment, as in *assess rareness*, whereas *-ity* derivatives follow verbs of featuring, as in *become a rarity*. A review of some pairs will spell out the distinction:

(11) oddness vs oddity

    a. She resents the oddness of her friend.
    b. Well, a man over six feet is an oddity.

The two nouns under (11) are derived from the adjectival root *odd,* which means 'peculiar, unusual, or out of the ordinary'. Yet, each noun represents a different construal of the root, and so has meaning of its own. In (11a), the noun *oddness* means 'the trait of being odd'. It means the friend is strange or unexpected. *Oddness* is preceded by verbs like *deprecate, disapprove, frown, object, resent*; and adjectives like *apparent, monumental, profound, sheer, unnatural*, etc. In (11b), the noun *oddity* means 'the entity that is odd'. An oddity is a person or thing that is strange or unusual. *Oddity* is preceded by verbs like *observe, notice, perceive, recognise, watch* and adjectives like *coincidental, historical, physical, psychological, statistical*, etc.

(12) rareness vs rarity

    a. The expert assesses the rareness of the antiques.
    b. His paintings are a great rarity on the art market.

The two nouns under (12) are derived from the adjectival root *rare,* which means 'not common or very unusual'. Yet, each noun represents a different construal of the root, and so has meaning of its own. In (12a), the noun *rareness* means 'the trait of being rare'. It means the antiques are scarce, not easy to find or obtain. *Rareness* is preceded by verbs like *assess, evaluate, measure, value, weigh;* adjectives like *alleged, comparative, considerable, relative, utmost;* and followed by *of* plus nouns like *reference, oeuvre*, etc. In (12b), the noun *rarity* means 'the entity that is rare'. A rarity is a person or thing that is interesting or valuable because it is an exception. *Rarity* is preceded by verbs like *be, become, feature, highlight, make* and adjectives like *actual, fantastic, great, phenomenal, real*, etc.

(13) realness vs reality

  a. They were convinced of the realness of the story.
  b. A paperless office is still far from being a reality.

The two nouns under (13) are derived from the adjectival root *real*, which means 'existing in fact, not imaginary'. Yet, each noun represents a different construal of the root, and so has meaning of its own. In (13a), the noun *realness* means 'the trait of being real'. It means the story is true or actual. *Realness* is preceded by verbs like *assess, evaluate, judge, rate, test*; adjectives like *incredible, positive, supreme, thrilling, ultimate*; and expressions like *kind of, level of, sense of, type of*, etc. In (13b), the noun *reality* means 'the entity that is real'. A reality is a thing that is actually experienced or seen, in contrast to what people might imagine. *Reality* is preceded by verbs like *be, become, create, grow, turn* and adjectives like *actual, basic, new, practical, virtual*, etc.[6]

3.4.4   The status–trait distinction: *-cy vs -ness*

As noted earlier, the suffix *-cy* indicates status, the position that an entity enjoys or its standing in relation to others. For its part, the suffix *-ness* indicates trait, a distinguishing feature of an entity's nature. A search of the BNC concordances and UK pages in Google, in the case of nouns ending in *-ness*, confirms the fact that nouns ending in the two suffixes have different behaviour. Those ending in *-cy* are treated as entities. As evidence, they come after verbs denoting concealment, as in *veil secrecy*, or protection, as in *safeguard privacy*. By contrast, nouns ending in *-ness* are treated as concepts. As evidence, they occur after verbs denoting meditation, as in *contemplate privateness*, or comprehension, as in *grasp secretness*. As for the adjectives, *-cy* derivatives accompany non-scalar words, as in *perfect accuracy*, while *-ness* derivatives accompany scalar words, as in *great secretness*. A check of some pairs will elucidate the distinction:

(14) accuracy vs accurateness

  a. They began to examine the accuracy of the figures.
  b. They consider the accurateness of the information.

The two nouns are derived from the adjectival root *accurate*, which means 'correct, exact, and without any mistakes'. Nonetheless, the construal of the root in each noun is different, and so causes a distinction in their use. In (14a), the noun *accuracy* means 'the status of being accurate'. Accuracy is a standard with which things show accordance. *Accuracy* is preceded by verbs like *assess, examine, check, prove, test* and adjectives like *absolute, complete, impeccable, remarkable, total*, etc. In (14b), the noun *accurateness* means 'the trait of being accurate'. It means the information is right, exact or precise. *Accurateness* is preceded by verbs like *assume, consider, reckon, suspect, understand* and adjectives like *historical, necessary, philosophical, technical, uncanny*, etc.

(15) privacy vs privateness

> a. The laws are designed to safeguard people's privacy.
> b. In fact, art captures the privateness of human nature.

The two nouns are derived from the adjectival root *private*, which means 'belonging to or concerning an individual person'. Nonetheless, the construal of the root in each noun is different, and so causes a distinction in their use. In (15a), the noun *privacy* means 'the status of being private'. Privacy is a stage in which one is in seclusion from company or observation. *Privacy* is preceded by verbs like *invade, preserve, respect, safeguard, violate*; adjectives like *complete, individual, personal, strict, total*; expressions like *archive, email, invasion of, intrusion of, right of*; and followed by nouns like *code, intrusion, issues, laws, practices*, etc. In (15b), the noun *privateness* means 'the trait of being private'. It means the human nature is concealed or hidden, secluded from the presence or view of others. *Privateness* is preceded by verbs like *capture, envisage, feature, realise, visualise*; adjectives like *basic, essential, inherent, intense, true*; and expressions like *degree of, element of, moment of, quality of, sense of*, etc.

(16) secrecy vs secretness

> a. The content of the report is shrouded in secrecy.
> b. Due to its secretness, the cure remains a rumour.

The two nouns are derived from the adjectival root *secret*, which means 'kept from knowledge or view'. Nonetheless, the construal of the root in each noun is different, and so causes a distinction in their use.

In (16a), the noun *secrecy* means 'the status of being secret'. Secrecy is something that is being kept secret. *Secrecy* is preceded by verbs like *be cloaked in, be shrouded in, be veiled in, maintain, swear somebody to*; adjectives like *absolute, excessive, official, strict, unnecessary*; and phrases like *a blanket of, a cloak of, a veil of*, etc. In (16b), the noun *secretness* means 'the trait of being secret'. It means the treatment is not known by other people. *Secretness* is preceded by verbs like *apprehend, comprehend, fathom, grasp, understand* and adjectives like *deep, great, super, taut, top*, etc.[7]

3.4.5   The status–mode distinction: *-cy* vs *-ity*

With nouns formed on the same root, the *-cy* indicates status, namely the relative position of an entity within a group, whereas the *-ity* indicates mode, namely a possible, customary, or preferred way of doing something. A check of the UK pages on the Internet and of the concordance lines in the corpus confirm the fact that *-cy* derivatives collocate with verbs of diagnosing, as in *detect a malignancy*, or resilience, as in *restore normalcy*; and with classifying adjectives, as in *political normalcy*. By contrast, *-ity* derivatives collocate with verbs of reflection, as in *radiate benignity*, or promotion, as in *strengthen normality*; and with scalar adjectives, as in *great malignity*. A study of some pairs will explicate the distinction:

(17) benignancy vs benignity

    a. He would newer be able to repay their benignancy.
    b. Most of her friends take advantage of her benignity.

The two nouns are derived from the adjectival root *benign*, which means 'pleasant and kind'. Still, the root is construed differently, and so each noun has its own sense. In (17a), the noun *benignancy* means 'the status of being benign'. A benignancy is a kind act or a generous deed. *Benignancy* is preceded by verbs like *give, make, offer, pay back, repay* and adjectives like *altruistic, complaisant, munificent, philanthropic, seasonal*, etc. In (17b), the noun *benignity* means 'the mode of being benign'. It means she manifests kindness in dealing with people. *Benignity* is preceded by verbs like *beam with, exude, ooze, radiate, reflect*; adjectives like *divine, gracious, noble, paternal, wise*; and the expression *an air of*.

(18) malignancy vs malignity

    a. Tests detected a malignancy that had to be removed.
    b. His malignity wrecked the lives of innocent people.

The two nouns are derived from the adjectival root *malign*, which means 'evil in intent, effect, or character'. Still, the root is construed differently, and so each noun has its own sense. In (18a), the noun *malignancy* means 'the status of being malign'. A malignancy is a cancerous tumour. *Malignancy* is preceded by verbs like *detect, diagnose, find, identify, pinpoint*; adjectives like *burning, common, low-grade, renewed, unrecognised*; and expressions like *indicative of, no sign of, no evidence of, suggestive of*, etc. In (18b), the noun *malignity* means 'the mode of being malign'. It means his behaviour is driven by intense hatred or the desire to harm others. *Malignity* is preceded by verbs like *display, exhibit, manifest, reveal, show* and adjectives like *deep, excessive, fiendish, great, utter*, etc.

(19) normalcy vs normality

    a. After a state of tension, they yearned for a return to normalcy.
    b. They attempt to strengthen normality between their countries.

The two nouns are derived from the adjectival root *normal*, which means 'ordinary or usual'. Still, the root is construed differently, and so each noun has its own sense. In (19a), the noun *normalcy* means 'the status of being normal'. A normalcy is a situation in which every thing is normal. *Normalcy* is preceded by verbs like *re-establish, reinstate, restore, return to, revive* and adjectives like *economical, growing, political, social, stable*, etc. In (19b), the noun *normality* means 'the mode of being normal'. It means the relationship conforms to a norm, rule, principle, standard, or pattern. *Normality* is preceded by verbs like *advance, boost, develop, promote, strengthen*; adjectives like *domestic, exuberant, relative, surface, weak*; and expressions like *a period of, a sign of, a standard of, semblance of*, etc.[8]

3.5 Summary

In this chapter, the goal has been to explore the approach suggested here in the semantic interpretation of complex nouns derived from adjectives. Using data offered in the British National Corpus and Internet pages, I based the analysis on three arguments. In section 3.2, the argument was on suffixal polysemy. The numerous senses of a de-adjectival suffix constitute a semantic network which is organised around a primary sense. The *prototype*, in turn, interacts with a set of cognitive principles to derive a set of additional distinct senses. In section 3.3, the argument was on suffixal domain. De-adjectival nominal suffixes do not exist independently of each other, but rather belong to a domain in which each suffix designates a particular facet of it.

In section 3.4, the argument was on non-synonymy. A noun pair sharing the same root and ending in different suffixes is not synonymous. The distinction resides in the alternative ways the speaker construes their common root and consequently uses different morphemes to express them. In deriving each noun, the suffix shifts the meaning of the root to a certain direction, and so encodes the intended construal. The resulting difference is backed up by the discriminating collocates of each pair member, which corpus data show. In Cognitive Semantics, formal differences correlate with semantic differences.

Notes

1. Marchand (1969: 249–50) claims that nouns in -*a/ence* are de-verbal nouns expressing the idea of action, whereas nouns in -*a/ency* are de-adjectival nouns expressing the state or quality. For example, *insistence* belongs to *insist*, whereas *insistency* belongs to *insistent* and *compliance* belongs to *comply*, whereas *compliancy* belongs to *compliant*. Further, Marchand, as well as other standard works on word formation, treats the suffixes -*ce* as -*ance* and -*cy* as -*ancy*. In this work, I treat them as -*ce* and -*cy*. The reason is that the suffixes are not necessarily added to roots ending in -*ant* or -*ent*, such as *preference* from *prefer*, *defence* from *defend*, *advocacy* from *advocate*, and *captaincy* from *captain*.
2. The same distinction applies to other nominal pairs ending in -*ce* and -*cy*, which dictionaries often give as alternatives. These are *brilliance/brilliancy*, *competence/competency*, *consistence/consistency*, *consonance/consonancy*, *insistence/insistency*, *relevance/relevancy*, *transparence/transparency*, *excellence/excellency*, etc. Let us explain one example. The nouns *competence/competency* are derived from the adjectival root *competent*, which means 'able to do something well'. Although they are derived from the same root, they are used in different contexts. In *He tried to acquire some linguistic competence*, the noun *competence* means 'the state of being competent', i.e. capable. In *He challenged the competency of the charges*, the noun *competency* means 'the status of being competent', i.e. fitness. In a legal sense, it means the status of being physically and intellectually fit.
3. The same distinction applies to other nominal pairs ending in -*ity* and -*ness*, which dictionaries simply cross-reference one to the other as equivalents. These are *fatalness/fatality*, *obliqueness/obliquity*, *saneness/sanity*, etc. Let us explain one example. The nouns *obliqueness/obliquity* are derived from the adjectival root *oblique*, which means 'having angle or being indirect'. A closer look at their meanings can make a difference in how each is properly used. In *His story-telling has no obliqueness, everything is slowly explained*, the noun *obliqueness* means 'the trait of being oblique', i.e. angular. In *There is no doubt the book has an ironic obliquity*, the noun *obliquity* means 'the mode of being oblique', i.e. done in a way that lacks clarity or explicitness.
4. In the preceding discussions, the meanings of the noun pairs have been identified by the same domain. The meanings of a few noun pairs, however, can be established by means of different domains which they activate. This is in line with the cognitive principle that a semantic unit can be conceptualised against more than one domain. A sample of the noun pairs includes *authenticity*

vs *authentication*, *deformity* vs *deformation*, *diversity* vs *diversion*, *duplication* vs *duplicity*, *facility* vs *facilitation*, *liquidity* vs *liquidation*, *profanity* vs *profanation*, *reciprocity* vs *reciprocation*, etc.

Let us take some examples. The de-adjectival suffix *-ity* evokes the domain of *characterisation* (mode), whereas the de-verbal suffix *-ion* evokes the domain of *process* (action). The two nouns *reciprocity* and *reciprocation* relate to *reciprocate*, but they have separate meanings. In *Over the years, they achieved a satisfactory reciprocity*, the noun *reciprocity* refers to the mode of being reciprocal. *Reciprocity* is a condition in which two people or countries exchange help or advantages. In *Indeed, reciprocation is perhaps the operational basis for friendship*, the noun *reciprocation* refers to the act of doing something in return. *Reciprocation* is the act of behaving or feeling towards somebody in the same way as s/he behaves or feels towards you.

To confirm the analysis, let us examine another nominal pair. The two nouns *deformity* and *deformation* relate to *deform*, but each has its own use. In *The injury resulted in a deformity of the hip joint*, the noun *deformity* refers to the mode of being deformed. *Deformity* is a condition in which a part of the body is not the normal shape because of injury, illness, or because it has grown wrongly. In *The deformation of the bones was caused by poor diet*, the noun *deformation* refers to the act of deforming. *Deformation* is the act of causing a change in the normal shape of something as a result of injury or illness.

5. In the interpretation of some noun pairs, suffixes belonging to different domains can be involved, as in *barbarity* vs *barbarism*, *duality* vs *dualism*, *fatality* vs *fatalism*, *humanity* vs *humanism*, *liberality* vs *liberalism*, *nationality* vs *nationalism*, *opportunity* vs *opportunism*, *modernity* vs *modernism*, *nudity* vs *nudism*, *reality* vs *realism*, etc.

Let us take some examples. The de-adjectival suffix *-ity* actuates the domain of *characterisation* (mode), whereas the suffix de-nominal *-ism* actuates the domain of *representation* (belief). The two nouns *humanity* and *humanism* relate to *humane*, but each has a distinct meaning. In *The judge was praised for his courage and humanity*, the noun *humanity* refers to the mode of being humane. *Humanity* is the condition of being kind to people or animals by making sure that they do not suffer. In *They aspire for a society built on the principles of humanism*, the noun *humanism* refers to the philosophy of asserting the intrinsic worth of humans and rejecting religious beliefs. *Humanism* is a system of thought which considers solving human problems by means of reason rather than religious beliefs.

To consolidate the analysis, let us scrutinise another nominal pair. The two nouns *liberality* and *liberalism* relate to *liberal*, but they emphasise different aspects of it. In *She is known for the liberality of her views*, the noun *liberality* refers to the mode of being liberal. *Liberality* is a condition in which one has respect for political, religious, or moral views, even if one does not agree with them. In *The motion proposed preferred Liberalism to Conservatism as the better future for the country*, the noun *liberalism* refers to the philosophy of open-mindedness in opinions and beliefs. *Liberalism* is a system of thought and behaviour in which people are receptive to new ideas and suggestions, and avoid imposing their own values and principles on others.

6. The meaning of some noun pairs can be conceptualised against two different domains, as in *abstractness* vs *abstraction*, *appropriateness* vs *appropriation*,

conciseness vs *concision, considerateness* vs *consideration, corruptness* vs *corruption, preciseness* vs *precision, tenseness* vs *tension,* etc.

Let us take some examples. The de-adjectival suffix *-ness* evokes the domain of *characterisation* (trait), whereas the de-verbal suffix *-ion* evokes the domain of *process* (action). The two nouns *considerateness* and *consideration* relate to *consider,* but the meanings they express are different. In *When he got down to Punctuality and Considerateness as a Driver, he decided to give up and improvise,* the noun *considerateness* refers to the trait of being considerate. *Considerateness* is the quality of being thoughtful of the rights and feelings of others. In *Could you turn your music down and show a little consideration for the neighbours?* the noun *consideration* refers to the act of considering. *Consideration* is the act of showing concern for or sensitivity towards the feelings of others.

To support the analysis, let us review another nominal pair. The two nouns *tenseness* and *tension* relate to *tense,* but each has its own peculiarity. In *The atmosphere in the meeting was characterised by tenseness,* the noun *tenseness* refers to the trait of being tense. *Tenseness* is a situation in which people are nervous or worried, and unable to relax. In *Walking is excellent for releasing tension,* the noun *tension* refers to the act of feeling anxious. *Tension* is the act of feeling nervous or worried about something that is happening or might happen in the future, which makes it impossible for one to relax.

7. Some noun pairs activate facets of different domains for their interpretation, as in *ascendancy* vs *ascension, expectancy* vs *expectation, occupancy* vs *occupation, precipitancy* vs *precipitation,* etc.

    Let us take some examples. The suffix de-adjectival *-cy* evokes the domain of *characterisation* (status), whereas the de-verbal suffix *-ion* evokes the domain of *process* (action). The two nouns *ascendancy* and *ascension* relate to *ascend,* but they are distinct in meaning. In *They are in danger of losing their political ascendancy,* the noun *ascendancy* refers to the status of being ascendant. *Ascendancy* is the position where one has power or influence over somebody or something. In *Finally, she achieved her ascension to the throne,* the noun *ascension* refers to the act of ascending. *Ascension* is the act of moving up or of reaching a high position.

    To corroborate the analysis, let us analyse another nominal pair. Both *expectancy* and *expectation* relate to *expect,* but they have different meanings. In *There was an air of expectancy among the waiting crowd,* the noun *expectancy* refers to the status of being expectant. *Expectancy* is expecting or hoping that something, especially something good or exciting, will happen. In *There was a general expectation that he would win,* the noun *expectation* refers to the act of expecting. *Expectation* is the act of anticipation or forecasting that something will happen in the future.

8. In some noun pairs, the suffix *-cy* stands in contrast to the suffix *-ure.* For instance, the de-adjectival suffix *-cy* evokes the domain of *characterisation* (status), whereas the de-verbal suffix *-ure* evokes the domain of *entity* (state). The two nouns *candidacy* and *candidature* relate to *candidate,* but they demonstrate a difference in meaning. In *He announced his candidacy for the post,* the noun *candidacy* refers to the status of being a candidate. *Candidacy* is the relative position which an entity reaches. In *They supported him during his candidature against the strong challenger,* the noun *candidature* refers to the state of being a candidate. *Candidature* is a condition which an entity is in at a given time, which is subject to change.

4
De-Nominal Nominalisers

In this chapter, I discuss the semantics of de-nominal nominalisers. More specifically, I discuss the meanings of morphemes and how they combine to form nouns. During the investigation, I examine three tenets of Cognitive Semantics. To that end, I structure the chapter as follows. In section 4.1, I say what a de-nominal suffix is and enumerate the mechanisms that condition its integration with a root to form a noun. I section 4.2, I argue that a de-nominal suffix has a core sense which leads, through extension, to the creation of other peripheral senses. In section 4.3, I argue that the meaning of a de-nominal suffix crucially depends on its function in the domain in which it is embedded. In section 4.4, I argue that although the members of a noun pair are closely related, they do not necessarily have identical meanings. Each represents a different construal. To demonstrate non-synonymy, I resort to their distinctive collocates. This is done by examining actual data offered in the corpus. In section 4.5, I sum up the most important points of the chapter.

4.1 Introduction

A de-nominal suffix is a word-final element that is added to a noun to form another noun. It is a bound morpheme because it cannot exist on its own; it needs a free morpheme to complete its meaning. The integration of the two morphemes is established by means of what Langacker (1987: 277–327) calls *valence* relations. First, the integration is established by the semantic and phonological correspondences between them. Second, the integration is established by asymmetry in dependence. The free morpheme functions as autonomous, whereas the bound morpheme functions as dependent. Third, the integration is established by asymmetry in determinacy. The bound morpheme functions as a profile determinant of the composite structure. As a word class indicator, it changes the class of the lexical item to which it is appended: from concrete to abstract or from abstract to concrete. As a meaning indicator, it contributes to the semantic make-up of the lexical item to which it is linked. Fourth, the integration is established by asymmetry in function. The bound morpheme functions as head, while the free morpheme as complement. In some derivational cases, the root undergoes a phonetic change as in *ageism* from *ageist*, whereas in others it preserves its phonetic shape as in *citizenry* from *citizen*.

4.2 Semantic networks

In this section, I discuss the impact of the *category* theory on the semantic behaviour of de-nominal suffixes. The meaning of a de-nominal suffix, I argue, is modelled in terms of a network of senses, which language users intuitively organise with respect to a prototypical sense. The prototypical sense is the best example of the network; it exhibits the common properties of the category. It is the sense that comes to mind first or is the easiest to recall. The other, peripheral, senses build around the prototypical sense; they are assimilated to the category according to how closely they resemble the prototype. The relations between the senses resemble those between family members, which share some but not all of the features. Like members of a family, the peripheral senses share the general properties of the category, but they differ in specific details. *Category* refers to a cognitive ability which upholds the unity of a lexical item. It presents the senses in order by starting from a basic sense and linking all the other ones to it.

To capture the semantic behaviour of a de-nominal suffix, I ground the description in the cognitive model of *animacy*. The model is scalar in dimension in that the entity described can be of two categories: animate and inanimate. The root acts as a reference point which facilitates access to such categories. Let me take an example of the suffix -*ship*. In a prototypical formation, an animate entity denoted by the nominal root is in focus. In *professorship*, the combination means a position held by an individual. In *internship*, the combination means the time an individual spends in a given field. In *comradeship*, the combination means the feeling an individual has. In a peripheral formation, an inanimate entity denoted by the nominal root is in focus. In *warship*, the combination means a vehicle. In *fellowship*, the combination means an amount of money. In *censorship*, the combination means a suppression policy.

In what follows, I present synchronic descriptions of the de-nominal nominalisers in English.

4.2.1 *-age*

The suffix *-age* came into the language through loans from French. Prototypically, the suffix *-age* is appended to nominal roots to form nouns. Based on the nature of the combining root, the suffix expresses a range of meanings:

a. 'a collection of things indicated by the nominal root'. This meaning comes about when the suffix is appended to nominal roots referring to concrete entities, i.e. material objects. For example, *baggage* is a collection of bags that travellers take on a flight, *herbage* is a collection of plants grown for cows, and *wreckage* is a collection of the broken parts of a vehicle or building. Additional examples include *coinage, flowerage, fruitage, leafage, plumage*, etc. In rare extensions, the derived nouns refer to a body of people. For example, *clientage* is a body of people who regularly visit a shop, and *the peerage* is the group of people who are peers, either because of their families or because they are life peers.

b. 'a quantity of the thing indicated by the nominal root'. This meaning comes about when the suffix is appended to nominal roots referring to units of measurement. For example, *dosage* is the amount of medicine that a person takes over a period of time, *mileage* is the number of miles that a vehicle can travel, *tonnage* is the total amount that something weighs. Additional examples include *acreage, gallonage, percentage, voltage, yardage*, etc.

c. 'the cost of the thing indicated by the nominal root'. This meaning comes about when the derived nouns refer to charges or fees paid for services. For example, *corkage* is the charge paid for drinking wine in a restaurant that one has bought somewhere else, *postage* is the fee paid for sending a letter by post, and *storage* is the price charged for keeping goods in a storehouse. Additional examples include *cartage, dockage, poundage, tankage, towage*, etc.

d. 'a place indicated by the nominal root'. This meaning comes about when the derived nouns refer to names of places. For example, *anchorage* is a place where ships or boats can anchor, *hermitage* is a place where a hermit lives or lived, and *orphanage* is a home for children whose parents are dead. Additional examples include *harborage, parsonage, vicarage*, etc.

Peripherally, the suffix -*age* is appended to verbal roots to form nouns expressing a distinct but related range of meanings:

a. 'the action indicated by the verbal root'. This meaning comes about when the suffix is appended to verbal roots that are transitive. The event involves two participants: namely, an agent and a patient. For example, *blockage* is the action of blocking something from moving, *carriage* is the action of transporting goods from one place to another, and *coverage* is the action of reporting news in newspapers and on the radio and television.

b. 'the result indicated by the verbal root'. This meaning comes about when the suffix is appended to verbal roots that are intransitive. The event involves only one participant: namely, a patient. The agent is not mentioned. For example, *shrinkage* is the result of a fabric becoming smaller in size, and *slippage* is the result of something being reduced in the rate, amount or standard.

c. 'the action or the result indicated by the verbal root'. This meaning comes about when the suffix is appended to verbal roots that are (in)transitive. The event is interpretable in two ways: one with agent, another without the agent. For example, *breakage* is the action of breaking a vase or the result of a vase being broken, *drainage* is the action of draining a pool or the result of a pool being drained, *leakage* is the action of leaking or the result of liquid being leaked, and *stoppage* is the action of stopping a car or the result of a car being stopped.

A graphical representation of the multiple senses of the noun-forming suffix -*age* is offered in Figure 4.1. Note that the solid arrow represents the prototypical sense, whereas the dashed arrows represent the semantic extensions.

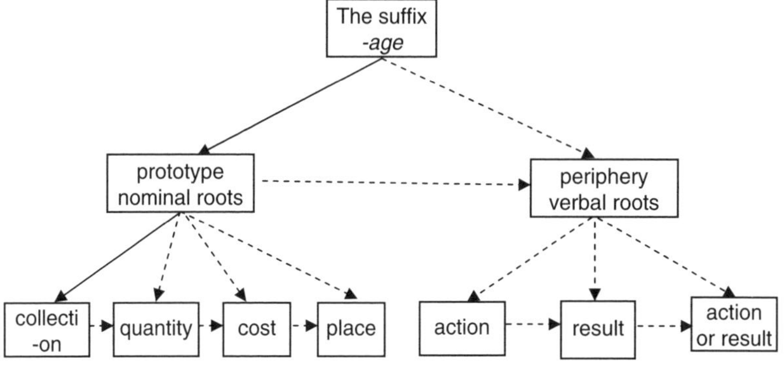

Figure 4.1 The semantic network of the noun-forming suffix -*age*

4.2.2   *-dom*

Prototypically, the suffix *-dom* is tacked on to nominal roots to form nouns. Depending on the nature of the joining root, the suffix expresses a variety of meanings:

a. 'the territory ruled by the person specified by the nominal root'. Nouns formed in this way refer to the area, province, or realm of whatever is indicated by the nominal root. For example, *dukedom* is a region or territory owned by a duke, *earldom* is a land or province ruled by an earl or countess, and *kingdom* is a realm or country ruled by a king or queen.
b. 'the land inhabited by the people specified by the nominal root'. Nouns formed in this way refer to the inhabitants of a region characterising them as a community. For example, *Yankeedom* is a land or region inhabited by Yankees.
c. 'a group of people united by the thing specified by the nominal root'. Nouns formed in this way refer to people united by a common interest. For example, *dogdom* is a group of people who are interested in dogs, *fandom* is a group of people who support a particular sport, and *moviedom* or *filmdom* is a group of people who are employed in the movie industry.

Peripherally, the suffix *-dom* is tacked on to other roots to form nouns which has the meaning 'the state of being specified by the nominal root'. Nouns formed in this way refer to the experience of whatever is indicated by the roots, be they nouns or adjectives. In some derived nouns, the suffix conveys the idea of high standards. For example, *freedom* is the state of being free, *martyrdom* is the state of being a martyr, and *stardom* is the state of being a star, i.e. a celebrity. In other derived nouns, the suffix conveys a tinge of depreciation or mockery. For example, *boredom* is the state of being bored, *thraldom* is the state of being a thrall, i.e. a slave, and *whoredom* is the state of being a whore.

A graphical representation of the multiple senses of the noun-forming suffix *-dom* is offered in Figure 4.2. Note that the solid arrow represents the prototypical sense, whereas the dashed arrows represent the semantic extensions.

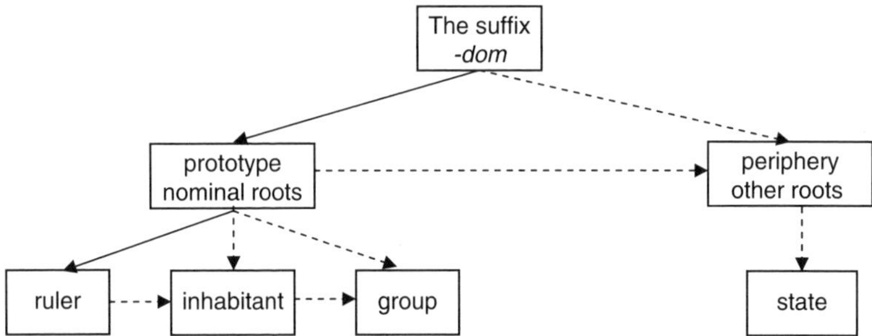

Figure 4.2   The semantic network of the noun-forming suffix *-dom*

4.2.3   *-hood*

Prototypically, the suffix *-hood* combines with nominal roots to form nouns. Relative to the nature of the joining root, the suffix receives multiple definitions:

a   'the condition of being what is referred to by the nominal root'. The nouns derived imply conditions of human life, social statuses, or legal rights. For example, *maidenhood* is the condition of being an unmarried woman, *nationhood* is the condition of being an independent nation, *statehood* is the condition of being a separate state. More examples include *adulthood, boyhood, fatherhood, manhood, parenthood, widowhood, womanhood*, etc.

b. 'a union of people sharing the thing referred to by the nominal root'. The nouns derived imply ideas or aims. For example, *brotherhood* is a union that includes men who are united for a common purpose, *priesthood* is a union that includes the priests of a religion, and *sisterhood* is union that includes women who have shared goals, experiences or viewpoints.

c. 'the period of time referred to by the nominal root'. The nouns derived imply important stages in one's life march. For example, *babyhood* is the period of time when one is a baby, *childhood* is the period of time when one is a child, and *girlhood* is the period of time when one is a girl.

Peripherally, the suffix *-hood* combines with adjectival roots to form nouns. The suffix means 'an instance of the quality referred to by the adjectival root'. For example, *falsehood* is an instance of a lie or untruth, and *hardihood* is an instance of boldness or bravery.

A graphical representation of the multiple senses of the noun-forming suffix *-hood* is offered in Figure 4.3. Note that the solid arrow represents the prototypical sense, whereas the dashed arrows represent the semantic extensions.

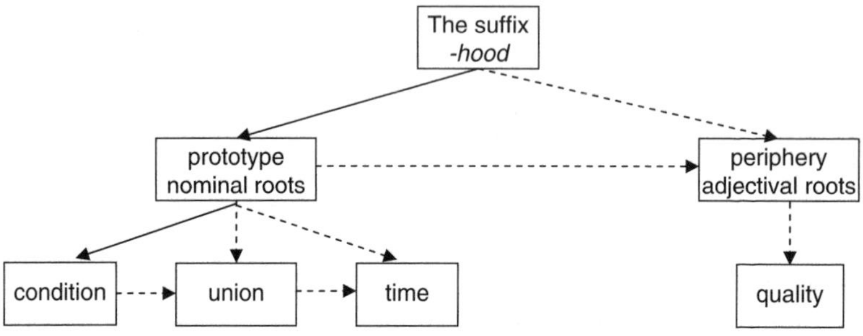

Figure 4.3 The semantic network of the noun-forming suffix *-hood*

4.2.4 *-ism*

Prototypically, the suffix *-ism* is attached to nominal roots to form abstract nouns. The meanings the suffix has are as follows:

a. 'the belief embodied in the theory named by the nominal root'. In this derivation, the suffix is attached to nominal roots and implies beliefs, doctrines or philosophies. Some beliefs are approving. For example, *feminism* is the belief that women should have the same rights as men, *liberalism* is the belief that calls for freedom and change, especially in politics, and *pacifism* is the belief that disputes should be settled by peaceful means. Other beliefs are disapproving. For example, *anarchism* is the belief that laws and government are not necessary, *conservatism* is the belief that dislikes change, and *racism* is the belief that the qualities of one's own race are better than others. Further examples include *ageism, atheism, defeatism, fascism, sexism*, etc.

b. 'the philosophy descended from the person named by the nominal root'. In this derivation, the suffix is attached to nominal roots referring to the founders of the beliefs, doctrines, or philosophies. For example, *Calvinism* descends from John Calvin's philosophy, which holds that God controls what happens on Earth; *Machiavellism* descends from Machiavelli's philosophy, which believes that craft and deceit are justified in pursuing political power; and *Platonism* descends from Plato's philosophy, which asserts the relationship between abstract entities and their corresponding forms in the material world.

c. 'the practice based on the belief named by the nominal root'. In this derivation, the suffix is attached to nominal roots and implies characteristic behaviour or typical manner. Some practices are approving. For example, *heroism* is the practice of doing things that are extremely brave, *patriotism* is the practice of loving and being proud of one's country, and *symbolism* is the practice of using symbols in art, literature, or films to represent ideas. Other practices are disapproving. For example, *despotism* is the practice of cruelly ruling people by having unlimited power over them, *extremism* is the practice of going beyond moderation to extreme positions, especially on political issues, and *vandalism* is the practice of deliberately damaging things, especially public property. Further examples include *barbarism, cynicism, hooliganism, scepticism, terrorism,* etc.[1]

Peripherally, the suffix *-ism* is attached to other roots to form abstract nouns. The roles the suffix plays in deriving the nouns are as follows:

a. 'the linguistic usage featured by the thing named by the adjectival root'. In this derivation, the suffix is attached to adjectival roots and refers to a speech style or a distinctive word. For example, *archaism* is a word or phrase that is no longer used, *vulgarism* is a word or expression that is crude or indecent, and *witticism* is a remark that is clever and humorous. Further examples include *colloquialism, neologism, Latinism, solecism, truism,* etc. Similar nouns are formed with proper names to identify a regional or language-specific expression. For example, *Americanism* is an American word, phrase, or usage; *Scotticism* is a Scottish pronunciation, figure of speech, or the like; *Gallicism* is an expression or idiom in French; and *Hellenism* is an idiom, phrase, or the like in Greek.

b. 'the quality of being which is named by the adjectival root'. In this derivation, the suffix is attached to adjectival roots implying characteristics. For example, *anomalism* is the quality of being anomalous, *modernism* is the quality of being modern, and *exoticism* is the quality of being exotic. Further examples include *humanism, idealism, nationalism, optimism, realism,* etc.

c. 'the act named by the verbal root'. In this derivation, the suffix is attached to verbal roots ending in *-ise* to form nouns referring to the process described by the verb or to an instance of that process. For example, *criticism* is the act of criticising people because of a disapproval of their behaviour, *exorcism* is the act of forcing an evil spirit to leave a person or place by using prayers or magic, and *plagiarism* is the act of presenting other people's ideas as one's own. Further examples include *baptism, hypnotism, magnetism, mechanism, specialism*, etc.

A graphical representation of the multiple senses of the noun-forming suffix *-ism* is offered in Figure 4.4. Note that the solid arrow represents the prototypical sense, whereas the dashed arrows represent the semantic extensions.

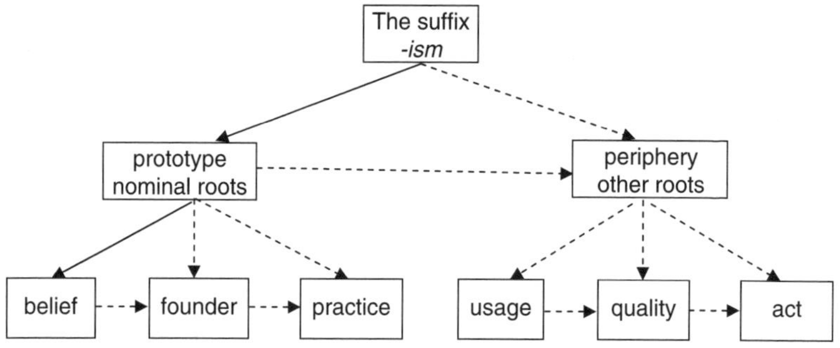

Figure 4.4   The semantic network of the noun-forming suffix *-ism*

4.2.5   *-ship*

The suffix *-ship* is tacked on to nominal roots, prototypically personal, to form nouns. The suffix gets rough glosses like:

a. 'the position of being what is signalled by the nominal root'. Nouns so formed denote the rank, office or occupation which an individual holds in a given field. For example, *editorship* is the position of being an editor at a newspaper or magazine, *headship* is the position of being the head in a school, and *leadership* is the position of being a leader of an organisation. Additional examples are *authorship, chancellorship, directorship, lectureship, professorship, tutorship*, etc.

b. 'the period of time spent on the thing signalled by the nominal root'. Nouns so formed denote the time one is requested or entitled to spend in a given field. For example, *apprenticeship* is the period of time when one works as an apprentice, *courtship* is the period of time when people have a romantic relationship with the intention of getting married, *governorship* is the period of time when someone is a governor, and *internship* is the period of time when one does a job as part of becoming qualified to do it.

c. 'the fact of being what is signalled by the nominal root'. Nouns so formed imply having the the feeling or the condition of the thing mentioned, conveying thus an abstract meaning. For example, *companionship* is the fact of being someone's companion in travel, *friendship* is the fact of being someone's friend in life, and *partnership* is the fact of being someone's partner in business. Additional examples are *acquaintanceship*, *citizenship*, *comradeship*, *ownership*, *relationship*, etc.

d. 'a group of people signalled by the nominal root'. Nouns so formed denote a body of people having a special bond. For example, *kinship* is a group of people who belong to the same family, *membership* is a group of people who belong to the same organisation, and *readership* is a group of people who regularly read the same newspaper or magazine.

The suffix *-ship* is tacked on to nominal roots, peripherally non-personal, to form nouns. The suffix gets rough glosses like:

a. 'an allowance of the thing signalled by the nominal root'. For example, *fellowship* is an amount of money given to postgraduates to enable them to study a subject at an advanced level, *scholarship* is an amount of money given by a school, college, university, or other organization to persons with great ability, to cover their studies, and *sponsorship* is an amount of money given to a person, organization, activity or event.

b. 'the policy or regime of the thing signalled by the nominal root'. Nouns so formed denote the practice or system of doing what the root signals. For example, *censorship* is the policy of suppressing published or broadcast material, especially something regarded as objectionable, and *dictatorship* is the policy of ruling a country with absolute power or despotic control.[2]

A graphical representation of the multiple senses of the noun-forming suffix *-ship* is offered in Figure 4.5. Note that the solid arrow represents the prototypical sense, whereas the dashed arrows represent the semantic extensions.

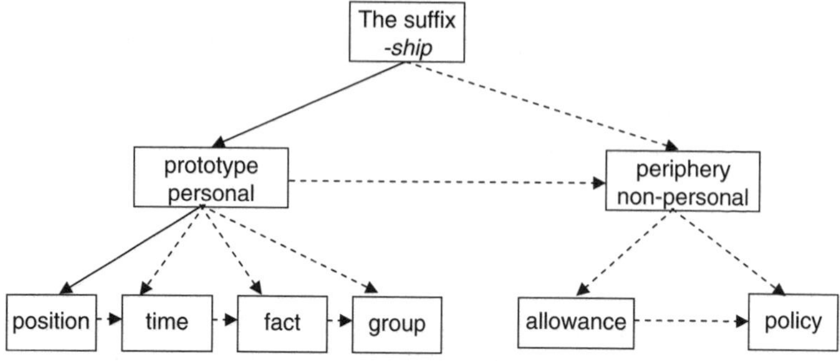

Figure 4.5   The semantic network of the noun-forming suffix *-ship*

4.2.6   *-(e)ry*

The suffix *-ery*, or its contracted form *-ry*, is prototypically used to form
nouns from nominal roots. The principal semantic patterns are:

a. 'a set of things expressed by the nominal root'. The nominal roots
   denote names of substances from which nouns standing for collections of objects are formed. For example, *jewellery* is a set of objects
   that are made from gold, silver, or precious stones; *pottery* is a set of
   objects that are made out of clay by hand; and *weaponry* is a set of
   objects that are made from metals. Similar examples are *chandlery,*
   crockery, cutlery, gadgetry, machinery, stationery, etc.
b. 'a body of people expressed by the nominal root'. The nominal roots
   denote common names from which nouns standing for collections
   of people are formed. For example, *merchantry* is a body of people
   who are merchants, *peasantry* is a body of people who are peasants,
   and *tenantry* is a body of people who occupy rented property. Similar
   examples are *ancestry, citizenry, yeomanry,* etc.
c. 'the place connected with the thing expressed by the nominal root'.
   Some places pertain to objects. For example, *perfumery* is a place where
   perfumes are made and/or sold, and *winery* is a place where wine is
   made. Some nouns derive from verbs. For example, *brewery* is a place
   where beer is made, *eatery* is a place where food is served, and *refinery*
   is a place where oil is made pure. Some places pertain to plants. For
   example, *grapery* is a building where grapes are grown, and *grocery* is
   a store where food and other supplies for household use are sold.
   Some places pertain to people. For example, *nunnery* is a home for
   female members of a religious order, and *nursery* is a place where
   babies are taken care of while their parents are at work. Some places

pertain to animals. For example, *fishery* is a place where fish are caught and sold, and *piggery* is a place where pigs are bred and raised.

The suffix *-ery*, or its contracted form *-ry*, is peripherally used to form nouns from other roots. The marginal semantic patterns are:

a. 'the attitude that shows the thing expressed by the adjectival root'. In this case, the suffix combines with adjectives to form nouns which refer to a style of behaviour. For example, *bravery* is the attitude that shows courage, *savagery* is the attitude that shows cruelty, and *treachery* is the attitude that shows betrayal. More examples are *foolery, knavery, prudery, snobbery*, etc. In some cases, the root is a noun. For example, *drudgery* is the attitude that shows boredom, *thuggery* is the attitude that shows violence, and *trickery* is the attitude that shows deception.
b. 'the practice of doing the thing expressed by the verbal root'. In this case, the suffix combines with verbs to form nouns which imply morally neutral behaviour. For example, *cookery* is the practice of preparing and cooking food, *joinery* the practice of making the wooden parts of a building, and *jugglery* is the practice of keeping objects moving through the air by throwing and catching them quickly. Some nouns imply morally objectionable behaviour. For example, *bribery* is the practice of giving someone money in return for help, *forgery* is the practice of forging a document or a painting, *robbery* is the practice of stealing money or goods from a place.

A graphical representation of the multiple senses of the noun-forming suffix *-(e)ry* is offered in Figure 4.6. Note that the solid arrow represents the prototypical sense, whereas the dashed arrows represent the semantic extensions.

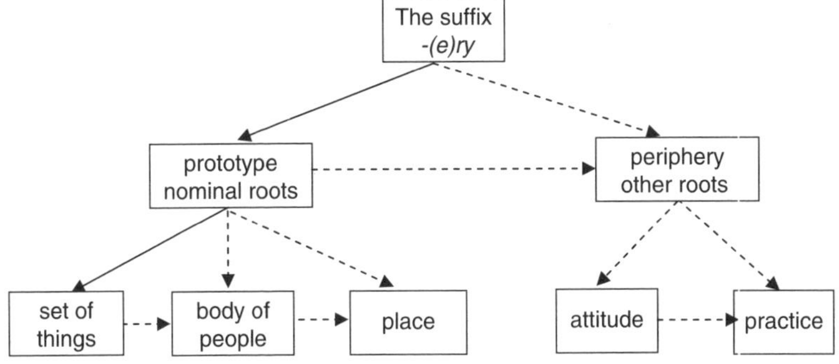

Figure 4.6   The semantic network of the noun-forming suffix *-ery*

Before going any further, let us draw some conclusions from the pre-ceding discussions. One conclusion is that each suffix forms a category of its own, which includes its multiple senses. Another conclusion is that the senses of a suffix gather around one representative sense, referred to as the *prototype*. A further conclusion is that the category of a suffix is a powerful conceptual framework which allows us to see how the different senses are related to one another. A look at the categorial descriptions of the suffixes shows where the senses converge and where they diverge. By convergence, I mean that the suffixes perform the same kind of function or create the same kind of word. On the basis of such converging senses, the suffixes can be grouped into sets, referred to as *domains*. It is within these domains that the suffixes can stand against each other as rivals. So, a *domain* is concerned with a knowledge configuration in which suffixes gather, showing similarity on the surface but dissimilarity below the sur-face. Two suffixes may stand for one concept but differ in the specifics. The elaboration of this cognitive tenet will be the task of the next section.

4.3   Knowledge configurations

In this section, I discuss the impact of the *domain* theory on the mean-ings of de-verbal suffixes. The meaning of a de-nominal suffix, I argue, cannot be known without taking into account the domain to which it belongs. A *domain* is a knowledge structure which comprises a set of lex-ical items. The meaning of any lexical item consists of the way the item contrasts with the other items in the domain. Meaning is constituted out of sense contrasts. The meaning of a lexical item is governed by its usage or the context in which it occurs. The participants in the domain then help to uncover the meanings of one another. De-nominal suffixes form a set in the sense that to understand the meaning of one suffix, it is necessary to understand the meaning of the others in the set. A *domain* has a twofold import. First, it houses the suffixes under one umbrella. Second, it diagnoses the specificity of the suffixes that make up the domain. A *domain* is a cognitive ability which singles out the individual behaviour of lexical items.

Applying the domain theory to the present topic, I argue that noun-forming nominalisers in English evoke, relative to their definitional analyses, the domain of *representation*, an area of knowledge that is con-cerned with the description of one or more members of the same group. As the definition reveals, the domain of *representation* incorporates two components: *individuality* and *collectivity*. *Individuality* involves one entity, a person or an object which is considered separately from the rest of the group. Morphologically, *individuality* is encoded by the nominal suffixes *-dom*, *-hood*, *-ism*, and *-ship*. They differ, I argue, in that *-dom* describes a place, *-hood* designates a condition, *-ism* stands for a belief, and *-ship* indicates a position. By contrast, *collectivity* involves a group of entities that share something in common. Morphologically, *collectivity* is encoded by the nominal suffixes *-age* and *-(e)ry*. They differ, I argue, in that *-age* refers to a small number of entities, whereas *-(e)ry* refers to a large number of entities.

For easy reference, I summarise in Table 4.1 the (sub)domains evoked by noun-forming suffixes in English.

Table 4.1   The (sub)domains evoked by noun-forming suffixes in English

Domain	**Subdomains**	**Exponents**	**Meaning differences**
	Individuality	*-dom*	place
		-hood	condition
		-ism	belief
Representation		*-ship*	position
	Collectivity	*-age*	a small number
		-(e)ry	a large number

In Table 4.1, I show how the *domain* theory applies to the description of noun-forming suffixes in English. The description comprises four steps. In the first step, I place all the nominal suffixes under one domain, which I name *representation*. In the second step, I group the suffixes into two subdomains, which I name *individuality* and *collectivity*. This is done relative to the definitions provided in the previous section. In the third step, I identify the suffixes that represent each subdomain. In the fourth step, I explain the rivalry between the suffixes by pinpointing the peculiarity of each suffix which makes it different from its counterpart. When and how to use a suffix is a matter decided by the speaker. The choice of the speaker comes under the rubric of *construal*. *Construal* is concerned with the ways the speaker conceives a situation and the right expressions s/he chooses to realise them. Two suffixes that stand as rivals construe a situation in different ways. The elaboration of this cognitive tenet will be the task of the following section.

4.4   Conceptual distinctions

In this section, I discuss the *construal* theory in morpho-lexicology, which suggests that the best method of finding out about meaning contrasts between morpho-lexical alternatives is to see how they differ in context where, referentially speaking, they could be seen as interchangeable. The choice of a derived noun, I argue, correlates with the particular construal imposed on its root. *Construal* refers to the particular image which the speaker selects to describe a particular situation for communicative purposes. Because the speaker can describe a given scene in multiple ways, language provides him/her with an army of symbolic resources to code them. Two expressions that are judged to be truth-conditionally the same turn out to be semantically different. The subtle differences in meaning can be expressed in language by using different constructions. Meaning cannot be reduced to a simple truth-conditional correspondence with the world. Meaning is a construal of the speaker's experience in specific ways.

The choice between members of a noun pair is not only a matter of conceptual content, but also of the way the speaker construes it. The construal that is at the disposal of the speaker here is called *perspective*. According to Langacker (1990), perspective refers to the viewpoint imposed on a scene which changes relative to one's intention or the requirement of the discourse. Two nouns may seem to be truth-functionally equivalent, but they are not randomly interchangeable. They certainly offer a distinction in meaning in each case. The distinction resides in the two perspectives the speaker takes on the scene, which are morphologically represented by rival suffixes. Two nouns may be derivationally related and so look alike. Even so, they are distinguishable in use. Each noun relates to a slightly different aspect of the root. Each noun represents a different perspective of the speaker who chooses a distinct morpheme for his/her conceptualisation. In each derivational case, it is the suffix that encodes the intended conceptualisation.

Below are the different perspectives taken on the roots, which are responsible for the semantic distinctions.

4.4.1 The territory–position distinction: *-dom* vs *-ship*

The suffixes *-dom* and *-ship* converge on forming nouns delineating mainly individual entities. Nonetheless, a perusal of concordances in the corpus and pages on the Internet shows that their paths diverge when it comes to precise details. The suffix *-dom* focuses on the territory, area, or sphere where one lives or works. The suffix *-dom* can, thus, be glossed as 'the territory ruled by the entity specified by the nominal root'. This sense can be substantiated by the accompanying collocates. Derived nouns in *-dom* collocate with verbs expressing construction or maintenance, adjectives expressing size or quality, and nouns expressing headquarters or institutions. Syntactically, such derived nouns accept prepositions of place, as in *in the kingdom*. By contrast, the suffix *-ship* focuses on the position, rank, or job which one holds. The suffix *-ship* can, thus, be glossed as 'the position of being the thing signalled by the nominal root'. This sense can be validated by the adjacent collocates. Derived nouns in *-ship* collocate with verbs expressing acquisition or practice, adjectives expressing importance or duration, and nouns expressing duties or rights. Syntactically, such derived nouns accept prepositions of time, as in *during the kingship*. Let us examine some nominal pairs to understand the distinction:

(1) chiefdom vs chiefship

    a. Each section of the chiefdom is ruled by a chief.
    b. She obtained the chiefship despite her wild past.

The two nouns under (1) are derived from the nominal root *chief*, which means 'a person with the highest rank in a company or an organisation'. Yet, construal makes a clear distinction between them in use. In (1a), the noun *chiefdom* means 'the territory where one is a chief'. It is the dominion or state controlled by a chief. *Chiefdom* is preceded by verbs like *build, construct, divide, end, reform*; adjectives like *immense, minor, newly-created, spacious, tiny*; and followed by nouns like *authorities, bases, centres, headquarters, institutions*, etc. In (1b), the noun *chiefship* means 'the position of being a chief'. It is duty or function of a chief. *Chiefship* is preceded by verbs like *attain, obtain, earn, secure, win*; adjectives like *brief, current, momentary, paramount, ultimate*; and followed by nouns like *chore, duty, errand, job, work*, etc.

(2) earldom vs earlship

    a. He held an important office in the earldom.
    b. After some dispute, he acquired the earlship.

The two nouns under (2) are derived from the nominal root *earl*, which means 'a nobleman of high rank'. Yet, construal draws a sharp demarcation between them in use. In (2a), the noun *earldom* means 'the territory where one is an earl'. It is the area or land governed by an earl. *Earldom* is preceded by verbs like *establish, keep up, occupy, restore, take possession of;* adjectives like *extant, extinct, feudal, huge, premier;* and followed by nouns like *associations, corporations, foundations, lands, societies,* etc. In (2b), the noun *earlship* means 'the position of being an earl'. It is job or rank of an earl. *Earlship* is preceded by verbs like *acquire, claim, hold, inherit, receive;* adjectives like *crucial, fair, eternal, momentous, permanent;* and followed by nouns like *assignments, functions, obligations, responsibilities, tasks,* etc.

(3) kingdom vs kingship

    a. He was a prince in a kingdom that knew his worth.
    b. She passed the kingship directly to her elderly son.

The two nouns under (3) are derived from the nominal root *king,* which means 'the male ruler of an independent state that has a royal family'. Yet, construal maintains a noticeable difference between them in use. In (3a), the noun *kingdom* means 'the territory where one is a king'. It is the country or realm ruled by a monarch. *Kingdom* is preceded by verbs like *abolish, expand, found, reside in, sustain;* adjectives like *enormous, independent, separate, small, united;* and followed by nouns like *agencies, businesses, cities, organisations, regions,* etc. In (3b), the noun *kingship* means 'the position of being a king'. It is the authority or power of a monarch. *Kingship* is preceded by verbs like *cede to, descend, gain, pass to, succeed to;* adjectives like *ancient, everlasting, medieval, significant, traditional;* and followed by nouns like *burdens, duties, limits, powers, rights,* etc.[3]

4.4.2 The condition–position distinction: *-hood* vs *-ship*

The suffixes *-hood* and *-ship* work together in forming nouns sketching out largely individual entities. Nevertheless, a review of concordance lines in the corpus and pages on the Internet shows that they follow different directions. The suffix *-hood* lays emphasis on the condition which one goes through. Accordingly, the suffix *-hood* can be defined as 'the condition of being the thing referred to by the nominal root'. This sense can be corroborated by the neighbouring collocates. Nouns derived by means of *-hood* collocate with verbs expressing experience or demonstration, adjectives describing character or personality, and nouns expressing concept or essence. Syntactically, such derived nouns are considered uncountable. By contrast, the suffix *-ship* lays emphasis on the duty which one does or the status which one has. Accordingly, the suffix *-ship* can be defined as 'the position of being the thing signalled by the verbal root'. This sense can be verified by the co-occurring collocates. Nouns derived by means of *-ship* collocate with verbs expressing acquisition or practice, adjectives expressing grace or intelligence, and nouns expressing affection or rite. Syntactically, such derived nouns are considered countable. Let us probe some nominal pairs to make the distinction plain:

(4) fatherhood vs fathership

    a. The prospect of fatherhood is a lifelong responsibility.
    b. The old man provides a fathership for the orphan boy.

The two nouns under (4) are derived from the nominal root *father*, which means 'a male parent'. Still, construal confines them to distinct uses. In (4a), the noun *fatherhood* means 'the condition of being a father'. It refers to the qualities that befit a father. *Fatherhood* is preceded by verbs like *become, conceive, display, experience, imagine*; adjectives like *dubious, early, fulfilled, joyful, lovely*; and followed by nouns like *concept, event, idea, matter, prospect*, etc. In (4b), the noun *fathership* means 'the position of being a father'. It is the high social status given to a man. *Fathership* is preceded by verbs like *embody, furnish with, lavish on, provide, symbolise*; adjectives like *affectionate, compassionate, holy, sympathetic, tender*; and followed by nouns like *affection, care, devotion, love, passion*, etc.[4]

(5) ladyhood vs ladyship

    a. She demonstrates real ladyhood.
    b. He humbly thanked her ladyship.

The two nouns under (5) are derived from the nominal root *lady*, which means 'a woman who has excellent manners and always behaves well'. Still, construal restricts them to separate uses. In (5a), the noun *ladyhood* means 'the condition of being a lady'. It is the qualities that are suitable for a lady. *Ladyhood* is preceded by verbs like *achieve, blossom into, demonstrate, evince, perceive*; adjectives like *angelic, charismatic, exquisite, real, young*; and followed by nouns like *air, core, essence, ideal, notion*, etc. In (5b), the noun *ladyship* means 'the position of being a lady'. It is the title of respect given to a woman. *Ladyship* is preceded by verbs like *achieve, get, have, receive, take*; adjectives like *elegant, good, gracious, sensible, wise*; and followed by personal nouns such as *Thatcher, Jane*, etc.

(6) queenhood vs queenship

    a. She exhibits queenhood in her attitude.
    b. She exercises queenship with prowess.

The two nouns under (6) are derived from the nominal root *queen*, which means 'the female ruler of an independent state that has a royal family'. Still, construal reserves them for independent uses. In (6a), the noun *queenhood* means 'the condition of being a queen'. It is the qualities that are typical of a queen. *Queenhood* is preceded by verbs like *contemplate, exhibit, feel, illustrate, live through*; adjectives like *attractive, beautiful, intrinsic, mature, natural*; and followed by nouns like *conception, essence, honour, pride, spirit*, etc. In (6b), the noun *queenship* means 'the position of being a queen'. It is the office or work of a queen. *Queenship* is preceded by verbs like *apply, carry out, exercise, perform, realise*; adjectives like *astute, brilliant, modern, resourceful, shrewd*; and followed by nouns like *ceremony, feast, practice, ritual, tradition*, etc.[5]

4.4.3 The territory–condition distinction: *-dom* vs *-hood*

In the previous sections, the suffixes *-dom* and *-hood* have been shown to contrast sharply with the suffix *-ship*. In this section, I put them side by side to see if they still retain their meanings. A check of concordances in the corpus and pages on the Internet shows that they do so. The suffix *-dom* stands for the territory that someone rules or occupies. The suffix *-dom* can, hence, be paraphrased as 'the territory ruled by the entity specified by the nominal root'. Collocational evidence can back up this sense. Nouns derived via the suffix *-dom* collocate with verbs expressing construction or maintenance, adjectives expressing size or quality, and nouns expressing headquarters or institutions. For syntactic evidence, such derived nouns are countable. By contrast, the suffix *-hood* describes the condition of experiencing something. The suffix *-hood* can, hence, be paraphrased as 'the condition of being the thing referred to by the nominal root'. Collocational evidence can bear out this sense. Nouns derived via the suffix *-hood* collocate with verbs expressing experience or demonstration, adjectives describing character or personality, and nouns expressing concept or essence. Let us delve into a nominal pair to unravel the distinction:

(7) princedom vs princehood

    a. They scored a quick victory over the princedom of Tatar.
    b. He manifests inherent princehood when he faces people.

The two nouns under (7) are derived from the nominal root *prince*, which means 'the son or grandson of a king or queen'. Nevertheless, construal links them with different uses. In (7a), the noun *princedom* means 'the territory where one is a prince'. It is the country or state ruled by a prince. *Princedom* is preceded by verbs like *create, declare, destroy, run, seize*; adjectives like *civil, independent, private, royal, secular*; and followed by nouns like *bureaus, departments, offices, units, zones*, etc. In (7b), the noun *princehood* means 'the condition of being a prince'. It is the qualities that make a prince. *Princehood* is preceded by verbs like *demonstrate, display, improve, manifest, upgrade*; adjectives like *charismatic, fairy, inherent, magical, natural*; and followed by nouns like *attribute, gift, pattern, principle, stamp*, etc.

4.4.4   The condition–belief distinction: *-hood* vs *-ism*

When they stand as rivals, the suffixes *-hood* and *-ism* contrast quite clearly. The suffix *-hood* indicates the particular state that something or someone is in, and so can be reworded as 'the condition of being the thing referred to by the nominal root'. By contrast, the suffix *-ism* indicates beliefs or ways of behaving, and so can be reworded as 'the belief in being the thing named by the nominal root'. A probe of the concordance lines in the corpus and pages on the Internet confirm the difference in meaning. The confirmation is provided by the collocations. Nominal derivatives in the suffix *-hood* collocate with verbs expressing experience or demonstration, adjectives describing character or personality, and nouns expressing concept or essence. By contrast, nominal derivatives in the suffix *-ism* collocate with verbs denoting adherence or compliance, adjectives describing degrees of belief, and nouns signifying ways of behaving. An example illustrating the distinction is given below:

(8) bachelorhood vs bachelorism

    a. Michael grows into bachelorhood with graceless ease.
    b. Excessive tidiness had been added to his bachelorism.

The two nouns under (8) are derived from the nominal root *bachelor*, which means 'a man who has never been married'. However, construal marks a certain distance between them in use. In (8a), the noun *bachelorhood* means 'the condition of being a bachelor'. It is the qualities that a bachelor has. *Bachelorhood* is preceded by verbs like *abandon, enjoy, give up, grow into, value*; adjectives like *bitter, contented, enforced*, *fretful, horrible*; and followed by nouns like *ambition, dream, era, phase, time*, etc. In (8b), the noun *bachelorism* means 'the belief in being a bachelor'. It is the peculiarity of a bachelor. *Bachelorism* is preceded by verbs like *adhere to, complain of, hold to, persist in, savour of*; adjectives like *liberal, moderate, popular, radical, youthful*; and followed by nouns like *fashion, manner, tone, style, vein*, etc.

4.4.5 The position–doctrine distinction: *-ship* vs *-ism*

When they are in competition, the suffixes *-ship* and *-ism* characterise the root differently. The suffix *-ship* characterises the profession which one has or the rank which one enjoys. So, it can be defined as 'the position of being the thing signalled by the nominal root'. By contrast, the suffix *-ism* indicates the belief which one holds or the practice which one does. So, it can be defined as 'the belief in being the thing named by the nominal root'. A survey of the concordance lines in the corpus and pages on the Internet demonstrates the difference in meaning. One can prove the difference by looking at the collocates. Derivatives ending in the suffix *-ship* collocate with verbs expressing acquisition or practice, adjectives expressing importance or duration, and nouns expressing duties or rights. By contrast, derivatives ending in the suffix *-ism* collocate with verbs denoting adherence or compliance, adjectives describing degrees of belief, and nouns signifying ways of behaving. In the light of this, consider the following distinction:

(9) attorneyship vs attorneyism

    a. She was appointed to an attorneyship in court.
    b. He conveys great attorneyism in legal matters.

The two nouns under (9) are derived from the nominal root *attorney*, which means 'someone whose job is to give advice to people about the law and speak for them in court'. Nonetheless, construal applies them to different contexts. In (9a), the noun *attorneyship* means 'the position of being an attorney'. It is the job or work of an attorney. *Attorneyship* is preceded by verbs *appoint, notch up, pursue, train, work*; adjectives like *entitled, competent, masterful, qualified, vital*; and followed by nouns like *ability, expertise, knowledge, proficiency, skill*, etc. In (9b), the noun *attorneyism* means 'the doctrine of the attorney'. It is the set of beliefs held by an attorney. *Attorneyism* is preceded by verbs like *abide by, convey, heed, observe, practise*; adjectives like *absolute, great, impartial, public, realistic*; and followed by nouns like *approach, culture, form, issue, tendency*, etc.[6]

4.4.6 The condition–body distinction: *-hood* vs *-age*

The suffixes *-hood* and *-age* compete to form nouns from the same root, but then they go in different directions. The suffix *-hood* underlines the qualities befitting someone. Thereupon, it can be defined as 'the condition of being the thing referred to by the nominal root'. By contrast, the suffix *-age* underlines a group of people taken collectively. Thereby, it can be defined as 'a body of the thing indicated by the nominal root'. A scan of the concordance lines in the corpus and pages on the Internet vindicates the difference in meaning. To ascertain the difference, one needs to examine the collocates. Derivatives in the suffix *-hood* collocate with verbs expressing experience or demonstration, adjectives describing character or personality, and nouns expressing concept or essence. By contrast, derivatives in the suffix *-age* collocate with verbs implying identification or etymology, adjectives describing origin or nationality, and nouns implying analysis or assessment. In this regard, consider a distinction such as the following:

(10) parenthood vs parentage

    a. The prospect of parenthood filled them with horror.
    b. She is of mixed Australian and Japanese parentage.

The two nouns under (10) are derived from the nominal root *parent*, which means 'a person's father or mother'. Despite that, construal imputes distinct applications to them. In (10b), the noun *parenthood* means 'the condition of being a parent'. It is the qualities of a parent. *Parenthood* is preceded by verbs like *brace for, entertain, face, reflect on, value*; adjectives like *adoptive, (in)experienced, lone, responsible, single*; and followed by nouns like *delights, joys, prospects, pressures, stresses*, etc. In (10a), the noun *parentage* means 'a body of parents'. It is a person's parents or ancestors, especially when regarded in terms of social characteristics or geographic origins. *Parentage* is preceded by verbs like *deny, dispute, identify, presume, share*; ordinary adjectives like *common, different, indeterminate, obvious, unknown*; nationality adjectives like *American, Indian, Italian, Spanish, Turkish*; and followed by nouns like *analysis, assessment, concern, evaluation, testing*, etc.[7]

4.4.7 The position–body distinction: *-ship* vs *-age*

There is such rivalry between the suffixes *-ship* and *-age* to form nouns from a common root. Yet, each displays different potential to win the rivalry. The suffix *-ship* depicts the position or rank which one holds. On this basis, it can be defined as 'the position of being the thing signalled by the nominal root'. By contrast, the suffix *-age* depicts a group of people taken collectively. On this basis, it can be defined as 'a body of the thing indicated by the nominal root'. A study of the concordance lines in the corpus and pages on the Internet supports the difference in meaning. To uncover the difference, one needs to scrutinise the collocations. Derivatives ending in the suffix *-ship* collocate with verbs expressing acquisition or practice, adjectives expressing importance or duration, and nouns expressing duties or strategies. By contrast, derivatives ending in the suffix *-age* collocate with verbs expressing enhancement or selection, adjectives describing extent or pattern, and nouns expressing connections or networks. In this respect, consider a distinction such as:

(11) clientship vs clientage

      a. Permanent clientship is a good thing.
      b. The restaurant has a regular clientage.

The two nouns under (11) are derived from the nominal root *client*, which means 'a person who is a customer of a shop, store, restaurant, organisation, etc'. In spite of that, construal assigns them discrete roles. In (11a), the noun *clientship* means 'the position of being a client'. It is the status of being a client. *Clientship* is preceded by verbs like *change, claim, confer on, exchange, improve*; adjectives like *demanding, important, modern, permanent, transitory*; and followed by nouns like *conditions, initiatives, policies, structures, systems*, etc. In (11b), the noun *clientage* means 'a body of clients'. It is the people who use the services of a professional person or organisation. *Clientage* is preceded by verbs like *attract, build up, expand, increase, select*; adjectives like *broad, contemporary, extensive, local, regular*; and followed by nouns like *connections, networks, relationships, systems, ties*, etc.[8]

4.4.8 The position–body distinction: *-ship* vs *-ery*

In the area of forming nouns from the same root, the suffixes *-ship* and *-ery* are considered contestants. In the course of the contest, the suffixes, however, expose different characters. The suffix *-ship* portrays the rank which one holds or the status which one has. As a result, it can be defined as 'the position of being the thing signalled by the nominal root'. By contrast, the suffix *-ery* portrays a group of people taken collectively. As a result, it can be defined as 'a body of the thing expressed by the nominal root'. An analysis of the concordance lines in the corpus and pages on the Internet bears out the difference in meaning. The difference is shown by means of the collocations. Derivatives ending in the suffix *-ship* collocate with verbs expressing acquisition or practice, adjectives expressing importance or duration, and nouns expressing duties or strategies. By contrast, derivatives ending in the suffix *-ery* collocate with verbs expressing announcements or encouragement, adjectives describing principles or tendencies, and nouns depicting category or cluster. In this connection, consider the following distinction:

(12) citizenship vs citizenry

    a. After careful thought, he chose to take Canadian citizenship.
    b. They encourage participation of the citizenry in the election.

The two nouns under (12) are derived from the nominal root *citizen*, which means 'a person who has the legal right to belong to a particular country'. Even so, in terms of construal they are not interchangeable. In (12a), the noun *citizenship* means 'the position of being a citizen'. It is the status of being a citizen. *Citizenship* is preceded by verbs like *acquire, change, grant, have, take*; adjectives like *active, dual, full, global, multiple*; and followed by nouns like *ceremonies, duties, obligations, pledges, rights* and adjectives of nationality, such as *Australian, British, Canadian, European, Swedish*, etc. In (12b), the noun *citizenry* means 'a body of citizens'. It is the people of a particular town, country, etc. *Citizenry* is preceded by verbs like *arouse, encourage, inform, mobilise, treat*; adjectives like *apathetic, civilised, democtratic, local, patriotic*; and nouns like *category, class, cluster, section, selection* plus *of*, etc.

4.5 Summary

In this chapter, the purpose has been to extend the approach to the semantic description of complex nouns that are derived from nominal roots. To shed light on this, I checked three arguments against data offered in the British National Corpus and Internet pages. In section 4.2, I argued that noun-forming suffixes form categories; a category is a network made up of a range of senses exhibiting minimal differences. For each suffix, I identified an archetypal sense and worked outwards from there to get to all the marginal senses. In section 4.3, I argued that noun-forming suffixes gather in domains; a *domain* is a knowledge representation in which its members share common properties but differ in specific details. In section 4.4, I argued that noun-forming suffixes are by no means in complementary distribution, and the nouns they form are not in free variation. The distinction between the noun pair is not merely a matter of formal constraints. Rather, it is a matter of meaning, which resides in the alternate ways the root is construed. In each construal, the root takes on a different suffix with its semantic substance. This is supported by the distinguishing collocates of each pair member, which the corpus data show. In cognitive semantics, meaning considerations control the preference of one lexical item over another.

Notes

1. In some rare derivations, the suffix *-ism* denotes businesses. For example, *journalism* is the business of collecting, writing, and publishing news stories and articles in newspapers and magazines or broadcasting them on the radio and television; and *tourism* is the business of providing services – such as transport, places to stay, or entertainment – for people who are on holiday.
2. When tacked on to a professional agent or the like, the suffix *-ship* denotes a skill or ability. This meaning is the chief productive use today. For example, *marksmanship* is the skill or ability to shoot a gun accurately, *musicianship* is the skill in playing a musical instrument or singing, and *statesmanship* is the skill of making good judgements. Extra examples are *craftsmanship, draftsmanship, horsemanship, penmanship, salesmanship, showmanship, sportsmanship, workmanship*, etc.
3. The same distinction applies to pairs like *dukedom* vs *dukeship*. Both are derived from the nominal root *duke*, which means 'a man with the highest social rank outside the royal family'. Yet, they differ in use. In *He set sail for the dukedom of Brittany*, the noun *dukedom* means 'the territory where one is a duke'. In *He received the dukeship of Brittany*, the noun *dukeship* means 'the position of being a duke'.
4. The same distinction applies to pairs like *cousinhood* vs *cousinship* and *sisterhood* vs *sistership*. Both *cousinhood* vs *cousinship* are derived from the nominal root *cousin*, which means 'a child of a person's aunt or uncle'. Yet, they differ in use. *Cousinhood* means 'the condition of being a cousin', whereas *cousinship* means 'the position of being a cousin'.
5. In this study, aspects of one domain are shown to be responsible for the interpretation of noun pairs. In some cases, aspects of two different domains interact to provide explanation for the meanings of noun pairs. This is in line with the cognitive principle that the set of domains which a semantic unit triggers provide the necessary context for its understanding. For instance, the de-nominal suffix *-ship* evokes the domain of *representation* (individuality), whereas the de-adjectival suffix *-ness* evokes the domain of *characterisation* (trait). The two nouns *hardship* and *hardness* relate to *hard*, but they represent different connotations. In *The town endured great hardship during the war*, the noun *hardship* refers to the position of being hard. Hardship is a situation that is difficult and unpleasant because one does not have enough money, food, clothes, etc. In *He is known for hardness of heart*, the noun *hardness* refers to the trait of being hard. *Hardness* is the quality of being tough and unyielding.

6. The meanings of some noun pairs are so flexible that they are capable of accepting two different domains for their characterisation, as in *activism* vs *activity, egocentrism* vs *egocentricity, formalism* vs *formality, individualism* vs *individuality, pluralism* vs *plurality*, etc.

   Let us take some examples. The de-nominal suffix *-ism* evokes the domain of *representation* (belief), whereas the de-adjectival suffix *-ity* evokes the domain of *characterisation* (mode). The two nouns *individualism* and *individuality* relate to *individual*, but there is a difference in meaning between them. In *Capitalism stresses innovation, competition, and individualism*, the noun *individualism* refers to the philosophy of asserting the self. *Individualism* is the belief that individual people in society should have the right to make their own decisions, etc. rather than be controlled by the government. In *She expresses her individuality through her clothes*, the noun *individuality* refers to the mode of being individualistic. *Individuality* is a condition that makes somebody or something different from others.

   To vindicate the analysis, let us check another nominal pair. The two nouns *formalism* and *formality* relate to *formal*, but each has a meaning that is different from the other. In *The defence of formalism is always that it serves to control an excess of feeling*, the noun *formalism* refers to the philosophy of strictly adhering to traditional or prescribed forms. *Formalism* is the doctrine of rigorous adherence to traditional forms, as in religious practice, or artistic expression. In *She greeted him with stiff formality*, the noun *formality* refers to the mode of being formal. *Formality* is a condition in which one strictly attends to propriety or ceremony, or rigidly observes rules or customs.

7. There exist some pairs with slight differences in meaning. One such pair is *personhood* vs *personage* but with a slight difference in meaning. In *They are in danger of losing personhood*, the noun *personhood* means 'the condition of being a person'. *In She became the most celebrated personage*, the noun *personage* means 'an important or famous person'.

   Another pair is *orphanhood* vs *orphanage*. In *She suffers from orphanhood*, the noun *orphanhood* means 'the condition of being an orphan'. In *She was brought up in an orphanage*, the noun *orphanage* means 'a home for children whose parents are dead'.

8. Another pair with a slight difference in meaning is *tutorship* vs *tutorage*. In *He accepted an offer of a tutorship in modern history at Oxford*, the noun *tutorship* means 'the position of being a tutor'. In *He has matured under the tutorage of Angelo Dundee*, the noun *tutorage* means 'the authority or solemnity of a tutor'.

5
Agent-Forming Nominalisers

In this chapter, I dwell on the semantics of agent-forming nominalisers. More specifically, I examine the meanings of morphemes and how they combine to form nouns. During the investigation, I verify three tenets of Cognitive Semantics. To that end, I organise the chapter as follows. In section 5.1, I say what an agent-forming suffix is and enumerate the mechanisms that condition its integration with a root to form a noun. In section 5.2, I argue that each agent-forming suffix has a core sense from which its other senses fan out. In section 5.3, I argue that the scope of meaning of an agent-forming suffix is demarcated by the type of semantic relations it has with its counterparts. In section 5.4, I argue that the members of a noun pair cannot be freely exchanged for each other despite the fact that they look alike. Each has a specific meaning which is the result of construal. To depict non-synonymy, I resort to their distinctive collocates. This is done by examining actual data offered in the corpus. In section 5.5, I repeat the main points of the chapter.

5.1 Introduction

An agent-forming suffix is a word-final element that is added to a root to form an agentive noun. Because it cannot occur alone, it is considered a bound morpheme. It integrates with a free morpheme to form a composite structure. For the integration to succeed, they should conform to what Langacker (1987: 277–327) calls *valence* conditions. First, they should show correspondence at both semantic and phonological poles. Second, they should show difference in dependence; the free morpheme occurs as autonomous while the bound morpheme as dependent. Third, they should show difference in determinacy; the bound morpheme acts as a profile determinant and so is primarily responsible for the character of the composite structure. It has a double import. Syntactically, it marks a change in the class of a lexical item from abstract to concrete. Semantically, it marks a shift in the meaning of the root. Fourth, they should show difference in status; the bound morpheme is the head, while the free morpheme is the complement. In some derivational cases, the root undergoes a phonetic change, as in *tactician* from *tactics*, whereas in others it preserves its phonetic shape, as in *adoptee* from *adopt*.

5.2   Semantic networks

In this section, I examine the impact of the *category* theory on the semantic description of agent-forming suffixes. An agent-forming suffix, I argue, is polysemous in that it exhibits a cluster of distinct but related senses, which are derived from a core, prototypical, sense. The core sense serves as a standard from which the other senses are derived via semantic extensions. The core sense has the common properties of the category; hence it is deemed the best represenstative of it. The core sense is the sense that comes to mind first or is the easiest to recall. The remaining, peripheral, senses have some but not all of the properties of the category; hence they are related to the core sense relative to their degrees of similarity to it. Like members of a large family, the peripheral senses are linked in a way that they resemble one another in a variety of ways, yet each has its own individuality. *Category* is then a powerful tool which reveals both the general as well as the specific properties of a given lexical item, via their relationships with one another.

To capture the semantic behaviour of an agentive suffix, I ground the description in two cognitive models. With verbal roots, I ground the description in the cognitive model of *transitivity*. Let me give an example of the suffix -*ee*. In a prototypical formation, the suffix is added to monotransitive verbs to denote a patient, as in *examinee*, and, in some cases, to denote ditransitive verbs, as in *presentee*. Peripherally, the suffix is added to verbs to denote an agent, as in *retiree*. With nominal roots, I ground the description in the cognitive model of *animacy*. Let me give an example of the suffix -(*i*)*an*. Prototypically, the suffix is added to roots denoting intellectual disciplines to form agentive nouns. In *beautician*, it is added to a name of a trade. In *statistician*, it is added to a name of science. Peripherally, the suffix is added to names of countries to form agentive nouns, as in *American*.

5.2.1 De-verbal agent suffixes

De-verbal suffixes are bound morphemes that are added to verbs to form agentive nouns. They are *-ant*, *-ee*, and *-er*.

5.2.1.1 *-ant*

Prototypically, the suffix *-ant*, and its variant *-ent*, is attached to verbal roots denoting action, to form adjectives. Relative to the nature of the combining root, the suffix expresses three meanings:

a. 'liable to do the action signalled by the verbal root'. This meaning emerges when the suffix is attached to transitive verbs. The adjectives so formed denote an action which involves both an agent and a patient. For example, *a defiant protester* is a protester who is liable to defy authority, *a resistant politician* is a politician who is liable to resist change, and *an observant guard* is a guard who is liable to observe things. Other examples are *acceptant, attendant, continuant, ignorant, reliant*, etc.
b. 'apt to do the action signalled by the verbal root'. This meaning emerges when the suffix is attached to intransitive verbs. The adjectives so formed denote an action which involves no patient. For example, *a compliant child* is a child who is apt to comply, and *an errant husband* is a husband who is apt to err, and *a hesitant leader* is a leader who is apt to hesitate. Other examples are *deviant, emigrant, repentant, resultant, triumphant*, etc.
c. 'being in the condition signalled by the verbal root'. This meaning emerges when the suffix is attached to (in)transitive. For example, *a dominant issue* is an issue that is more important than anything of the same type, *a radiant bride* is a bride who is obviously happy or beautiful, and *a vibrant performer* is a performer who is energetic, exciting, and full of enthusiasm.

Peripherally, the suffix *-ant* is attached to verbal roots to form agentive nouns. Relative to the nature of the combining root, the suffix expresses two meanings:

a. 'a person who performs the specific action signalled by the verbal root'. In these derivations, the agent nouns are humans. This meaning emerges when the suffix is attached to verbs to form agentive nouns, often used in technical or legal discourse. For example, *an applicant* is a person who applies for a job, *a complainant* is a person or an organization that takes legal action against another, and *a defendant* is a person or company that answers charges in a court. Other examples are *accountant, assailant, assistant, attendant, consultant, dependant, informant, inhabitant,* etc. Some verbal roots end in *-ate,* which they lose before the *-ant,* as in *celebrant, emigrant, immigrant, litigant, participant,* etc. Some agentive nouns end in *-ent.* For example, *a correspondent* is a person who reports on a particular subject or sends reports from a foreign country, *a president* is a person who leads a country or an organisation, and *a resident* is a person who lives in a given place.

b. 'a substance which performs the specific action signalled by the verbal root'. In these derivations, the agent nouns are non-humans. This meaning emerges when the suffix is attached to verbs to form names of instruments, often used to promote an action or serve a particular purpose. For example, *a disinfectant* is a substance which kills bacteria, especially in toilets and kitchens, *a pollutant* is a substance that contaminates the air, soil, or water, and *a relaxant* is a substance which reduces tension and strain, particularly in muscles. Other examples are *coolant, retardant,* etc. Some verbal roots end in *-ate,* which they lose before the suffix, as in *intoxicant, irritant, lubricant, precipitant,* etc. Some agentive nouns end in *-ent.* For example, *a repellent* is a substance which discourages insects, and *a solvent* is a substance which dissolves solids.

A graphical representation of the multiple senses of the de-verbal agent-forming suffix *-ant* is offered in Figure 5.1. Note that the solid arrow represents the prototypical sense, whereas the dashed arrows represent the semantic extensions.

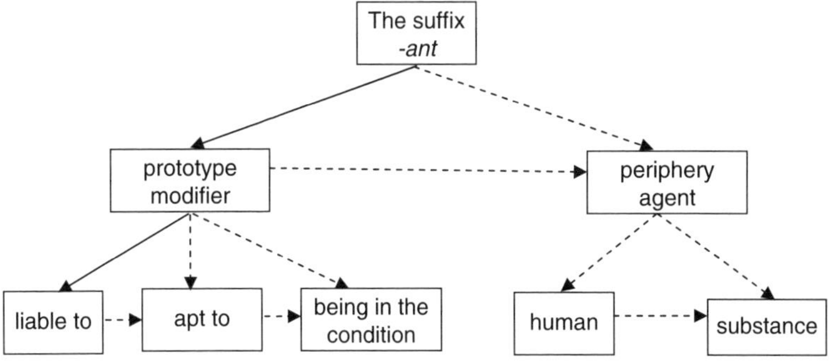

Figure 5.1   The semantic network of the de-verbal agent-forming suffix *-ant*

5.2.1.2   *-ee*[1]

Prototypically, the suffix *-ee* is added to verbal roots to form patientive nouns. The verbal roots can vary in terms of transitivity, and so the suffix means:

a. 'a person who is affected by the action named by the verbal root'. This meaning arises when the suffix is added to monotransitive verbs of affecting. The human person is the direct object of the verb, and so the target of the influence. For example, *an employee* is a person who is employed, *an interviewee* is a person who is interviewed, and *a trainee* is a person who is being taught how to do a particular job. Other examples are *adoptee, counselee, divorcee, examinee, rescuee,* etc. Some verbal roots end in *-ate* which they lose before the suffix as in *evacuee* and *nominee*. In all the examples, the person involved in the event is considered a volitional participant. However, in some examples the person involved in the event is considered a non-volitional participant. For example, a *biographee* is a person whose life is described in a biography, *a detainee* is a person who is kept in prison because of hos/her political views, *a draftee* is a person who is drafted for military service, and *an internee* is a person who is put into prison for political reasons, usually without a trial.

b. 'a person to whom something is transferred by the action named by the verbal root'. This meaning arises when the suffix is added to ditransitive or prepositional verbs denoting transfer of an entity, be it physical or verbal. The human person is the indirect object of the ditransitive or the prepositional verb, and so the receiver of the transaction. For example, *a grantee* is a person to whom something is given, *a payee* is a person to whom money is paid, and *a sendee* is a person to whom something is sent. Other examples are *awardee, assignee, chargee, dedicatee, depositee, presentee, promisee, releasee,* etc.

c. In rare formations, the verbal roots allow both interpretations. For example, a *transferee* is either a person who is transferred, or a person to whom a conveyance is made.

Peripherally, the suffix *-ee* is added to other roots to form various nouns. The suffix expresses the following senses:

a. 'a person who is granted the thing named by the nominal root'. This sense arises when the suffix is added to nominal roots to form patientive nouns. For example, *a patentee* is a person who is granted a patent, *a franchisee* is a person who is granted a franchise, *a mortgagee* is a person who is granted a mortgage, and *a trustee* is a person who is granted trust.

b. 'a person who has performed the action named by the verbal root'. This sense arises when the suffix is added to verbal roots to form agentive nouns. Although the pattern is rare, there exist some nouns in contemporary English. For example, *an attendee* is a person who has attended a meeting, *an escapee* is a person who has escaped from prison, and *a standee* is a person who stands on a bus. Other examples include *arrivee, devotee, recoveree, retiree, returnee*, etc.

c. 'a person who is associated with the thing named by the nominal root'. This sense arises when the suffix is added to nominal roots denoting place to form nouns. For example, *a townee* is a person who is associated with towns.

d. 'a thing that resembles the thing named by the nominal root'. This sense arises when the suffix is added to nominal roots to form inanimate nouns. For example, *a goatee* is a short-pointed beard on the chin like that of a goat.

e. 'a thing that is diminutive of the thing named by the nominal root'. This sense arises when the suffix is added to nominal roots to form inanimate nouns. For example, *a bootee* is a small woollen boot for a baby, and *a coatee* is a short close-fitting coat.

A graphical representation of the multiple senses of the de-verbal agent-forming suffix *-ee* is offered in Figure 5.2. Note that the solid arrow represents the prototypical sense, whereas the dashed arrows represent the semantic extensions.

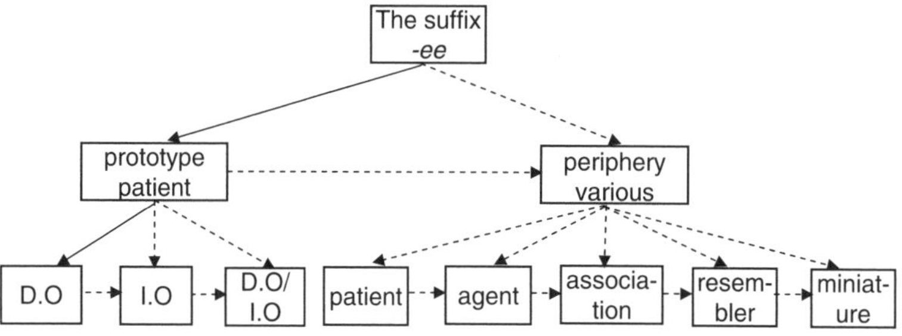

Figure 5.2 The semantic network of the de-verbal agent-forming suffix *-ee*

5.2.1.3 *-er*^{2}

The suffix *-er* takes other orthographic variants like *-or* and *-ar*. The form *-er* is by far the most frequent and has become a living formative. Prototypically, the suffix *-er* is added to verbal roots to form agentive nouns, exhibiting the following range of meanings:

a. 'a person who performs the action labelled in the verbal root'. This meaning results when the suffix is added to transitive verbs to form animate entities. In some formations, the agentive nouns are humans. For example, *a caterer* is a person who serves food, *a farmer* is a person who takes care of a farm, and *a manager* is a person who controls an organisation. Other examples are *baker, driver, reader, teacher, writer*, etc. Some agentive nouns end in *-or* as in *advisor, director, governor, instructor, supervisor*, etc. For example, *a governor* is a person who runs a political unit. Some others end in *-ar* as in *beggar, bursar, liar*, etc. For example, *a beggar is* a person who asks for money. In other formations, the agentive nouns are non-humans. For example, *a pointer* is a hunting dog trained to point towards the prey that is being hunted, *a retriever* is a large dog trained to find and bring back something, and *a trotter* is a horse that is trained for harness racing.

b. 'a person who does the activity labelled in the verbal root'. This meaning results when the suffix is added to intransitive verbs to form animate entities. For example, *a dreamer* is a person who dreams, *a runner* is a person who runs, and *a worker* is a person who works. Other examples are *gambler, hiker, jogger, jumper, surfer, talker, thinker, walker*, etc. Some agent nouns end in *-or*. For example, an *actor* is a person who acts.

c. 'a thing that is set to perform the action labelled in the verbal root'. This meaning results when the suffix is added to transitive verbs to form inanimate entities. For example, *a freezer* is a device which preserves food at a very cold temperature, *a lighter* is a device which provides a flame for a cigarette, and *a toaster* is a device which toasts bread. Other examples are *computer, duster, eraser, freighter, heater, pager, stapler, steamer*, etc. Some instruments end in *-or* like *accelerator, calculator, detonator, elevator, generator, refrigerator*, etc. For example, *a radiator* is a device which sends out heat. Some derived nouns stand for both animate and inanimate entities. For example, *a cleaner* is either a person who cleans a building or an instrument used for cleaning, and *an organisor* is either a person who organises a project or a calender used for planning.

d. 'a thing that does the thing labelled in the verbal root'. This meaning results when the suffix is added to (in)transitive verbs to form two types of agents. In some cases, the agents are material objects. Some signify devices. For example, *a beeper* is a device which makes a loud sound, *a buzzer* is a device which makes a buzzing sound, and *a timer* is a device which records time. Others signify garments. For example, *slippers* are soft comfortable shoes for wearing inside the house, *a stomacher* is an elaborately ornamented garment formerly worn over the stomach and chest, especially by women, and *waders* are rubber boots that cover the whole leg to keep a person dry in water. In other cases, the agents are immaterial objects. For example, *a clincher* is a fact which makes someone do something after a long consideration, *a reminder* is a written or spoken message which reminds someone to do something, and *a thriller* is a book, play or film which makes someone excited.

Peripherally, the suffix *-er* is added to other roots to form agentive nouns, exhibiting the following range of meanings:

a. 'a person who makes the object labelled in the nominal root'. This meaning results when the suffix is added to names of substances to denote occupations. For example, *a furrier* is a person who makes furry clothes, *a hatter* is a person who makes hats, and *a whaler* is a person who hunts whales. Other examples are *miller, sealer, slater, tinner*, etc.
b. 'a person who is associated with the thing labelled in the nominal root'. This meaning results when the suffix is added to names of sciences to denote professions. For example, *an astrologer* is a person who studies the movements of stars and planets, *an astronomer* is a person who makes observations about celestial phenomena, *a lawyer* is a person who gives advice to people about the law, and *a philosopher* is a person who studies or writes about the meaning of life.
c. 'a person who is from the place labelled in the nominal root'. This meaning results when the suffix is added to names of places to denote origin. For example, *a Berliner* is a person who is from Berlin, *a Hamburger* is a person who is from Hamburg, *a Londoner* is a person who is from London, and *a New Yorker* is a person who is from New York.
d. 'a person who has the attribute labelled in the nominal root'. This meaning results when the suffix is added to names of fruits or tissues to denote quality. For example, *a corker* is a person who is especially

attractive or amusing, *a miser* is a person who has a great desire to possess money and hates to spend it, and *a nutter* is a person who is crazy, foolish or strange.

e. 'a place which is used for the thing labelled in the nominal root'. This meaning results when the suffix is added to verbs of activities to denote location. For example, *a diner* is a railway carriage to dine in, *a kneeler* is something like a cushion or board to kneel on, and *a sleeper* is a railway carriage which contains beds for passengers to sleep in.

A graphical representation of the multiple senses of the de-verbal agent-forming suffix *-er* is offered in Figure 5.3. Note that the solid arrow represents the prototypical sense, whereas the dashed arrows represent the semantic extensions.

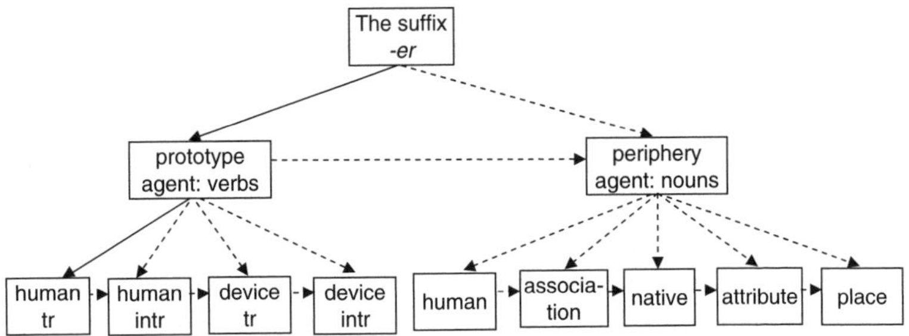

Figure 5.3   The semantic network of the de-verbal agent-forming suffix *-er*

5.2.2   De-nominal agent suffixes

De-nominal suffixes are bound morphemes that are added to nouns to form personal nouns. They are *-ian*, *-ist*, and *-ster*.[3]

5.2.2.1   *-(i)an*

Prototypically, the suffix *-(i)an* is added to nominal roots which refer to intellectual or artistic disciplines to coin agentive nouns. In such coinages, the suffix expresses two senses:

a. 'a person whose job involves the thing referred to in the nominal root'. This meaning occurs when the suffix is added to names of trades, ending mostly in *-ic* or *-ics*, to denote occupations. For example, *an electrician* is a person whose job is to put in and maintain electrical wires, *a magician* is a person whose job is to perform tricks for entertainment, and *an optician* is a person whose job is to examine people's eyes and sell glasses or contact lenses. Other examples are *beautician, clinician, musician, rhetorician, tactician, technician,* etc.

b. 'a person who is devoted to the knowledge field referred to in the nominal root'. This meaning occurs when the suffix is added to names of arts or sciences, ending mostly in *-ic* or *-ics*, to denote professions. For example, *a dietician* is a person who is devoted to dietetics, *a logician* is a person who is devoted to logic, and *a mathematician* is a person who is devoted to mathematics. Other examples are *academician, paediatrician, phonetician, physician, politician, statistician, theoretician,* etc.

Peripherally, the suffix *-ian* is added to nominal roots, which refer to names of countries, people or animals, to coin agentive nouns. In such coingaes, the suffix expresses three senses:

a. 'a person who is from the place referred to in the nominal root'. This meaning occurs when the suffix is added to names of cities and countries. For example, *an American* is a person who is from America, *an Arabian* is a person who is from Arabia, *a Cuban* is a person who is from Cuba, and *a Persian* is a person who is from Persia, Iran.

b. 'a person who is connected with the thing referred to in the nominal root'. This meaning occurs when the suffix is added to names of famous people to form agentive nouns having a link with the work or time of the person mentioned. For example, *an Elizabethan* is a person who is connected with the period of Elizabeth, *a Freudian* is a person who is connected with the psychoanalytic theories or practices of Freud, and *a Victorian* is a person who is connected with the time during which Queen Victoria was queen of Britain. Other examples are *Chaucerian, Darwinian, Edwardian, Georgian, Shakespearean,* etc.

c. 'a member of the group referred to in the nominal root'. This meaning occurs when the suffix is added to names of animals. For example, *a mammalian* is a member of the group of mammals, and *a reptilian* is a member of the group of reptiles.

A graphical representation of the multiple senses of the de-nominal agent-forming suffix *-(i)an* is offered in Figure 5.4. Note that the solid arrow represents the prototypical sense, whereas the dashed arrows represent the semantic extensions.

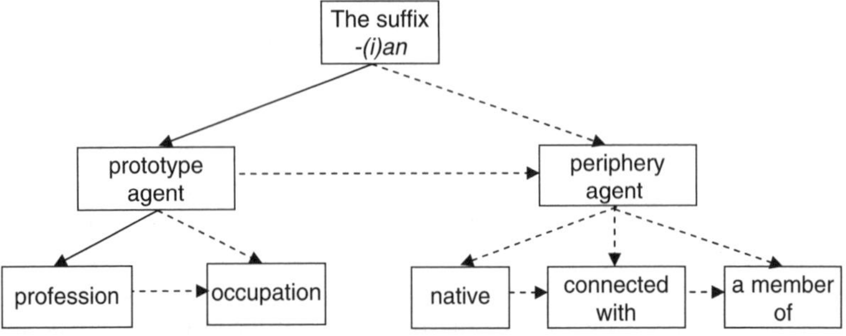

Figure 5.4   The semantic network of the de-nominal agent-forming suffix -*(i)an*

5.2.2.2   -*ist*

Prototypically, the suffix -*ist* is added to nominal roots to form agentive nouns. Relative to the nature of the joining root, the suffix has a variety of senses:

a. 'a person who is versed in the knowledge field indicated by the nominal root'. This sense ensues when the suffix is added to nominal roots referring to names of sciences. For example, *an anthropologist* is a person who is versed in anthropology, *a biologist* is a person who is versed in biology, and *a geologist* is a person who is versed in geology. As is clear, the personal nouns have counterparts in -*y*. Other examples are *botanist, ecologist, economist, pathologist, pharmacist, physiologist, psychologist, urologist,* etc.

b. 'a person who holds the thing indicated by the nominal root'. This sense ensues when the suffix is added to noiminal roots referring to beliefs, doctrines or philosophies. For example, *an extremist* is a person who has extreme opinions, *an idealist* is a person who has ideal principles, and *a nationalist* is a person who advocates political independence for his country. Other examples are *apologist, classicist, defeatist, empiricist, isolationist, Marxist, philanthropist, pragmatist, reformist, socialist,* etc.

c. 'a person who handles the thing indicated by the nominal root'. This sense ensues when the suffix is added to noiminal roots referring to skills. For example, *an archivist* is a person who takes care of archives, *a motorist* is a person who drives a car, and *a novelist* is a person who writes novels. Other examples are *artist, balloonist, columnist, dentist, dramatist, florist, humorist, journalist, lobbyist, lyricist,* etc. Some nouns like *anglicist, linguist, physicist, psychiatrist, semanticist* have counterparts in -*ics*. Some nouns are inanimate. For example *a stockist* is a shop that sells a particular type of goods.

d. 'a person who plays the instrument indicated by the nominal root'. This sense ensues when the suffix is added to roots referring to musical instruments. For example, *a cellist* is a person who plays the cello, *a pianist* is a person who plays the piano, and *a violinist* is a person who plays the violin. Other examples are *cymbalist, guitarist, harpist, trombonist,* etc. *Drummer* and *trumpeter* are exceptions.

Peripherally, the suffix *-ist* is added to nominal roots to form agentive nouns which describe a person as 'having the disapproving trait indicated by the nominal root' in the sense of showing hate or opposition. The nouns so formed have a cognate in *-ism*. For example, *an ageist* is a person who is prejudiced against the elderly, *a racist* is a person who is prejudiced against other races, and *a sexist* is a person who is prejudiced against the members of the other sex.

A graphical representation of the multiple senses of the de-nominal agent-forming suffix *-ist* is offered in Figure 5.5. Note that the solid arrow represents the prototypical sense, whereas the dashed arrows represent the semantic extensions.

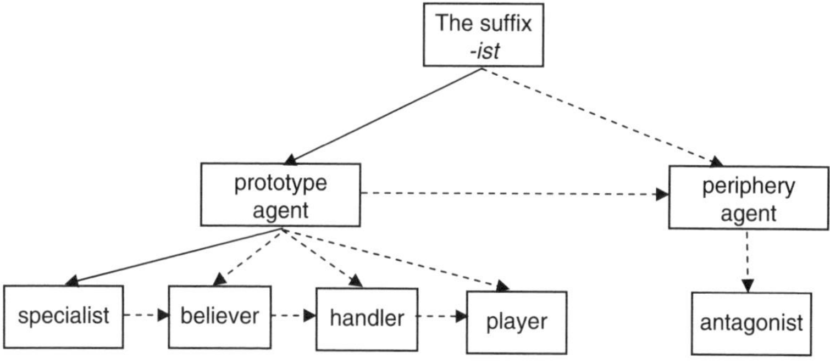

Figure 5.5   The semantic network of the de-nominal agent-forming suffix *-ist*

5.2.2.3   *-ster*[4]

Originally the suffix *-ster* was used, as Marchand (1969: 348) describes, in forming feminine agent nouns. In modern English, it is used in forming male agents, whereas the suffix *-ess* is used to form female agents as in *seamstress*, a woman whose occupation is sewing.

Prototypically, the suffix *-ster* is added to nominal roots to form agentive nouns having connotations of shadiness or illegal dealings. The nouns so formed denote occupation or habitual behaviour. The suffix means 'a person who performs the habitual action signified by the nominal root'. For example, *a fraudster* is a person who obtains money by deceiving people, *a gamester* is a person who habitually gambles, and *a mobster* is a person who is involved in organised crime. Other examples include *gangster, huckster, lewdster, ringster, trickster*, etc. Peripherally, the suffix *-ster* is added to a few nominal roots to form agentive nouns having a normal character. The suffix expresses three senses:

a. 'a person who is skilled at the thing signified by the nominal root'. The nouns so formed denote professions. For example, *a dabster* is a person who is skilled at doing a business, *a dopester* is a person who is skilled at making analyses and predictions, as of the outcome of an athletic or political contest, *a pollster* is a person who is skilled at conducting a public survey of facts or opinions, and *a tipster* is a person who is skilled at selling information, especially tips to betters.
b. 'a person who writes the thing signified by the nominal root'. For example, *a punster* is a person who writes puns, *a rhymester* is a person who writes poor verses, and *a songster* is a person who writes songs.
c. 'a vehicle that is signified by the nominal root'. For example, *a dragster* is a long narrow fast car which has been specially built to take part in drag races, *a roadster* is a car without a roof and with only two seats, and *a sportster* is a sports car. Some agent nouns denote either the vehicle or its user. For example, a *speedster* is a fast driver or vehicle, and a *teamster* is a person who drives a team or truck as a job.

A graphical representation of the multiple senses of the de-nominal agent-forming suffix *-ster* is offered in Figure 5.6. Note that the solid arrow represents the prototypical sense, whereas the dashed arrows represent the semantic extensions.

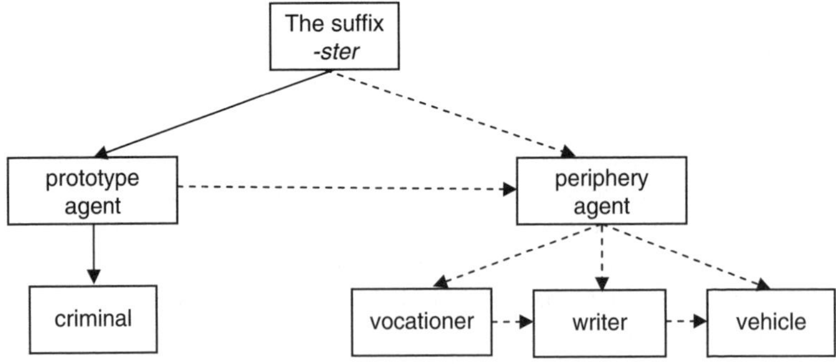

Figure 5.6 The semantic network of the de-nominal agent-forming suffix *-ster*

Before going any further, let us draw some conclusions from the preceding discussion about the suffixes. One conclusion is that each suffix forms a category of its own, which includes its multiple senses. Another conclusion is that the senses of a suffix gather around one representative sense, referred to as the *prototype*. A further conclusion is that the category of a suffix is a powerful conceptual framework which allows us to see how the different senses are related to one another. A look at the categorial descriptions of the suffixes shows where the senses converge and where they diverge. On the basis of the converging senses, the suffixes can be grouped into sets, referred to as *domains*. It is within these domains that the suffixes can stand against each other as rivals. So, a *domain* is concerned with a knowledge configuration in which suffixes gather showing similarity on the surface but dissimilarity below the surface. Two suffixes may stand for one concept but differ in the specifics. The elaboration of this cognitive tenet will be the task of the next section.

5.3   Knowledge configurations

In this section, I concentrate on the issue of the *domain* theory in morpho-lexicology, where it is used to characterise the meanings of agent-forming suffixes. According to this theory, the meaning of an agent-forming suffix, I argue, can be defined in terms of the domain which it activates. The basic idea is that one cannot understand the meaning of a suffix independently of the semantic knolwdge it evokes, which usually involves other suffixes. A *domain* is a coherent structure which relates suffixes together, captures their semantic specifications, and shows how they correspond to different aspects. Suffixes are organised as knowledge configurations in which each has a specific role to play and a specific task to fulfil. The notion of *domain* shows that what may appear to be hard-to-predict variations among lexical items can be treated as instances of regular linking relations. A *domain* is a device whereby the choice of a lexical item is guided by its meaning rather than by its formal property.

Extending the domain theory to morphology, I argue that agent-forming nominalisers in English activate, relative to their definitional analyses, the cognitive domain of *agenthood*. *Agenthood* is an area of knowledge which includes a person or thing that performs a particular action or specialises in a particular subject. As the definition reveals, the domain of agenthood incorporates two components: *performance* and *speciality*. *Performance* is the doing of an action or a piece of work.

Morphologically, *performance* is represented by the nominal suffixes *-ant*, *-er*, and *-ee*. They are considered de-verbal suffixes. They differ, I argue, in that *-ant* designates a performer of a potential technical action, *-er* designates a performer of a potential non-technical action, whereas *-ee* designates a performer of an actual action. By contrast, *speciality* is the subject that one knows a lot about or has a lot of experience of. Morphologically, *speciality* is represented by the nominal suffixes *-ist*, *-ian*, and *-ster*. They are considered de-nominal suffixes. They differ, I argue, in that *-ist* refers to a specialist who is versed in a positive thing, *-ian* refers to a specialist who is devoted to a positive thing, and *-ster* refers to a specialist who does something negative, mainly in return for money.

For easy reference, I summarise in Table 5.1 the (sub)domains evoked by agent-forming suffixes in English.

Table 5.1 The (sub)domains evoked by agent-forming suffixes in English

Domain	Subdomains	Exponents	Meaning differences
Agenthood	Performance	*-ant*	performer of a potential, specific action
		-er	performer of a potential, social, generic action
		-ee	performer of an actual action
	Speciality	*-ist*	inventor of a subject
		-ian	practitioner of a subject
		-ster	user of a skill

In Table 5.1, I show how the *domain* theory applies to the description of personal suffixes in English. The description comprises four steps. In the first step, I place all the personal suffixes under one domain, which I name *agenthood*. In the second step, I group the suffixes into two subdomains, which I name *performance* and *speciality*. This is done relative to the definitions provided in the previous section. In the third step, I identify the suffixes that represent each subdomain. In the fourth step, I explain the rivalry between the suffixes by pinpointing the peculiarity of each suffix, which makes it different from its counterpart. When and how to use a suffix is a matter decided by the speaker. The choice of the speaker comes under the rubric of *construal*. *Construal* is concerned with the ways the speaker conceives a situation and the right expressions s/he chooses to realise them. Two suffixes that stand as rivals construe a situation in different ways. The elaboration of this cognitive tenet will be the task of the following section.

5.4   Conceptual distinctions

In this section, I concentrate on the *construal* theory in morpholexicology. *Construal* is a language strategy which allows the speaker to conceptualise a situation in different ways and choose the linguistic structures to represent them in discourse. In Cognitive Semantics, the meaning of a linguistic expression, as Langacker (1997: 4–5) states, does not reside in its conceptual content alone, but includes the particular ways of construing that content. In this connection, the choice of a derived noun, I argue, coincides with the particular construal imposed on its root. What help the speaker to code the conceptualisations are the plentiful resources provided by language. Alternative expressions may appear to be truth-conditionally equivalent, but semantically they turn out to be non-equivalent. There are situations which favour the use of one over the other, relative to the needs of the discourse. Therefore, the specific experiences speakers conceptualise are reflected by the specific structures they choose from the repertoire of language.

The choice of a particular member of a noun pair is a response to the way the speaker construes the conceptual content of the root. The construal that is at the disposal of the speaker here is called *perspective*. According to Langacker (1990), *perspective* refers to the viewpoint imposed on a scene which changes relative to one's intention or the requirement of the discourse. Two nouns can be exchanged but the speaker should notice the difference in meaning that each makes. The difference in meaning is triggered by the difference in perspective which the speaker takes on the scene. For each perspective, the speaker opts for a different morpho-lexical form. That is, even if two nouns share a root they are certainly not synonymous in use. Each has its own meaning which is signalled by the particular suffix and which, for its part, correlates with the particular aspect of the meaning of the root. Consequently, the perspective embodied by a linguistic expression constitutes a significant facet of its meaning.

Below are the different perspectives taken on the roots, which are responsible for the semantic distinctions.

5.4.1   The specific–generic distinction: *-ant* vs *-er*

As illustrated earlier, the suffixes *-ant* and *-er* evoke the subdomain of *performance*. Nonetheless, each suffix focuses on a distinct facet of it. Examination of concordances in the corpus and pages on the Internet ascribes the difference to the scope of the performance. The suffix *-ant* focuses on the technical instance of performance, used in a specific or definite context. A specific instance pertains to a specialised subject or involves a technical field. A personal noun with suffix -*ant* can, thus, be glossed as 'a person who performs the specific action signalled by the verbal root'. As evidence, personal nouns ending in -*ant* collocate with words used in a penal code or in contexts having a methodical or systematic tinge. By comparison, the suffix -*er* focuses on the non-technical instance of performance, used in a generic or vague context. A generic instance involves an entity that is usable in a variety of contexts. A personal noun with suffix -*er* can, thus, be glossed as 'a person who performs the generic action labelled in the verbal root'. As evidence, personal nouns ending in -*er* collocate with words used in a general environment, or in contexts having a normal or casual tinge. To understand the distinction, we need to examine some nominal pairs:

(1) defendant vs defender

    a. The defendant has been convicted of a petty crime.
    b. She has finally found a defender of her viewpoints.

The two personal nouns under (1) involve the verbal root *defend*, which means 'to protect someone or something from harm or against attack'. Still, there is a distinction in their use, which rests on the way the root is construed. In (1a), the personal noun *defendant* means 'a person who performs the specific action of defending'. A *defendant* is a person who is required to defend a legal charge in a court of law. It collocates with nouns like *conviction, crime, evidence, hearing, trial*; adjectives like *arraigned, convicted, culpable, guilty, indicted*; and verbs used in the passive like *acquit, charge, convict, release, sue*, etc. In (1b), the personal noun *defender* means 'a person who performs the generic action of defending'. A *defender* is a person who defends someone or somewhere against attack. It collocates with nouns like *sports, faiths, policies, rights, viewpoints*; adjectives like *devoted, gallant, heroic, loyal, staunch*; and verbs like *guard, maintain, protect, support, uphold*, etc.

(2) informant vs informer

    a. The survey is based on information from 20 informants.
    b. Most police informers receive rewards for their tip-offs.

The two personal nouns under (2) link to the verbal root *inform*, which means 'to tell someone about particular facts'. In spite of that, each noun represents a particular construal, and so has a different use. In (2a), the personal noun *informant* means 'a person who performs the specific action of informing'. An *informant* is a person who gives a researcher useful linguistic or cultural information in answer to questions. It takes noun collocates like *information, investigation, question, survey, testimony*; adjective collocates like *aboriginal, born, endemic, indigenous, native*; and verb collocates like *apprise, brief, clue, enlighten, instruct,* etc. In (2b), the personal noun *informer* means 'a person who performs the generic action of informing'. An *informer* is a person who informs the police on the criminal activities of others, often for reward. It takes noun collocates like *government, mafia, police, secret agency, tip-off*; adjective collocates like *disgraceful, hateful, ignominious, notorious, shameful*; and verb collocates like *bug, monitor, snoop, spy, tap*, etc.

(3) occupant vs occupier

    a. The official occupants of the flat were an Italian family.
    b. The city occupiers were driven out after fierce fighting.

The two personal nouns under (3) contain the verbal root *occupy*, which means 'to exist in or use a place, or to move into and take control of a place'. Yet, they are used differently depending on the construal of the root. In (3a), the personal noun *occupant* means 'a person who performs the specific action of occupying'. An *occupant* is a person who has the legal rights to reside in a place, i.e. accommodation or vehicle, or hold a position. It allows noun collocates like *car, chair, flat, hotel, seat*; adjective collocates like *authorised, legal, licensed, official, sanctioned*; and verb collocates like *abide, dwell, hire, lease, rent*, etc. In (3b), the personal noun *occupier* means 'a person who performs the generic action of occupying'. An *occupier* is a person who does not have the legal rights to reside in a place, i.e. land, or takes possession of a property. It allows noun collocates like *city, country, land, premises, territory*; adjective collocates like *intrusive, meddlesome, obtrusive, presumptuous, trespassing*; and verb collocates like *breach, encroach on, intrude, trespass, violate*, etc.[5]

5.4.2 The potential–actual distinction: *-er* vs *-ee*

As expounded earlier, the suffixes *-er* and *-ee* signal the subdomain of *performance*. Nevertheless, each suffix emphasises a different aspect of it. Evaluation of concordance lines in the corpus and pages on the Internet relates the difference to the temporal aspect of the performance. The suffix *-er* lays emphasis on the potential aspect of performance. It denotes that the agent intends to perform an action, or looks forward to an upcoming event. Accordingly, a personal noun with suffix *-er* means 'a person who may perform the action labelled in the nominal verbal root'. As evidence, personal nouns ending in -*er* collocate with events of generic nature or contexts implying future events. By contrast, the suffix -*ee* lays emphasis on the actual aspect of performance. It denotes that the agent has already performed an action, or is engaged in performing it. Accordingly, a personal noun with suffix -*ee* means 'a person who has performed the action named by the verbal root'. As evidence, personal nouns ending in -*ee* collocate with events of specific nature or contexts implying past events. To make the distinction plain, we need to probe some nominal pairs:

(4) attender vs attendee

    a. He was a regular attender of all craft exhibitions.
    b. She was registered as an attendee of the seminar.

The two personal nouns under (4) encompass the verbal root *attend*, which means 'to go to or be present at an event'. Despite having the same root, each noun has a construal that provides a solution to its individual use. In (4a), the personal noun *attender* means 'a person who may perform the action of attending'. An *attender* is a person who may attend an event. It patterns with noun collocates like *ceremony, exhibition, gallery, meeting, party*; and adjective collocates like *assiduous, constant, frequent, persistent, regular*, etc. In (4b), the personal noun *attendee* means 'a person who has performed the action of attending'. An *attendee* is a person who has attended an event. It patterns with noun collocates like *conference, course, lecture, seminar, tutorial*; and adjective collocates like *current, former, one-time, matriculated, registered*, etc.[6]

(5) escaper vs escapee

    a. He looks more like a prospective escaper from a junk shop.
    b. The escapees were recaptured after several days on the run.

The two personal nouns under (5) relate to the verbal root *escape*, which means 'to get free from something, or to avoid something'. However, an understanding of construal makes a distinguishable difference in how they are used. In (5a), the personal noun *escaper* means 'a person who may perform the action of escaping'. An escaper is a person who may escape or intends to escape from a place or a situation to avoid danger or embarrassment. Its common collocates include nouns like *country, famine, fire, regime, war*; and adjectives like *eventual, expected, prospective, subsequent, ultimate,* etc. In (5b), the personal noun *escapee* means 'a person who has performed the action of escaping'. An *escapee* is a person who has escaped from a place, especially a prison, or from a chaser. Its common collocates include nouns like *captor, guard, jail, officer, prison;* and adjectives like *evasive, ongoing, momentary, recent, unexpected,* etc.

(6) returner vs returnee

    a. The training courses may be of interest to you as a returner.
    b. The organisation distributes winter clothing to the returnees.

The two personal nouns under (6) derive from the verbal root *return,* which means 'to go or come back, as to a previous place or condition'. Even so, they are used in different contexts, and so should not be confused. In (6a), the personal noun *returner* means 'a person who may perform the action of returning'. A *returner* is a person who may return to a place after some time. Its collocational patterns comprise of nouns like *clinic, office, school;* and adjectives like *accustomed, habitual, inveterate, steady, unfailing,* etc. In (6b), the personal noun *returnee* means 'a person who has performed the action of returning'. A *returnee* is a person who has returned to a place where one was before. Its collocational patterns comprise of nouns like *city, country, home;* and adjectives like *banished, deported, expelled, ousted, repatriated,* etc.[7]

5.4.3 The inventive–implementive distinction: *-ist* vs *-ian*

As elucidated earlier, the suffixes *-ist* and *-ian* evoke the subdomain of *speciality.* Even so, each suffix singles out a discrete aspect of it. Scrutiny of concordances in the corpus and pages on the internet imputes the difference to the nature of the specialisation. The suffix *-ist* describes someone as inventing a new concept or originating a novel idea. A personal noun with suffix *-ist* can, hence, be defined as 'a person who is versed in the knowledge field indicated by the nominal root'. As evidence, personal nouns ending in *-ist* collocate with nouns like biology, education, military, politics, or theology, and adjectives denoting creativity. By contrast, the suffix *-ian* describes someone as implementing a concept or pursuing an activity. A personal noun withsuffix *-ian* can, hence, be defined as 'a person who is devoted to the knowledge field referred to by the nominal root'. As evidence, personal nouns ending in *-ian* collocate with words used in religion, such as *books, ceremonies,* *doctrines*, and *teachings*; words used in art, such as *painting, drawing*, and *sculpture*; and adjectives denoting assiduity. To unravel the distinction, we need to delve into some nominal pairs:

(7) historicist vs historian

>   a. She was a pioneer historicist who argued for idealism.
>   b. He used to be an amateurish historian of medieval art.

The two personal nouns under (7) represent the nominal root *history*, which means 'the branch of knowledge that deals with past events'. Nevertheless, each noun symbolises a certain construal, and so has its individual sense. In (7a), the personal noun *historicist* means 'a person who is versed in the field of history'. A *historicist* is a person who is an authority on history, one who sees history as a standard of value or a determinant of events. It frequently associates with nouns and verbs derived from such nouns, like *argument, conception, formulation, proposition, theory*; and adjectives like *ace, consummate, expert, pioneer, versed*, etc. In (7b), the personal noun *historian* means 'a person who is devoted to the field of history'. A *historian* is a person who studies or writes about history, one who compiles a chronological record of historical events. It frequently associates with nouns like *art, family, space travel, theatre, war*; adjectives like *amateurish, inexperienced, non-professional, novice, unskilled*; and verbs like *compile, collect, describe, record, trace*, etc.

(8) theologist vs theologian

>   a. He teaches theology at Oxford. He is a theologist.
>   b. He studies theology at Oxford. He is a theologian.

The two personal nouns under (8) contain the nominal root *theology*, which means 'the study of religion and religious belief, or a set of beliefs about a particular religion'. After all, their uses are dissimilar when it comes to how the root is construed. In (8a), the personal noun *theologist* means 'a person who is versed in the field of theology'. A *theologist* is a person who is skilled in theology, a system of religious doctrine. It tends to co-occur with adjective collocates like *creative, innovative, original, proficient, premier*; and verb collocates like *intuit, preach, sermonise, speculate, surmise*, etc. In (8b), the personal noun *theologian* means 'a person who is devoted to the field of theology'. A *theologian* is a person who studies theology or uses a religious theory. It tends to co-occur with noun collocates like *Bible, gospel, sermon, faith, church*; and adjective collocates like *Anglican, Calvinist, Catholic, Christian*, etc.

(9) theorist vs theoretician

    a. The theorist speculated that a virus caused the disease.
    b. The theoretician displayed some paintings in the show.

The two personal nouns under (9) involve the nominal root *theory*, which means 'the body of principles that underlies an area, especially when seen as distinct from actual practice'. Though they are related in derivation, their meanings are quite different. In (9a), the personal noun *theorist* means 'a person who is versed in the field of theory'. A *theorist* is a person who speculates, formulates or invents a theory; a person who develops ideas about a particular subject so as to explain why things happen. It attracts noun collocates and verbs derived from them like *assumption, conception, hypothesis, speculation, supposition*; and adjectives denoting creativity, etc. In (9b), the personal noun *theoretician* means 'a person who is devoted to the field of theory'. A *theoretician* is a person who studies or uses the theoretical framework of a subject, a person who is given to theory. It attracts noun collocates like *drawings, paintings, photographs, sculpture, statue*; adjectives denoting persistence; and verbs like *exhibit, display, show, unveil*, etc.[8]

5.4.4   The social–vocational distinction: *-er* vs *-ster*

As explained earlier, the suffixes *-er* and *-ster* signal the domain of *agenthood*. However, each suffix selects a varied subdomain of it. Investigation of concordance listings in the corpus and pages on the Internet attribute the difference to the nature of the agenthood. The suffix *-er* characterises someone who performs a funny act, or someone who turns his/her hand to a trade for social interaction. Thereupon, a personal noun with suffix *-er* means 'a person who performs the social action labelled in the nominal root'. The suffix is neutral in connotation. As evidence, personal nouns ending in *-er* collocate with words denoting traits of approving nature. By contrast, the suffix *-ster* characterises someone who performs a vocational act, or someone who depends on a trade as a means of livelihood. Thereupon, a personal noun with suffix *-ster* means 'a person who performs the vocational action signified by the nominal root'. In the majority of cases, the suffix is derogatory in connotation. As evidence, personal nouns ending in *-ster* collocate with words denoting more or less traits of disapproving nature. To decode the distinction, we need to inspect some nominal pairs:

(10) joker vs jokester

    a. Michael is a bit of a practical joker.
    b. He was a gift for a comical jokester.

The two personal nouns under (10) derive from the noun *joke*, which means 'something, such as an amusing story or trick, that is said or done in order to make people laugh'. Even though they stem from the same root, the nouns don't mean the same thing. In (10a), the personal noun *joker* means 'a person who performs the social action of joking'. A *joker* is a person who does something to confuse someone else and make other people laugh. Most often, it collocates with adjectives like *funny, playful, practical, witty*, etc. In (10b), the personal noun *jokester* means 'a person who performs the vocational action of joking'. A *jokester* is a person who is skilled at telling amusing stories or performing comical acts to make people laugh. Most often, it collocates with adjectives like *clownish, comical, hilarious, jocular, waggish*, etc.

(11) tipper vs tipster

    a. The waiters liked him for being a big tipper.
    b. Jim Taylor is the season's top racing tipster.

The two personal nouns under (11) embody the nominal root *tip*, which means 'small gift, usually money, given in appreciation for a service rendered'. Although the nouns are similar in derivation, they are distinctive in use. In (11a), the personal noun *tipper* means 'a person who performs the social action of tipping'. A tipper is a person who leaves some money for the person who has provided him/her with a service. It shows a tendency to co-occur with noun collocates like *barber, hairdresser, porter, taxi driver, waiter*; adjective collocates like *big, generous, munificent, openhanded, unsparing*; and verb collocates like *pay*, etc. In (11b), the personal noun *tipster* means 'a person who performs the vocational action of tipping'. A tipster is a person who sells tips or information, especially to horserace betters or financial speculators. It shows a tendency to co-occur with noun collocates like *football, game, racing, sports, TV*; adjective collocates like *astute, shrewd, smart, top, visionary*; and verb collocates like *advise, favour, inform, say, tell*, etc.

(12) tricker vs trickster

> a. He often plays tricks on his friends. He is a bit of a tricker.
> b. The cheque book trickster was trapped by his finger print.

The two personal nouns under (12) embrace the nominal root *trick*, which means 'an action which is intended to deceive, either as a form of entertainment or as a way of cheating someone'. Still, each noun is distinct in construal, and so has a distinct role to play in the language. In (12a), the personal noun *tricker* means 'a person who performs the social action of tricking'. A *tricker* is a person who plays jokes on others for the sake of amusement. It pairs with adjective collocates like *artless, cheerful, harmless, innocent, light-hearted*; and verb collocates like *have somebody on, kid, pull somebody's leg, tease, wind somebody up*, etc. In (12b), the personal noun *trickster* means 'a person who performs the vocational action of tricking'. A *trickster* is a person who plays tricks on others for the sake of deception. It pairs with adjective collocates like *deceitful, misleading, sinful, vicious, wicked*; and verb collocates like *cheat, deceive, falsify, forge, mislead*, etc.[9]

5.4.5   The mechanical–inventive distinction: *-er* vs *-ist*

As clarified earlier, the suffixes *-er* and *-ist* embody the domain of *agenthood*. All the same, each picks a separate subdomain of it. Consideration of concordances in the corpus and pages on the internet associates the difference with animacy. The suffix *-er* depicts something that is designed for a particular function, a device that is made to do a particular type of work. Consequently, a personal noun with suffix *-er* means 'a device that is set to perform the action labelled in the verbal root'. As evidence, personal nouns ending in *-er* favour nouns denoting instruments and adjectives denoting colour, cost, fashion, make, or size. By contrast, the suffix *-ist* depicts someone who has the type of job that needs a high level of proficiency, someone who excels at doing a particular type of work. Consequently, a personal noun with suffix *-ist* means 'a person who is versed in the knowledge field indicated by the nominal root'. As evidence, personal nouns ending in *-ist* favour nouns denoting humans and adjectives denoting craftsmanship. To clarify the distinction, we need to go over some nominal pairs:

(13) copier vs copyist

> a. As Kim's business grew, she rented a new xerox copier.
> b. Of all landscape painters, Tom is the most gifted copyist.

The two personal nouns under (13) contain the verbal root *copy*, which means 'to make identical version of something', but they are not alike in use. In (13a), the personal noun *copier* means 'a device that is set to perform the action of copying'. A *copier* is a machine that makes exact copies of writing or pictures on paper by photographing them. Collocationally, it associates with nouns like *colour, fax, office, photo, xerox;* and adjectives like *bulky, digital, expensive, fashionable, new,* etc. In (13b), the personal noun *copyist* means 'a person who is versed in the field of copying'. A *copyist* is a person who makes copies of written documents or works of art. Collocationally, it associates with nouns like *cartoon, fiction, handwriting, painting, symphony;* and adjectives like *adept, gifted, professional, proficient, trained,* etc.

(14) cycler vs cyclist

    a. A thermal cycler maintains specific temperatures in a laboratory.
    b. Mike Drummond is more of a race cyclist than a mountain biker.

The two personal nouns under (14) embrace the verbal root *cycle*, which means 'to travel by means of a bicycle, motorcycle, or the like', but they are not compatible in use. In (14a), the personal noun *cycler* means 'a device that is set to perform the action of cycling'. A *cycler* is a device that makes something happen regularly. It commonly co-occurs with nouns like *image, light, text, wallpaper, water;* and adjectives like *costly, grey, fast, sizeable, thermal,* etc. In (14b), the personal noun *cyclist* means 'a person who is versed in the field of cycling'. A *cyclist* is a person who rides a bicycle on a professional basis. It commonly co-occurs with nouns like *bike, champion, helmet, race, riding;* and adjectives like *accomplished, experienced, Olympic, professional, ranked,* etc.

(15) styler vs stylist

    a. The new styler is attractively designed in gold and black.
    b. To have the mane tamed, you need to go to a hair stylist.

The two personal nouns under (15) encompass the verbal root *style*, which means 'to shape or design something such as a person's hair or an object', but they are not interchangeable in use. In (15a), the personal noun *styler* means 'a device that is set to perform the action of styling'. A *styler* is an electronical appliance used for setting or styling hair. Primarily, it is associated with nouns like *fleece, fur, garment, hair, pile*; and adjectives like *black, cheap, new-fashioned, plastic, small*, etc. In (15b), the personal noun *stylist* means 'a person who is versed in the field of styling'. A *stylist* is a person whose job is to shape or design something. Primarily, it is associated with nouns like *brush, curler, hair, lotion, trim*; and adjectives like *adroit, competent, dexterous, expert, talented*, etc.[10]

5.5 Summary

In this chapter, the objective has been to look in some detail at the semantics of complex nouns derived from nominal roots, looking specifically at pairs of nouns that share the same content but end in different agent-forming suffixes. To that end, I validated three arguments against data offered in the British National Corpus and Internet pages. In section 5.2, I argued that agent-forming suffixes are polysemous in the sense that they are associated with a number of related but distinct senses. Their senses are organised around a central sense from which the set of additional senses are derived. In section 5.3, I argued that agent-forming suffixes gather in domains, a *domain* is a concept in which the members converge by sharing general properties but diverge in the minute details. In section 5.4, I argued that neither are agent-forming suffixes in complementary distribution nor are the nouns they derive in free variation. The two derived nouns represent two different conceptualisations of their common root. Each conceptualisation is coded by a different suffix. This is evidenced by the distinguishing collocates of each pair member, which the corpus data show. In Cognitive Semantics, there is a strong correspondence between semantic properties and their morphological exponents.

Notes

1. For more on the suffix *-ee*, see papers of Barker (1998) and Portero Munoz (2003), which are rooted in other frameworks.
2. A number of papers have been written on *-er*. For detailed discussions, see Levin & Rappaport (1988), Ryder (1991, 1999), and Panther & Thornburg (2002), among others.
3. Another agent-forming suffix is *-eer*. Prototypically, the suffix is attached to nominal roots to denote humans. The suffix means:

   (i) 'a person who is engaged in the thing expressed by the nominal root'. Very often, a derogatory shade of meaning is attached to such nouns. For example, a *patrioteer* is a person who is engaged in extreme nationalism, a *profiteer* is a person who is engaged in profit-making by taking advantage of a situation in which other people are suffering, and a *racketeer* is a person who is engaged in illegal activities such as bribery, fraud, or intimidation to make a profit. However, a few nouns have a normal tinge. For example, an *engineer* is a person who is engaged in designing and constructing machines or buildings, an *auctioneer* is a person who is engaged in calling out the prices that people offer at an auction, and a *mountaineer* is a a person who is engaged in climbing mountains as a sport or job.

(ii) 'a person who writes the thing expressed by the nominal root'. This meaning arises when the suffix is attached to roots used in the arts. For example, a *fictioneer* is a person who writes fictions, a *pamphleteer* is a person who writes or publishes polemical pamphlets, a *sloganeer* is a person who writes slogans, and a *sonneteer* is a person who writes sonnets.

(iii) 'a person who designs or operates the thing expressed by the nominal root'. This meaning arises when the suffix is attached to roots used in the military. For example, a *cannoneer* is a person who fires a cannon, a *charioteer* is a person who drives a chariot, and a *rocketeer* is a person who designs space rockets.

Peripherally, the suffix is attached to nominal roots to denote inanimate objects. The suffix means 'a thing that is expressed by the nominal root'. For example, a *gazetteer* is a dictionary of geographical names, and a *muffineer* is a dish for keeping muffins in.

4. For a detailed semantic discussion of the suffix *-ster*, see Lubbers' (1965) paper.

5. The same distinction applies to pairs like *commandant/commander*, *servant/server*, etc. Let us explain one pair. Both *commandant* and *commander* are derived from the verb *command*, which means 'to lead and control, or to order and direct'. Yet, they differ in their use. In *He is the commandant of a naval base*, the personal noun *commandant* means 'a person who performs the specific action of commanding'. A *commandant* is an officer who is in charge of a military organisation, or a military force. In *He is the commander of the organisation*, the personal noun *commander* means 'a person who performs the general action of commanding'. A *commander* is a person in an official position of authority who can command or control others.

6. Likewise, the suffix *-ee* competes with the suffix *-ant* in *attendant*. In *The pool attendant keeps a constant watch on the swimmers*, the personal noun *attendant* means 'a person who performs the specific action of attending'. An *attendant* is a person who serves people at a car park, cloakroom, garage, lavatory, museum, petrol pump, pool, wedding, or on an aircraft, etc.

An interesting pair ending in *-ant* vs *-ee* is *cohabitant/cohabitee*. Both are derived from the verb *cohabit*, which means 'to live together as, or as if, a married couple'. Yet, they differ in their use. In *Is Mr Jones one of the cohabitants at this address?* the personal noun *cohabitant* means 'a person who performs the specific action of cohabiting'. A *cohabitant* is a person who officially lives with another in the same place. In *She got infected through a smoking cohabitee*, the personal noun *cohabitee* means 'a person who has performed the action of cohabiting'. A *cohabitee* is a person who has lived with someone else in a place.

7. The same distinction applies to pairs like *devoter/devotee, stander/standee*, etc. Let us explain one pair. Both *stander* and *standee* are derived from the verb *stand*, which means 'to be in a vertical state or to maintain an erect position on one's feet' Yet, they differ in their use. In *A crowd of sitters and standers*, the personal noun *stander* means 'a person who may perform the action of standing'. A *stander* is a person who stands. In *Three standees are occupying the standing room*, the personal noun *standee* means 'a person who has performed the action of standing'. A *standee* is a person who is standing in an auditorium or in a bus, etc.

8. The same distinction applies to the pair *physicist/physician*, which is different in root and meaning. In *The physicist deals with all aspects of matter and energy*, the noun *physicist* means 'a person who is versed in the field of physics'. A *physicist* is a person who specialises in physics. In *The physician diagnoses and heals human diseases*, the noun *physician* means 'a person who is devoted to the field of medicine'. A physician is a person who practises general medicine as distinct from surgery.

9. The same distinction applies to the pair *ganger/gangster*. Both personal nouns are derived from the noun *gang*, which means 'a group of people who work together for social or criminal purposes'. Yet, they differ in their use. In *The ganger and the workers are always in dispute*, the personal noun *ganger* means 'a person who performs the social action of ganging'. A *ganger* is a person who supervises a gang of workers, as in a factory. In *The gangster was trapped by his finger print*, the personal noun *gangster* means 'a person who performs the vocational action of ganging'. A *gangster* is a person who belongs to an organised gang of criminals.

10. The same distinction applies to the pair *conformer/conformist*. Both personal nouns are derived from the verb *conform*, which means 'to be or act in accordance with an established standard or norm'. Yet, they differ in their use. In *The furrows in the rock need a conformer*, the personal noun *conformer* means 'a device that is set to perform the action of conforming'. A *conformer* is a device used to bring something into harmony or back into its shape. In *A conformist is a man who conforms to the values of a society*, the personal noun *conformist* means 'a person who is versed in the field of conforming'. A *conformist* is a person who complies with accepted standards or established practices.

    Another pair with a slight difference in meaning is *astrologer/astrologist*. Both personal nouns are derived from the noun *astrology*, which means 'the study of the positions of the heavenly bodies in relation to each other, in the attempt to predict their influence on human affairs'. Yet, they differ in their use. In *The astrologer studies the movements of planets*, the personal noun *astrologer* means 'a person who performs the generic action of astrology'. An *astrologer* is a person who studies celestial bodies. In *The astrologist forecasts radical changes on the social arena*, the personal noun *astrologist* means 'a person who performs the specific action of astrology'. An *astrologist* is an expert who foretells the future by interpreting the movements of the planets, i.e. forecaster.

6
Conclusions

This chapter has two subject matters. One is the contributions made by the study. The other is the comparisons made with the other theoretical paradigms. To that end, I organise the chapter as follows. In section 6.1, I sum up the significant contributions, which come in two types: theoretical and empirical. As can be seen, the integration of theoretical and empirical models proved to be influential in describing linguistic structure. In section 6.2, I set the theory of Cognitive Semantics or Cognitive Grammar (two sides of the same coin) in a broader context with a view to drawing out explicit comparisons with other theories of language. As can be seen, the tools provided by Cognitive Semantics appeared to be powerful in accounting for language mysteries. A remaining challenge for the cognitive enterprise is to find solutions to problems in areas beyond grammar and morphology.

6.1 Significant contributions

This study has dealt with the semantics of noun formation in English; namely, the process of deriving a noun by adding a suffix to the final position of a root. The general goal of the book has been to demonstrate the significance of meaning as a determiner in the combination of morpho-lexical items. The meaning of a complex noun has been shown to consist of the meanings of the root and of the suffix. The specific goal of the book has been to demonstrate the semantic substance that the nominal suffixes add to the overall meanings of nouns. To identify the nuances expressed by the nominal suffixes, they have been treated as alternatives and manifested in noun pairs. To account for the alternations, the book has integrated the insights of both theoretical and empirical methods into the investigation. The theoretical method makes the necessary assumptions, while the empirical method provides the tools to verify them. The book has shown how the two methods can coexist to give a detailed description of the way language works. Based on their key tenets, the book has put forward a number of hypotheses and checked their validity through extensive illustrations and substantial evidence.

6.1.1 Theoretical contributions

To achieve its goals, the book has adopted the theoretical framework of Cognitive Semantics. The book has made three contributions and used three tenets throughout the analysis to achieve them.

6.1.1.1 Multiplicity of suffix meaning

The first theoretical contribution the book has made to the area of morpho-lexicology is shown by the use of the cognitive tenet of *category*. According to this tenet, all lexical items of language are attributed semantic values, which motivate their syntactic behaviour. The linguistic form of a lexical item is motivated by its semantic organisation; thus, form and meaning are inseparable. Their internal structures consist of the multiple senses which gather around a centre. The book has explored this tenet in relation to the description of nominal suffixes and argued that a nominal suffix has a distinctive meaning, and therefore has a special role to play in the language. A nominal suffix does not only serve the function of changing the speech part of a word, but also gives it a certain type of semantic information. A nominal suffix forms a category which involves prototypical as well as peripheral senses. The prototype of a nominal suffix is usually the most frequent sense and the first sense which is learnt in acquiring a language. The periphery of a nominal suffix comprises its other senses, regular and irregular, which are linked to the prototype via extensions.

For easy reference, I summarise in Table 6.1, Table 6.2, Table 6.3, and Table 6.4 the multiple senses of the noun-forming suffixes in English. Note that ■ represents the prototype, ◆ represents direct extensions, and ● represents indirect extensions.

Table 6.1 The multiple senses of de-verbal nominalisers in English

Suffix	Prototype	Periphery
-al	■ 'relating closely to the thing named by the nominal root', as in *an environmental issue* ◆ 'showing the proportion of the thing named by the nominal root', as in *an occasional vacation* ◆ 'showing the location of the thing named by the nominal root', as in *a coastal town* ◆ 'showing the character of the thing named by the nominal root', as in *a brutal dictator*	● 'the act of doing the process named by the verbal root', as in *approval*
-ce	■ 'the state indicated by the adjectival root', as in *brilliance* ◆ 'the amount indicated by the adjectival root', as in *abundance* ◆ 'the thing indicated by the adjectival root', as in *protuberance*	● 'the act of doing the process indicated by the verbal root', as in *defiance*
-ion	■ 'the act of doing the process referred to in the verbal root', as in *construction*	● 'the result of the process referred to by the verbal root', as in *alienation*
-ment	■ 'the result of the process referred to by the verbal root', as in *elopement*	● 'the act of doing the process referred to in the verbal root', as in *enrichment* ● 'the state referred to in the verbal root', as in *amazement* ● 'the means, instrument or agent referred to in the verbal root', as in *attachment* ● 'the location referred to in the verbal root', as in *embankment*

Table 6.2   The multiple senses of de-adjectival nominalisers in English

Suffix	Prototype	Periphery
-cy	■ 'the state indicated by the adjectival root', as in *complacency* ◆ 'an example of the state indicated by the adjectival root', as in *dependency* ◆ 'a period of time indicated by the adjectival root', as in *infancy*	● 'the practice, rank, job or office indicated by the nominal root', as in *accountancy* ● 'the act of doing the process indicated by the verbal root', as in *advocacy*
-ity	■ 'the quality or property designated by the adjectival root', as in *agility* ◆ 'the mode of dealing with the situation designated by the adjectival root', as in *brutality* ◆ 'the entity described by the adjectival root', as in *oddity*	● 'the fact of being what the root describes', as in *prosperity*
-ness	■ 'the trait denoted by the adjectival root', as in *awareness* ◆ 'the property denoted by the adjectival root', as in *awkwardness* ◆ 'an instance or example of the quality denoted by the adjectival root', as in *illness*	● 'the characteristic denoted by the adjectival root', as in *blindness*

Table 6.3   The multiple senses of de-nominal nominalisers in English

Suffix	Prototype	Periphery
-age	■ 'a collection of things indicated by the nominal root', as in *baggage* ◆ 'a quantity of the thing indicated by the nominal root', as in *dosage* ◆ 'the cost of the thing indicated by the nominal root', as in *corkage* ◆ 'a place indicated by the nominal root', as in *anchorage*	● 'the action indicated by the verbal root', as in *blockage* ● 'the result indicated by the verbal root', as in *leakage* ● 'the action or the result indicated by the verbal root', as in *breakage*
-dom	■ 'the territory ruled by the person specified by the nominal root', as in *kingdom*	● 'the state of being specified by the nominal root', as in *stardom*

(Continued)

Table 6.3   (*Continued*)

Suffix	Prototype	Periphery
	◆ 'the land inhabited by the people specified by the nominal root', as in *Yankeedom* ◆ 'a group of people united by the thing specified by the nominal root', as in *dogdom*	
-hood	■ 'the condition of being referred to by the nominal root', as in *maidenhood* ◆ 'a union of people sharing the thing referred to by the nominal root', as in *brotherhood* ◆ 'the period of time referred to by the nominal root', as in *babyhood*	● 'an instance of the quality referred to by the adjectival root', as in *falsehood*
-ism	■ 'the belief embodied in the theory named by the nominal root', as in *feminism* ◆ 'the philosophy descended from the person named by the nominal root', as in *Calvinism* ◆ 'the practice based on the belief named by the nominal root', as in *heroism*	● 'the linguistic usage featured by the thing named by the adjectival root', as in *archaism* ● 'the quality of being which is named by the adjectival root', as in *anomalism* ● 'the act named by the verbal root', as in *criticism*
-ship	■ 'the position of being what is signalled by the nominal root', as in *editorship* ◆ 'the period of time spent on the thing signalled by the nominal root', as in *apprenticeship* ◆ 'the fact of being what is signalled by the nominal root', as in *companionship* ◆ 'a group of people signalled by the nominal root', as in *kinship*	● 'an allowance of the thing signalled by the nominal root', as in *fellowship* ● 'the policy or regime of the thing signalled by the nominal root', as in *censorship*
-(e)ry	■ 'a set of things expressed by the nominal root', as in *jewellery* ◆ 'a body of people expressed by the nominal root', as in *merchantry* ◆ 'the place connected with the thing expressed by the nominal root', as in *perfumery*	● 'the attitude that shows the thing expressed by the adjectival root', as in *bravery* ● 'the practice of doing the thing expressed by the verbal root', as in *cookery*

Table 6.4 The multiple senses of agent-forming suffixes in English

Suffix	Prototype	Periphery
-ant	■ 'liable to do the action signalled by the verbal root', as in *a defiant protester* ◆ 'apt to do the action signalled by the verbal root', as in *a compliant child* ◆ 'being in the condition signalled by the verbal root', as in *a dominant issue*	● 'a person who performs the specific action signalled by the verbal root', as in *a complainant* ● 'a substance which performs the specific action signalled by the verbal root', as in , *a disinfectant*
-ee	■ 'a person who is affected by the action named by the verbal root', as in *a draftee* ◆ 'a person to whom something is transferred by the action named by the verbal root', as in *a grantee*	● 'a person who is granted the thing named by the nominal root', as in *a patentee* ● 'a person who has performed the action named by the verbal root', as in *an attendee* ● 'a person who is associated with the thing named by the nominal root', as in *a townee* ● 'a thing that resembles the thing named by the nominal root', as in *a goatee* ● 'a thing that is diminutive of the thing named by the nominal root', as in *a bootee*
-er	■ 'a person who performs the generic action labelled in the verbal root', as in *a caterer* ◆ 'a person who does the activity labelled in the verbal root', as in *a dreamer* ◆ 'a thing that is set to perform the action labelled in the verbal root', as in *a freezer* ◆ 'a thing that does the thing labelled in the verbal root', as in *a beeper*	● 'a person who makes the object labelled in the nominal root', as in *a furrier* ● 'a person who is associated with the thing labelled in the nominal root', as in *an astrologer* ● 'a person who is from the place labelled in the nominal root', as in *a Berliner* ● 'a person who has the attribute labelled in the nominal root', as in *a nutter.* ● 'a place which is used for the thing labelled in the nominal root', as in *a diner*

(Continued)

Table 6.4   (Continued)

Suffix	Prototype	Periphery
-(i)an	■ 'a person whose job involves the thing referred to in the nominal root', as in *an electrician*	● 'a person who is from the place referred to in the nominal root', as in *an American*
	◆ 'a person who is devoted to the knowledge field referred to in the nominal root', as in *a dietician*	● 'a person who is connected with the thing referred to in the nominal root', as in *an Elizabethan* ● 'a member of the group referred to in the nominal root', as in *a mammalian*
-ist	■ 'a person who is versed in the knowledge field indicated by the nominal root', as in *an anthropologist* ◆ 'a person who holds the thing indicated by the nominal root', as in *an extremist* ◆ 'a person who handles the thing indicated by the nominal root', as in *an archivist* ◆ 'a person who plays the instrument indicated by the nominal root', as in *a cellist*	● 'having the disapproving trait indicated by the nominal root', as in *an ageist*
-ster	■ 'a person who performs the habitual action signified by the nominal root', as in *a fraudster*	● 'a person who is skilled at the thing signified by the nominal root', as in *a dabster* ● 'a person who writes the thing signified by the nominal root', as in *a punster* ● 'a vehicle that is signified by the nominal root', as in *a dragster*

6.1.1.2   Specificity of suffix meaning

The second theoretical contribution the book has made to the area of morpho-lexicology is shown by the use of the cognitive tenet of *domain*. In view of this tenet, the meanings of lexical items are described relative to the cognitive domain to which they belong. The lexical items of a language have inter-locking senses such that one cannot understand an item without understanding the others. A domain is a context of background knowledge with regard to which the specific meanings of lexical items are identified. The book has explored this tenet with reference to the description of nominal suffixes and argued that nominal suffixes form domains where they are related in such a way that in some respects they are similar, while in others they are different. A *domain* represents a concept in which different types of relationships hold between its members, and these relationships are defined in terms of their minimally-divergent semantic roles. Each member identifies one aspect of the domain which is precisely different from the other. Suffixes do not exist in isolation in the mind of the speaker, but togather form structured sets.

For easy reference, I summarise in Table 6.5 the subdomains which the nominal suffixes in English evoke.

Table 6.5   The (sub)domains evoked by nominalisers in English

Domains	Subdomains	Exponents	Meaning differences
process	action	*-al*	denotes a sequential act
		-ion	denotes a whole act
	result	*-ce*	denotes an instance of a result
		-ment	denotes a type of a result
characterisation	apparent	*-ce*	denotes the state in which an entity is
	features	*-cy*	denotes the status which an entity reaches
	inherent	*-ness*	denotes the trait distinguishing an entity
	features	*-ity*	denotes the mode distinguishing an entity
representation	individuality	*-dom*	place
		-hood	condition
		-ism	belief
		-ship	position
	collectivity	*-age*	a small number
		-(e)ry	a large number
agenthood	performance	*-ant*	performer of a potential, specific action
		-er	performer of a potential, social, generic action
		-ee	performer of an actual action
	speciality	*-ist*	inventor of a subject
		-(i)an	practitioner of a subject
		-ster	user of a skill

6.1.1.3   Conditionality of noun alternation

The third theoretical contribution the book has made to the area of morpho-lexicology is shown by the use of the cognitive tenet of *construal*. By virtue of this tenet, no two expressions are synonymous even if they are derived from the same source. Derivationally-similar expressions are not transformationally related but are conceptually motivated. Two expressions may share the same conceptual content, but differ in terms of the construal imposed on that content. Each expression is a vehicle of a certain semantic structure, and so the alternatives available to the speaker should not be treated on an equal footing. The book has explored this tenet with regard to the description of noun pairs and has argued that such nouns, which are formed by means of the nominal suffixes, are by no means synonymous. Each noun has its own individuality that requires recognition. Each noun has the distinction of being suitable for a particular situation. Their interchange is conditional, depending upon the type of construal the speaker employs to describe a scene. The different dimensions of construal represent the contrasts between the nominal alternatives.

6.1.2   Empirical contributions

To achieve its goals, the book has adopted the empirical framework of Usage-based Linguistics. The book has made two contributions and used two formats throughout the analysis to achieve them.

6.1.2.1   Semantic distinctions

The first empirical contribution the book has made to the area of morpho-lexicology is realised by the discovery of the semantic distinctions between expressions. A semantic distinction is a situation where two expressions can appear in the same environment, but with a change in meaning. The two expressions are not in free variation; i.e. the use of one for another without a plan is incorrect. They are in complementary distribution, where one expression can be found in a particular environment, while the other can be found in the opposite environment. The book has explored this tenet with regard to the description of noun pairs and argued that such nouns share the same content but represent two different conceptualisations. Each noun describes the same situation, but does so in its own way. The choice between them is a function of meaning. In each conceptualisation, the speaker opts for a different suffix, as a different suffix is associated with a different nuance of meaning. When a root accepts two suffixes, it has two meanings and so two resulting structures. In each structure, the suffix serves to highlight a different facet of the root.

6.1.2.2 Discriminating collocations

The second empirical contribution the book has made to the area of morpho-lexicology is reflected by the identification of the discriminating collocations of expressions. A *discriminating collocation* is a lexical item that co-occurs with an expression and serves to single out its meaning. The functional property of a discriminating collocation is to contribute to the meaning of the key expression. The constituents of a collocation are in a direct syntactic relation with each other, with the syntactic relation indicating a potential semantic relation. The book has explored this tenet with regard to the description of noun pairs and argued that such nouns co-occur with different types of collocates, whether they are verbs, adjectives, or nouns, or whether they precede or follow them. Therefore, supposedly synonymous nouns are not at all equivalent in meaning when their actual patterns of use are analysed. There are systematic differences in the use of these seemingly similar nouns. The non-synonymy is realised by observing their real linguistic behaviour, which is in turn realised by the discriminating collocates which each noun takes.

For easy reference, I summarise in tabular forms the semantic distinctions which nominal suffixes exhibit and the discriminating collocates which the noun alternatives take. The lists of collocates contained in the tables are not exhaustive but include the most obvious examples which associate with the semantic distinctions and so serve to disengage the noun alternatives. As mentioned earlier, the evidence, represented by collocational data, is drawn from a variety of sources such as the BNC, the Internet, dictionaries, and a pool of native speakers.

Table 6.6 Discriminating collocates of noun alternatives sharing verbal roots

Semantic distinctions	Lexical items	Discriminating collocates
sequential	dispersal	enforce, govern, lead to, protest, result in; explosive, gradual, quick, rapid, violent; people, animals, flora, objects
whole	dispersion	achieve, control, prevent, trace, reduce; atmospheric, digital, practical, spatial, wide; air, gas, light, odour, pigment; power, income, returns, material, installations
	disposal	attend to, begin, complete, involve, resolve; illegal, improper, proper, routine, steady; furniture, refuse, rubbish, sewage, waste

(Continued)

Table 6.6   (*Continued*)

Semantic distinctions	Lexical items	Discriminating collocates
	disposition	analyse, exhibit, find out, make, show; administrative, dynamic, final, regular, tactical; books, fleet, goods, records, troops
	recital	give, offer, play, present, stage; brief, long, poor, short, smooth; guitar, organ, piano, violin
	recitation	begin, chant, do, give, start; beautiful, holy, live, popular, vocal; facts, narrative, poetry, prayers, story
instance	deterrence	create, guarantee, maintain, require, select; absolute, dynamic, effective, massive, strategic; burglary, entry, nuclear, smoking, theft
type	determent	consider, constitute, discuss, enhance, stimulate; basic, main, major, potential, primary; devices, methods, policy, steps, tactics
	governance	build, design, enhance, improve, implement; democratic, effective, good, innovative, wise; codes, ethics, guidelines, issues, principles
	government	establish, form, influence, rock, lobby; central, federal, interim, local, stable; grants, loans, offices, resources, services
	sustenance	acquire, distribute, lack, procure, receive; daily, essential, poor, rich, scant; allowances, costs, expenses, productions, subscriptions
	sustainment	absorb, afford, consume, need, provide; basic, external, important, main, substantial; issues, plans, programmes, strategies, technologies
sequential	acquittal	obtain, gain, lead to, result in, secure; complete, formal, full, initial, official; defendant, journalist, officer, presenter, suspect
instance	acquittance	give out an, send somebody an, sign; counterfeited, forged, genuine, sealed, true; crime, debt, obligation, trespass, violation
	referral	make, provide, receive, require, warrant; initial, lengthy, proposed, urgent, voluntary; dietition, chiropodist, health professional, practitioner, specialist

Table 6.6 (*Continued*)

Semantic distinctions	Lexical items	Discriminating collocates
	reference	endorse, make, provide, quote, receive; easy, general, particular, scant, special; copy, guide, material, number, source
	transferral	arrange, inspect, request, start, undergo; accurate, complete, direct, immediate, initial; commodities, stationery items
	transference	control, make, monitor, observe, oversee; annual, efficient, genuine, radical, simple; authority, energy, power, ownership, responsibility
sequential	appraisal	carry out, give, make, obtain, receive; brief, critical, detailed, serious, thorough; performance, project, proposal, research, work
type	appraisement	conduct, file, make, pass over, require; compulsory, independent, judicial, technical, unfair; assets, estates, liabilities, stock, work
	committal	articulate, discharge, draw up, seal, sign; brief, impeccable, strong, summary, suspended; application, hearing, order, proceedings, warrant
	commitment	demonstrate, display, make, reaffirm, show; complete, firm, great, long, real; economic recovery, environment, power sharing, soccer, social order
	deferral	consider, extend, grant, issue, offer; constant, indefinite, long-term, perpetual, routine; decision, marriage, payment
	deferment	apply for, deliver, grant, issue, secure; appropriate, long-term, proposed, temporary, typical; aid, debt, fee, loan, service
whole	domination	be free from/of, come under, establish, fall under, maintain, seek; class, colonial, economic, imperial, political; conference, league, party, relationship, world
instance	dominance	achieve, confirm, exercise, foster, retain; clear, overwhelming, growing, increasing, total; art, news media, painting, political interests, spoken language

(*Continued*)

Table 6.6   (*Continued*)

Semantic distinctions	Lexical items	Discriminating collocates
	observation	carry out, do, make, permit, trigger; clinical, close, direct, empirical, psychological; classroom, participant; carriage, cell, coaches, post
	observance	enforce, ensure, foster, practise, secure; austere, close, faithful, rigid, strict; custom, feast, law, Memorial Day, national holiday
	toleration	contain, encourage, inhibit, oppose to, permit; dangerous, grudging, limited, popular, quiet; drug, means, noise, tourists, traveller
	tolerance	have, exercise, lack, practise, show; mere, political, racial, religious, social; aggressive behaviour, errors, opinion, practices, sexual behaviour
whole	excitation	cause, discharge, produce, transmit, trigger electrical, electronic, molecular, physical, sexual, wave; coil, filter, nerve, pulse, spectrum
type	excitement	communicate, discover, enjoy, experience, share; breathless, great, intense, new, pure; Christmas, development, event, media, rehearsal; a quiver of, an amount of, a sense of, a feeling of, a surge, of, a bit of, a whoop of
	medication	give, need, receive, stop, take; heavy, mild, prescribed, regular, safe; abuse, information, practice, programme, regulation
	medicament	check, drink, give, swallow, use; effective, new, powerful, useful, vital; consumption, distribution, preparation, prescription, technology
	reconciliation	achieve, bring about, call for, hinder, promote; full, lasting, personal, political, royal; conference, forum, policy, process, talk
	reconcilement	establish, make, obtain, prepare, reach; easy, full, internal, national, partial; account, deposit, fund, interest, payment

Table 6.7 Discriminating collocates of noun alternatives sharing adjectival roots

Semantic distinctions	Lexical items	Discriminating collocates
state	belligerence	approve, bear, stand, sustain, tolerate; childish, open, sinful, vicious, wicked; message, remark, response, style
status	belligerency	abandon, end, oppose to, renounce, terminate; audacious, foolhardy, illegal, reckless, unlawful; Cuban, Indian, Korean, Portuguese, Sudanese
	dependence	display, exhibit, have, manifest, show; absolute, complete, growing, necessary, total; economical, financial, institutional, physical, psychological; charity, foreign aid, fossil fuels, mechanical strength, oil, parents
	dependency	become, remain; colonial, overseas, regional, self-governed, separate; British, Danish, French, Japanese, Norwegian; concept, culture, programme, territory, theory
	emergence	indicate, mark, see, signal, witness; abrupt, gradual, rapid, swift, sudden; dynamic economy, free trade, high speed train, professional consultants, single market
	emergency	cope with, deal with, handle, respond to, take care of; major, minor, serious, unexpected, unforeseen; aid, assistance, funds, relief, supply, laws, legislation, measures, procedures, regulations, kit, medicine, tool, treatment centres, vehicles
	insurgence	attest, betoken, bespeak, see, testify; absurd, extreme, incredible, radical, unthinkable
	insurgency	crush, launch, plot, quell, suppress; armed, civil, ethnic, military, popular; communist, guerrilla, Tamil
	permanence	assure, guarantee, guard, preserve, secure; essential, inevitable necessary, practical, virtual
	permanency	acquire, achieve, become, gain, obtain; apparent, considerable, great, prominent, sizeable, framework, planning, policy, principles, programme
trait	acuteness	lack, need, own, possess, require; connate, especial, innate, native, natural; argument, conception, debate, inquiry, observation

(Continued)

Table 6.7   (*Continued*)

Semantic distinctions	Lexical items	Discriminating collocates
mode	acuity	cultivate, develop, increase, improve, raise; auditory, hearing, psychological, rhythmic, visual; eyesight, senses
	crudeness	criticise, denounce, object, reject, spurn; occasional, original, relative, startling, terrible
	crudity	detect, examine, note, notice, perceive; adult, appalling, casual, childish, maximum; comment, language, message, method, remark
	falseness	diagnose, identify, pinpoint, recognise, see; apparent, awful, awkward, infinite, integral
	falsity	demonstrate, expose, indicate, manifest, reveal; assumptions, ideas, beliefs, claims, statements
	laxness	criticise, decry, punish, report, reproach, apparent, excessive, moral, shameful, unprecedented
	laxity	endure, experience, face, know, sustain; certain, mindless, relative, simple, soft
	sensitiveness	analyse, define, expound, identify, specify; abnormal, excessive, quick, unusual, vivid
	sensitivity	express, display, pose, reflect, show; deep, extreme, great, heightened, optimum, cold, danger, distress, trauma, values
trait	oddness	deprecate, disapprove, frown, object, resent; apparent, monumental, profound, sheer, unnatural
existent	oddity	observe, notice, perceive, recognise, watch; coincidental, historical, physical, psychological, statistical
	rareness	assess, evaluate, measure, value, weigh; alleged, comparative, considerable, relative, utmost; reference, oeuvre
	rarity	be, become, feature, highlight, make; actual, fantastic, great, phenomenal, real
	realness	assess, evaluate, judge, rate, test; incredible, positive, supreme, thrilling, ultimate; kind of, level of, sense of, type of
	reality	be, become, create, grow, turn; actual, basic, new, practical, virtual

Table 6.7 (*Continued*)

Semantic distinctions	Lexical items	Discriminating collocates
status	accuracy	assess, examine, check, prove, test; absolute, complete, impeccable, remarkable, total
trait	accurateness	assume, consider, reckon, suspect, understand; historical, necessary, philosophical, technical, uncanny
	privacy	invade, preserve, respect, safeguard, violate; complete, individual, personal, strict, total; archive, email, invasion of, intrusion of, right of; code, intrusion, issues, laws, practices
	privateness	capture, envisage, feature, realise, visualise; basic, essential, inherent, intense, true; degree of, element of, moment of, quality of, sense of
	secrecy	be cloaked in, be shrouded in, be veiled in, maintain, swear somebody to; absolute, excessive, official, strict, unnecessary; a blanket of, a cloak of, a veil of
	secretness	apprehend, comprehend, fathom, grasp, understand; deep, great, super, taut, top
status	benignancy	detect, diagnose, identify, recognise, spot; artificial, bright, environmental, imperturbable, seasonal
mode	benignity	beam with, exude, ooze, radiate, reflect; divine, gracious, noble, paternal, wise; the expression an air of
	malignancy	detect, diagnose, find, identify, pinpoint; burning, common, low-grade, renewed, unrecognised; indicative of, no sign of, no evidence of, suggestive of
	malignity	display, exhibit, manifest, reveal, show; deep, excessive, fiendish, great, utter
	normalcy	re-establish, reinstate, restore, return to, revive; economical, growing, political, social, stab
	normality	advance, boost, develop, promote, strengthen; domestic, exuberant, relative, surface, weak; a period of, a sign of, a standard of, semblance of

Table 6.8　Discriminating collocates of noun alternatives sharing nominal roots

Semantic distinctions	Lexical items	Discriminating collocates
territory	chiefdom	build, construct, divide, end, reform; immense, minor, newly-created, spacious, tiny; authorities, bases, centres, headquarters, institutions
position	chiefship	attain, obtain, earn, secure, win; brief, current, momentary, paramount, ultimate; chore, duty, errand, job, work
	earldom	establish, keep up, occupy, restore, take possession of; extant, extinct, feudal, huge, premier; associations, corporations, foundations, lands, societies
	earlship	acquire, claim, hold, inherit, receive; crucial, fair, eternal, momentous, permanent; assignments, functions, obligations, responsibilities, tasks
	kingdom	abolish, expand, found, reside in, sustain; enormous, independent, separate, small, united; agencies, businesses, cities, organisations, regions
	kingship	cede to, descend, gain, pass to, succeed to; ancient, everlasting, medieval, significant, traditional; burdens, duties, limits, powers, rights
condition	fatherhood	become, conceive, display, experience, imagine; dubious, early, fulfilled, joyful, lovely; concept, event, idea, matter, prospect
position	fathership	embody, furnish with, lavish on, provide, symbolise; affectionate, compassionate, holy, sympathetic, tender; affection, care, devotion, love, passion
	ladyhood	achieve, blossom into, demonstrate, evince, perceive; angelic, charismatic, exquisite, real, young; air, core, essence, ideal, notion
	ladyship	achieve, get, have, receive, take; elegant, good, gracious, sensible, wise; Thatcher, Jane
	queenhood	contemplate, exhibit, feel, illustrate, live through; attractive, beautiful, intrinsic, mature, natural; conception, essence, honour, pride, spirit

Table 6.8 (*Continued*)

Semantic distinctions	Lexical items	Discriminating collocates
	queenship	apply, carry out, exercise, perform, realise; astute, brilliant, modern, resourceful, shrewd; ceremony, feast, practice, ritual, tradition
territory	princedom	create, declare, destroy, run, seize; civil, independent, private, royal, secular; bureaus, departments, offices, units, zones
condition	princehood	demonstrate, display, improve, manifest, upgrade; charismatic, fairy, inherent, magical, natural; attribute, gift, pattern, principle, stamp
condition	bachelorhood	abandon, enjoy, give up, grow into, value; bitter, contented, enforced, fretful, horrible; ambition, dream, era, phase, time
belief	bachelorism	adhere to, complain of, hold to, persist in, savour of; liberal, moderate, popular, radical, youthful; fashion, manner, tone, style, vein
position	attorneyship	appoint, notch up, pursue, train, work; entitled, competent, masterful, qualified, vital; ability, expertise, knowledge, proficiency, skill
doctrine	attorneyism	abide by, convey, heed, observe, practise; absolute, great, impartial, public, realistic; approach, culture, form, issue, tendency
condition	parenthood	brace for, entertain, face, reflect on, value; adoptive, (in)experienced, lone, responsible, single; delights, joys, prospects, pressures, stresses
body	parentage	deny, dispute, identify, presume, share; common, different, indeterminate, obvious, unknown; American, Indian, Italian, Spanish, Turkish; analysis, assessment, concern, evaluation, testing
position	clientship	change, claim, confer on, exchange, improve; demanding, important, modern, permanent, transitory; conditions, initiatives, policies, structures, systems

(*Continued*)

Table 6.8   (*Continued*)

Semantic distinctions	Lexical items	Discriminating collocates
body	clientage	attract, build up, expand, increase, select; broad, contemporary, extensive, local, regular; connections, networks, relationships, systems, ties
position	citizenship	acquire, change, grant, have, take; active, dual, full, global, multiple; ceremonies, duties, obligations, pledges, rights; Australian, British, Canadian, European, Sweden
body	citizenry	arouse, encourage, inform, mobilise, treat; apathetic, civilised, democratic, local, patriotic; category, class, cluster, section, selection, plus *of*

Table 6.9   Discriminating collocates of noun alternatives denoting agenthood

Semantic distinctions	Lexical items	Discriminating collocates
specific	defendant	conviction, crime, evidence, hearing, trial; arraigned, convicted, culpable, guilty, indicted; acquit, charge, convict, release, sue
generic	defender	sports, faiths, policies, rights, viewpoints; devoted, gallant, heroic, loyal, staunch; guard, maintain, protect, support, uphold
	informant	information, investigation, question, survey, testimony; aboriginal, born, endemic, indigenous, native; apprise, brief, clue, enlighten, instruct
	informer	government, mafia, police, secret agency, tip-off; disgraceful, hateful, ignominious, notorious, shameful; bug, monitor, snoop, spy, tap
	occupant	car, chair, flat, hotel, seat; authorised, legal, licensed, official, sanctioned; abide, dwell, hire, lease, rent
	occupier	city, country, land, premises, territory; intrusive, meddlesome, obtrusive, presumptuous, trespassing; breach, encroach on, intrude, trespass, violate

Table 6.9   (*Continued*)

Semantic distinctions	Lexical items	Discriminating collocates
potential	attender	ceremony, exhibition, gallery, meeting, party; assiduous, constant, frequent, persistent, regular
actual	attendee	conference, course, lecture, seminar, tutorial; current, former, one-time, matriculated, registered
	escaper	country, famine, fire, regime, war; eventual, expected, prospective, subsequent, ultimate
	escapee	captor, guard, jail, officer, príson; evasive, ongoing, momentary, recent, unexpected
	returner	clinic, office, school; adjectives like accustomed, habitual, inveterate, steady, unfailing
	returnee	city country, home; banished, deported, expelled, ousted, repatriated
inventive	historicist	argument, conception, formulation, proposition, theory; ace, consummate, expert, pioneer, versed
implementive	historian	art, family, space travel, theatre, war; amateurish, inexperienced, nonprofessional, novice, unskilled; compile, collect, describe, record, trace
	theologist	creative, innovative, original, proficient, premier; intuit, preach, sermonise, speculate, surmise
	theologian	Bible, gospel, sermon, faith, church; Anglican, Calvinist, Catholic, Christian
	theorist	assumption, conception, hypothesis, speculation, supposition; adjectives denoting creativity
	theoretician	drawings, paintings, photographs, sculpture, statue; adjectives denoting persistence; exhibit, display, show, unveil
social	joker	funny, playful, practical, witty
vocational	jokster	clownish, comical, hilarious, jocular, waggish
	tipper	barber, hairdresser, porter, taxi driver, waiter; big, generous, munificent, openhanded, unsparing; pay
	tipster	football, game, racing, sports, TV; astute, shrewd, smart, top, visionary; advise, favour, inform, say, tell

(*Continued*)

Table 6.9 (*Continued*)

Semantic distinctions	Lexical items	Discriminating collocates
	tricker	artless, cheerful, harmless, innocent, light-hearted: have somebody on, kid, pull somebody's leg, tease, wind somebody up
	trickster	deceitful, misleading, sinful, vicious, wicked; cheat, deceive, falsify, forge, mislead
mechanical	copier	colour, fax, office, photo, xerox; bulky, digital, expensive, fashionable, new
inventive	copyist	cartoon, fiction, handwriting, painting, symphony; adept, gifted, professional, proficient, trained
	cycler	image, light, text, wallpaper, water; costly, grey, fast, sizeable, thermal
	cyclist	bike, champion, helmet, race, riding; accomplished, experienced, Olympic, professional, ranked
	styler	fleece, fur, garment, hair, pile; black, cheap, new-fashioned, plastic, small
	stylist	brush, curler, hair, lotion, trim; adroit, competent, dexterous, expert, talented

6.2 Explicit comparisons

As is clear, the present study has taken a synchronic approach to language, concentrating the discussion on Modern English. The discussion has been about nominal pairs sharing the same roots. The discussion has been rooted in Cognitive Semantics. To bring out its effectiveness, it is important to compare it with other language theories. The comparison covers only the two themes that have been at the centre of the study, namely, meaning and alternation. In this respect, two key questions arise. The first question is: do the other theories have the hypotheses that are critical to the meaning of morpho-lexemes? The second question is: are the other approaches well-equipped to successfully solve the problems associated with alternation in morpho-lexicology? To answer the questions, I will first address the issue of linguistic meaning and then consider the issue of linguistic alternation. The purpose is to show how Cognitive Semantics defines itself against the other language theories. For sources that provide general accounts, see Croft & Cruse (2004) and Evans & Green (2006).

6.2.1 Meaning

In the present study, meaning has been defined as the semantic content associated with a symbol. It has a linguistic form, an orthographic representation, with which it pairs. The issue of meaning has been explained in terms of three theories. The first theory is about *category*, which accounted for the internal structures of linguistic items. A nominal suffix has been found to consist of multiple senses which gather around a centre but exhibit minimal differences. The second theory is about *domain*, which illustrated the distinctive uses of linguistic items. The meanings of nominal suffixes have been found to arise from their relations of similarity and contrast with one another in the same conceptual area. The third theory is about *construal*, which clarified how semantic distinctions constrain lexical projections. The noun pairs formed by nominal suffixes have been found to display subtle differences in meaning, which are due to the particular ways of construing their common roots. The usage-based methodology backed the framework by identifying the discriminating collocations that accompany the members of the pairs, and thus confirm the differences in their meanings.

One striking aspect of the present study is that it is the first to employ cognitive assumptions in investigating the issue of meaning in morpho-lexicology. As the preceding chapters have demonstrated, the adoption of the Cognitive Semantics framework has offered a revelatory account of the issue of linguistic meaning. It is hoped that this new way of describing morpho-lexicology can be exploited to tackle other areas within language. Linguists working in other theoretical paradigms have also shed some light on linguistic meaning, and posited different kinds of theories to account for it. Yet, their theories mainly deal with sentence meaning, rather than word meaning. In what follows, I examine in some detail how the other theories of language treat the issue of linguistic meaning, and examine the hypotheses they hold in its investigation. In the course of the examination, I sketch out some of the differences between Cognitive Semantics and such language theories. The differences revolve around the fundamental assumptions characterising the present study, which distinguish it from the others.

6.2.1.1 Check-list theory

The theory of *category* is a reaction against the *classical* or *check-list* theory of linguistic meaning, which goes back to Aristotle. According to this theory, categories should be clearly defined, mutually exclusive, and collectively exhaustive. Categories are discrete entities characterised by a set of properties which are shared by their members. These properties establish the conditions which are both necessary and sufficient for definition and membership. A necessary condition is one that must be satisfied for category membership. A sufficient condition is one that, if satisfied, guarantees category membership. The conditions are binary, i.e. a yes-or-no matter. An entity is a category member if it fulfils all the conditions. An entity is not a category member if it fails to satisfy any of the conditions. Categories have clear boundaries. All members of a category are of equal status. To illustrate this, consider the lexical concept *bird*. For an entity to be included in this category, it must fulfil such conditions as having a beak, wings and feathers, and being able to fly. A *sparrow* is included because it meets the conditions. A *penguin*, by contrast, is excluded because it cannot fly.

However, the *classical* theory of meaning is associated with some serious problems. First, it is difficult to identify a precise set of conditions that are necessary and sufficient to define a category. As the data have shown, there is no single set of conditions that is shared by each member of the category of any suffix. Second, not all categories have clear boundaries. As the data have shown, categories of suffixes display fuzzy boundaries. It is not necessary for a suffix sense to possess all the attributes for category membership. Third, category members are not equal; categories exhibit typicality. As the data have shown, a nominal suffix has given rise to a typical example, from which the other less typical examples are derived. The asymmetries between category members are called *typicality effects*. To solve the problems, Cognitive Semantics adopts the *prototype* theory of meaning, which emerged from the work of Rosch and her colleagues. According to Rosch (1978), humans categorise not by means of necessary and sufficient conditions, as assumed by the *classical* theory, but with reference to a *prototype*, an exemplar or a salient member of a category which assembles its key attributes.

6.2.1.2   Componential analysis theory

The theory of *domain* is a response to the *componential analysis* or *semantic decomposition* theory of linguistic meaning, adopted within the generative model. It appeared in Katz & Fodor (1963), and was refined in Katz & Postal (1964) and Katz (1972). According to this theory, the vocabulary of language can be defined in terms of semantic components or primitives. The meaning of words can be analysed as construed from basic semantic features or markers. For instance, the word *bachelor* can be analysed by using the components [+MALE, +ADULT, -MARRIED]. The core meaning of a word resides in the information represented by these components. For example, the word *bachelor* means 'unmarried adult male'. Linguistic meaning is then defined in terms of intrinsic or non-contextual components. This is the proper sphere of lexical semantics. Questions such as, how the outside world interacts with linguistic meaning? belong to the sphere of pragmatics. Such questions are considered by componential analysis theorists to be external to the concerns of linguistics.

While the *componential analysis* is useful for describing some aspects of phonology or syntax, and for analysing kinship terms, it is not a representation of how language works. In fact, the theory has been criticised in two important ways. The first criticism has to do with the identification of the semantic components. No linguist has ever been able to develop a complete list of such components. If semantic components were to exist, they would number in the thousands. Besides, it proves impossible to agree on the number of components needed for precise definition of words. The second criticism has to do with the use of metalanguages. The devices used, symbols and diagrams, are ad hoc and unsystematic, at best another arbitrary language. Attaching a set of components to a word is not semantic analysis in the deepest sense. Translating from the object language into an arbitrary invented language does not advance semantic analysis very far. Cognitive Semantics rejects the idea that word meaning can be modelled by strict definitions based on semantic decomposition. As the data have shown, nominal suffixes could only be understood relative to the domains in which they are embedded.

6.2.1.3   Truth-conditional theory

The theory of *construal* is a reply to the *truth-conditional* or *objectivist* theory of linguistic meaning, developed within the generative model. This theory holds that a truth bearer, e.g. a statement, is true if it corresponds to a state of affairs holding in the world. It assumes an objective external reality against which descriptions in language can be judged true or false. This is achieved by first translating natural language sentences into a logical metalanguage, and then by establishing how the logical form derived corresponds to a particular model of reality. To judge a statement, the state of affairs in the world must hold for it to be true. For example, to know the meaning of a sentence like *It is cloudy* one has to know what the world will have to be like for the sentence to be true. A look at the sky is enough to tell you whether the statement is true or not. Linguistic meaning then is defined in terms of the conditions that hold for the sentence to be true. In that light, if two sentences express the same state of affairs in the world, or have the same content, they are considered equal.

This view can only account for the meaning of a subset of utterance types. It cannot account for expressions which do not express propositions like questions, commands, greetings and so on. It stands in direct opposition to the experientialist view adopted within Cognitive Semantics, which describes meaning in terms of human construal of reality. Meaning is a relationship between language and world, which is mediated by the human mind. Sweetser (1990: 4) writes: "By viewing meaning as the relationship between words and the world, truth-conditional semantics eliminates cognitive organisation from the linguistic system". As Talmy (2000: 4) asserts, there is a relationship between conceptual structure and human interaction with the external world of sensory experience. Conceptual structure is embodied, i.e. the nature of conceptual organisation arises from bodily experience. As the data have shown, the meanings associated with the nominal suffixes and the derived nouns have been shown to be manifestations of thoughts, i.e. of the way the speaker construes situations.

A related theory, with which the current study is inconsistent, is the *referential* or *denotational* theory of linguistic meaning, developed within the generative model. The basic premise of this theory is that the meaning of an expression refers to the entity picked out in the world. For example, if one uses the phrase *the bank*, one is likely referring to the edge of a river. In this way, the meaning of a lexical item derives from the kind of thing it refers to in the world. Jackendoff (1983:29) asserts that the semantic value of a lexical item is reduced to the observable features of a situation. This stance stems from the *objectivist* theory of meaning, which views meaning in terms of correlation between what is said and what is seen. This approach is irrelevant to the concerns of the current analysis for various reasons. It applies only to linguistic items which designate concrete entities. It ignores extra-linguistic information in the definition of a lexical item. It disregards the speaker's role in construing a situation. As the data have shown, a nominal suffix or a derived noun refers to an entity in a mental space, be it actual or hypothetical. Its meaning includes knowledge that goes beyond its reference.

6.2.2 Alternation

In the present study, alternation has been defined as the case where two, or more, constructions share the same root, but differ in meaning. The issue of alternation or the choice of an alternative has been found to be a matter of two keystones: *conceptual content* and *construal*.

Conceptual content is the semantic property inherent in the components of an expression. *Construal* is the way the speaker describes the content vis-à-vis the communicative needs. To make this clear, the study has applied it to the description of a complex noun. A root has multiple content. A suffix has content of its own. In the combining process, the suffix imposes its content on that of the root, and so gives the derived alternative a different meaning. The use of the suffix is the result of the particular construal the speaker employs to describe a scene. That is, when two rival suffixes attach to a root, each serves to highlight a different facet of the root's content and represent a different construal of a situation. Each of the resulting alternatives encodes, therefore, a distinct meaning. The distinction in meaning is confirmed by the discriminating collocations that accompany each alternative.

Another striking aspect of the present study is that it is the first to investigate the issue of linguistic alternation in morpho-lexicology. As the preceding chapters have manifested, the Cognitive Semantics framework has given a fascinating insight into the issue of alternation. It is hoped this way of accounting for distinction in morpho-lexicology can be extended to handle other areas within language. Researchers working in other theoretical paradigms have also paid attention to alternation. Yet, they have confined themselves to the area of grammar by studying pairs of grammatical constructions like active vs passive, *s*-genitive vs *of*, etc. In what follows, I look at how the other theoretical approaches to language consider the issue of alternation, and examine the hypotheses they form to investigate it. In general, I reveal the differences between Cognitive Semantics and the other approaches. The differences relate to whether lexical pairs derived from the same sources are considered similar or distinct in meaning. In particular, I want to show if the hypotheses of the other approaches can be extended to the area of morpho-lexicology. In this regard, my statements should be taken just as speculations.

6.2.2.1 Traditional approach

One hypothesis of the traditional approach pertains to the *notional* view of language, which emphasises the importance of meaning in describing linguistic structures. It is a view of language in which linguistic units are defined in terms of meaning rather than form. To traditionalists, meaning is uniquely and discretely associated with form. This line of thinking is followed in reference books on grammar. Jespersen (1970: 166) contends that every grammatical construction is associated with meaning of its own. The selection of a grammatical item is a matter of correlation between form and meaning. The grammarian Kruisinga (1931: 217–8), for instance, states that in cases where two grammatical constructions – e.g., the *to*-infinitive and the *-ing* gerund – are possible, the choice proceeds from the difference in their meaning. From this hypothesis with which the present analysis is in accord, one can deduce that lexical pairs sharing the same roots are also semantically unequal. Unfortunately, the traditional approach does not provide any mechanism for solving riddles surrounding the issue of lexical alternation in language, which could help to explain the data presented here.

Another hypothesis of the traditional approach pertains to the *intuitive* and *normative* views of language. An *intuitive* view is based on personal opinions, whereas a *normative* view is based on a set of rules. It is a view of language that ignores actual usage in favour of prescriptive rules derived from Latin and Greek. This line of thinking is followed in usage manuals. Fowler (1996), for instance, instructs speakers how a language should be used, rather than describe how it is used. The present analysis is in discord with such a hypothesis for various reasons. First, usage writers tackle words that are randomly selected and mostly unrelated by derivation. A look at the traditional literature is enough to find that there is no listing of existing lexical pairs in language. Second, they do not devise procedures that are necessary to disambiguate the lexical pairs. They provide only superficial knowledge of the distinctions, without going below the surface. Third, they prefer rules over usage. They place no emphasis on cognitive abilities, which are capable of capturing the semantic distinctions between lexemes.

6.2.2.2   Structural approach

One hypothesis of the structural approach concerns the negligence of meaning in shaping linguistic forms. To structuralists, there is no relationship between the meaning of a linguistic unit and the form it takes. The nature of this relationship is characterised as arbitrary or unmotivated. Saussure (1916:182) writes: 'The system of language is based on the irrational principle of the arbitrariness of signs'. Language is primarily considered as a self-regulating system of structures, with focus being laid on form rather meaning. Language regulates its own functions automatically, not by its users. The present account is incompatible with this hypothesis for two reasons. First, structuralists ignore the fact that linguistic forms are meaningful, and that they have special missions to convey in language. Second, they fail to recognise the fact that language is neither self-contained nor describable without essential reference to cognitive processing. Analysing grammatical units without reference to their semantic values is just like writing a dictionary without including the meanings of the words.

From this hypothesis, it emerges that lexical pairs sharing the same roots are purely coincidental. Alternation is random and constitutes a case of *synonymy*, where two lexical items have a similar range of reference but are differentiated by the speakers on stylistic grounds. On the basis of structural criteria, a nominal pair has two different morphological structures, which happen by chance and appear semantically similar. The choice of a lexical item is then treated as unexpected, in which the root and the suffix co-occur without a plan. This way of description is defended by Stageberg (1965: 94): 'The words with which derivational suffixes combine is an arbitrary matter. To make a noun from the verb *adore*, we must add *-ment*, and no other suffix will do, whereas the verb *fail* combines only with *-ure* to make a noun *failure*'. The present account is incompatible with this hypothesis. As the data have shown, alternation between lexical items has been found to be structured, not random.

Another hypothesis of the structural approach concerns the relationship between lexical items, where an item derives its meaning from *syntagmatic* and *paradigmatic* relations with other items in the language. A *syntagmatic* relation is a pattern of association between lexical items on a linear level. A *paradigmatic* relation is a pattern of association between lexical items on a vertical level. The meaning of a lexical item derives from the totality of relationships the item has with other items in the language. Lyons (1968: 443) remarks that the meaning of a lexical item is internally determined by the set of relations which hold between the item in question and other items in the same linguistic system. The present account is compatible with this hypothesis to some extent. The meaning of a lexical item is also understood in terms of how it functions together with and in contrast to other related items, but this is only one side of the story. The other side of the story, which is ignored, involves context. The context against which meanings are characterised is external to the linguistic system as such. Meanings are conceptual structures embedded in patterns of knowledge.

6.2.2.3 Transformational approach

One hypothesis of the transformational approach relates to the formal relationship between linguistic units. Grammatical constructions have the same deep structure, which determines their meaning. The surface differences between grammatical constructions are the result of different transformational rules. Since grammatical constructions are related by transformations, they are semantically equivalent. They are considered the output of phrase structure rules operating on lexical items. As such, they are not treated as meaningful elements. Such a position is advocated by linguists such as Chomsky (1957). The current study is inconsistent with this hypothesis. As the data have shown, the difference between linguistic items is not only a matter of form but rather of meaning. Morpho-lexical alternation should be described in terms of features present on the surface, which include not only phonological but also semantic information. The cognitive hypothesis is that each distinct sense of a word is associated with a distinction in form, and the form of the word is shaped by a conceptual motivation.

While modern generative approaches are still interested in the formal properties of linguistic elements, some included semantics in their analyses, where a level of semantic interpretation mediates the relationship between grammatical constructions. Lieber (2004) thinks that words are generated by means of lexical rules, in the formation of which semantics has a role to play. She treats affixes as lexical items on a par with stems. She attributes broad semantic content to affixes, whose function is to create new lexemes and extend the lexicon. Each affix contributes a distinct meaning to the complex word. Affixes differ from simple free forms in that they are subcategorised for attachment to items of specific categories. Lieber's view is insightful, but unfortunately it holds only for single words derived from roots. She doesn't provide any interpretation as to the use of alternative suffixes or alternative pairs of words. There is no mention of any sort of alternation between word pairs.

On the basis of the transformational hypothesis, it is claimed that lexical pairs sharing the same roots have the same deep structure, and so are semantically equivalent. Alternation constitutes a case of *free variation*, referring to the interchangeable relationship between two items, in which they may substitute for each other in the same environment, without causing a change in meaning. The selection of a lexical item is then treated as basically indiscriminate and unpredictable. This is so because the transformational approach deals with the structural specificity of language. According to Lees (1960), the relationship between linguistic constructions is captured in terms of a transformational rule, which relates members of a pair to the same underlying structure. Lexical pairs are treated as exchangeable, and the choice between them, which is purely formal, is the result of different transformations. The current study rejects this idea. As the data have shown, although lexical pairs are related by derivation, they are considered distinct variants.

Their disambiguation is a task that requires cues from semantics. Each variant has a specific function to carry out in the discourse.

6.2.2.4 Functional approach

One hypothesis of the functional approach belongs to the pragmatic view of language. Language is seen as a medium of social exchange rather than a set of abstract systems. Form-meaning relationship is perceived not as arbitrary but as iconic, i.e. motivated or transparent. There is similarity between the form of language and the meaning it stands for. Such a non-arbitrary relationship between form and function is, as Givón (1985) asserts, one of the idealised principles of Functional Grammar. Semantic relations are reflected in the formal patterns in which they are realised. Grammatical forms are interpreted largely in terms of the different ways in which they package information flow, and in terms of notions like *topicality*, *thematicity*, *givenness*, or *animacy*, on the basis of which speakers select the appropriate grammatical variant. In Halliday's (1985: 142) view, in communication the speaker chooses from the options available within the grammatical system the one that fits the speech situation. Accordingly, the choices are never completely synonymous. They are taken to be functional, that is to say, they serve different communication needs.

From a theoretical standpoint, this hypothesis is ideal, but from a practical one it is unfortunately restricted. A survey of the functional literature does not yield any work that has been done on morpho-lexical alternation. That's partly at least because there hasn't been much work on morphology generally. This is in a way odd because morphology involves meaning, which is what Functional Linguistics is interested in. For the majority of functional theorists, the bias, however, has been towards the clause and the text. Nouns have been looked at, in general, as examples of nominalisation, but there hasn't been any focus on cases where two nouns derive from the same root by means of two suffixes. Although the current solution embraces some of the insights of Functional Linguistics, it differs from it in two ways. First, the current solution links the choice to the human mind. The availability of linguistic constructions is the outcome of the human cognitive abilities and processing system. Second, by extending the analysis to the area of morpho-lexicology and elaborating on the semantics of the suffixes the current solution offers a unified treatment of the complexities of language.

Thus, in the functional approach neither is the semantic property of alternation addressed nor is the nature of the relationship between alternatives investigated. However, the functional hypothesis leads on to predict that lexical pairs sharing the same roots have meanings of their own, and are chosen for their own sake. Alternation is driven by function, where meaning determines the choice of a lexical item. The selection of a lexical item is a matter of communicative force. The demand of the discourse determines the form of the lexical item. This position is made explicit by Bolinger's (1968: 119–27) thesis: a difference in form correlates with a difference in meaning. Bolinger (1977: 1) goes on to say: 'if two ways of saying the same thing differ in their words or their arrangement they will also differ in meaning'. There is a direct correlation between a conceptual notion and its linguistic representation. The form of a lexical item is viewed as a consequence of the communicative need of the discourse. Each lexical item reflects a semantic distinction of its own. A lexical item is chosen for its own sake, not as a mechanical result of something else.

6.2.2.5   Construction-Grammar approach

In Construction Grammar – as in Cognitive Grammar, which is dependent on Cognitive Semantics – the fundamental unit of grammar is a symbolic unit. A symbolic unit has two poles: a semantic pole (meaning) and a phonological pole (form). Construction Grammar calls it a *construction*, whereas Cognitive Grammar calls it a *symbolic assembly*. A language system consists of such units stored whole rather than assembled. In Construction Grammar, as in Cognitive Grammar, knowledge of language consists of a structured inventory of constructions. These constructions form a complex network in which the constructions are related to one another by aspects of form and meaning. In Construction Grammar, as in Cognitive Grammar, knowledge of language emerges from language use. The speaker's knowledge of language is formed by abstracting symbolic units from situated usage events. Properties of language directly reflect human experiences. An important consequence of this thesis is that there is no distinction between knowledge of language (competence) and language use (performance). The upshot of the foregoing hypotheses is that knowledge of language is knowledge of how language is used.

Construction Grammar differs from Cognitive Grammar in the way the notion of *construction* is defined. Goldberg (1995: 4) defines a *construction* as any form-meaning pairing whose meaning cannot be predicted from its subparts. A *construction* is any symbolic unit, complex or otherwise, that is to some degree arbitrary in terms of meaning or structure. Goldberg focuses on the formal properties of the constructions that make up the structured inventory. Langacker (1987) defines a *construction* as any unit with complex symbolic structure, a sentence, phrase or a word, whose meaning is predicted to a large extent from the lexical items that are part of it. A *construction* is any unit with complex symbolic structure, regardless of whether its structure or meaning can be predicted from the properties of its subparts. Langacker focuses on the cognitive principles which give rise to linguistic organisation. That is, Langacker attempts to describe the cognitive mechanisms which motivate the formation of the symbolic units of language, their uses and the relationships that hold between them.

Construction Grammar is built only on sentence-level constructions like the ditransitive, caused-motion and resultative constructions, all of which are argued to have meaning independent of the lexical items that instantiate them. Meaning is governed by sentence-level constructions. According to Goldberg (1995: 1), sentence-level constructions themselves carry meaning independently of the words in the sentence. This entails that Construction Grammar cannot account for the area of morphology, which represents a significant subset of language. In Goldberg's model, a complex word does not count as a construction if some aspects of its meaning can be predicted from its subparts. By contrast, Cognitive Grammar is open to all types of constructions. In the present study, the focus has been on word-level constructions, where meaning is governed by the semantic properties of individual parts. As the data have shown, the components of a complex noun contribute a great deal to its meaning. The challenge then is for Construction Grammar to extend its thesis beyond grammar, from sentence-level to word-level constructions, or from verb-argument constructions to word pairs formed on the same root.

In spite of all this, let us speculate how a lexical pair sharing the same root can be accounted for, by analogy with the treatment of grammatical constructions. The question whether a given root may accept two or more alternating suffixes is also seen in terms of semantic compatibility. A root can accept a given suffix if there is compatibility in meaning between them. It can accept two suffixes if its meaning is compatible with the meanings of both suffixes. In this case, it results in two constructions. Given the thesis, each construction is directly associated with a particular meaning, which is not predictable from its component parts. In this case, some questions can be raised. The first question is: what is the semantic difference between the two constructions? The second question is: who is responsible for bringing about the semantic difference? The third question is: how can one provide evidence to support the difference? The ultimate question is: can Construction Grammar as a cognitive approach to language provide a plausible solution, or does it have the right tools for such a task?

6.2.2.6 Grammaticalisation approach

Grammaticalisation refers to a diachronic process of semantic change, whereby content words change into function words or existing grammatical units acquire further grammatical functions. The changes affect different areas of language, with the lexicon changing more rapidly than phonology, and the latter more rapidly than grammar. Grammaticalisation hinges on some central claims. One claim is that the change is gradual rather than discrete. The various expressions a language uses are seen as moving gradually along a continuum without changing their relative positions. As exemplified by Hopper & Traugott (1993: 7), the chain of grammaticality includes: content item > grammatical word > clitic > inflectional affix. Another claim is that the change is unidirectional, i.e. it goes in one direction. The direction of the change is from the lexical to the grammatical and not vice versa. For example, inflectional affixes do not give rise to prepositions or pronouns. A further claim is that the change is cyclic. Words enter the language as open-class lexical items, evolve into closed-class items, eventually leave the language via a process of loss and are replaced by new open-class items.

Grammaticalisation involves correlated changes in the sound, meaning, and grammar of a given symbolic unit. One pattern in grammaticalisation is form change associated with a linguistic item. Relating this to the present topic, it involves a pattern in which free morphemes become bound morphemes. For example, Modern English derivational suffixes *-hood* and *-dom* evolved from nouns meaning 'condition' and 'realm', respectively. As evidence, consider Hopper & Traugott's (1993: 41) examples: cild-had 'condition of a child' > childhood, Freo-dom 'realm of freedom' > freedom. Another pattern in grammaticalisation is meaning change associated with a linguistic form. The meaning change is described by Croft (2003: 262) as an instance of polysemy, a chain of related meanings or uses. Relating this to the present topic, it involves a pattern in which Modern English derivational suffixes have multiple meanings according to the context in which they are used. For example, the suffix *-ship* signals meanings like position, period of time, fact, people, allowance, policy, etc. This coexistence of related meanings which emerged at historically different periods is called *layering*.

As an alternative strategy to language description, Grammaticalisation offers some intriguing insights into the history of suffixes in English, tracing their development over time. A lexical pair like *dispersion* and *dispersal*, may have historical reasons, the *-ion* ending being much older – and coming via French into Middle English – than the *-al* ending, which came straight from Latin in the Renaissance. Once both forms were there, they started to have slightly different meanings. However, accounting for the meaning difference between the pair members lies outside the scope of Grammaticalisation. This is so because these are not lexical items becoming part of the grammar, but instances of word formation. In this respect, the Grammaticalisation approach faces some difficult questions. The first question is: can it identify the stages through which morpho-lexical variants go? The second question is: is it able to account for the alternation by providing historical evidence? The third question is: what role does the notion of *layering*, the synchronic presence of diachronic variants expressing the same meaning or linguistic function, play in this case?

6.2.2.7 Word-Grammar approach

Word Grammar is based on two widespread assumptions. One assumption is that language, like other parts of cognition, constitutes a network of units linked by relations. Hudson (1984: 1) writes, 'a language is a network of entities related by propositions'. The links in the network are organised in two ways. One way is *spreading activation*, where activation of one node spreads to the nodes to which it is directly linked. Activation in the network can spread across several links, so it does not require strict adjacency. The degree of semantic relatedness is determined by the degree of conceptual distance. The further apart two concepts are, the less likely they are to activate one another. A word like *ink*, for example, is primed by an immediately preceding word like *pen*, and not *king*. The link between the two words *ink* and *pen* lies in their meaning. The other way is *inheritance hierarchy*, where the entity that inherits the property of the network is directly linked to it. It is the one that involves the least conceptual distance. In Cognitive Grammar, language is also presented as a network of units, but the network may, as Langacker (1990: 2) claims, include both open- and closed-class elements.

The other assumption is that sentence structure consists of dependencies between individual words. Dependency requires two types of correlate features: semantic relations between the words' meanings and syntactic relations between the words themselves, such as word order or agreement. In *They longed for rain*, the verb *long* requires the preposition *for* as its dependent. So, the two words are directly linked in a dependency structure. So far as I know, the Word-Grammar literature does not address the notion of dependency within a complex word, i.e. the internal structure of single words. In Cognitive Grammar, the integration of component substructures is also influenced by semantic and phonological correspondences between them. However, the correspondence covers not only large constructions but also small ones. From the preceding Word-Grammar assumption, one predicts that the members of a pair are semantically distinct, but the way to account for the distinction is not presented. Then, Word Grammar faces a great challenge including the extension of the model to a fully developed account of alternation, subsuming cases where pairs of words are derived from the same roots.

Finally, it is to be noted that Usage-based Semantics is a reaction against the generative theory. The generative theory developed by Chomsky (1965: 51) makes a distinction between *competence* and *performance*. Every human is equipped with a language faculty, an innate cognitive subsystem, which gives rise to competence, unconscious knowledge of language. Knowledge of language arises from drawing out what is innate in the mind of the human. This view is referred to as *rationalist*. According to this view, competence determines performance. Because performance is affected by language-external factors, it fails to adequately reflect competence. The usage-based theory developed by Langacker (2000) rejects the distinction between competence and performance. It argues that knowledge of language is derived from patterns of language use. Knowledge of language is knowledge of how language is used. In the words of Tomasello (2003: 5), 'language structure emerges from language use'. Linguistic knowledge is constructed on the basis of experience. This view is referred to as *empiricist*. The uses of linguistic items are not arbitrary. They are constrained by meanings.

References

Books and articles

Adams, Valerie. 1973. *An Introduction to Modern English Word-Formation*. London: Longman.

Adams, Valerie. 2001. *Complex Words in English*. Essex: Longman.

Anderson, Stephen. 2001. *A-Morphous Morphology*. Cambridge: Cambridge University Press.

Anshen, Frank & Mark Aronoff. 1984. "Morphological productivity in historical perspective". Paper read at the 4th International Conference on Historical Linguistics: Historical Semantics/Historical Word-Formation. Blazejewko, Poland.

Aronoff, Mark. 1976. *Word Formation in Generative Grammar*. Cambridge MA: MIT Press.

Aronoff, Mark. 1980. "The relevance of productivity in a synchronic description of Word formation". In Jacek Fisiak (ed.). *Historical Morphology*. The Hague: Mouton. 71–82.

Aronoff, Mark & Sungeun Cho. 2001. "The semantics of *-ship* suffixation". *Linguistic Inquiry* 32: 167–73.

Aronoff, Mark & Kirsten Fudeman. 2005. *What is Morphology?* Oxford: Blackwell.

Baayan, Harald & Rochelle Lieber. 1991. "Productivity and English derivation: A corpus-based study". *Linguistics* 29: 801–43.

Barker, C. 1998. "Episodic *-ee* in English: A thematic role constraint on new word formation". *Language* 74: 695–727.

Bartsch, Sabine. 2004. *Structural and Functional Properties of Collocations in English: A Corpus Study of Lexical and Pragmatic Constraints on Lexical Co-Occurrence*. Tübingen: Gunter Narr Verlag.

Bauer, Laurie. 1983. *English Word-Formation*. Cambridge: Cambridge University Press.

Bauer, Laurie. 1988. *Introducing Linguistic Morphology*. Edinburgh: Edinburgh University Press.

Bauer, Laurie. 2001. *Morphological Productivity*. Cambridge: Cambridge University Press.

Beard, Robert. 1981. *The Indo-European Lexicon: A Full Synchronic Theory*. Amsterdam: North-Holland.

Beard, Robert. 1995. *Lexeme-Morpheme Base Morphology*. New York: State University of New York Press.

Beard, Robert & Bogdan Szymanek. 1988. *Bibliography of Morphology, 1960–1985*. Amsterdam: Benjamins.

Biber, Douglas, Susan Conrad & Randi Reppen. 1998. *Corpus Linguistics: Investigating Linguistic Structure and Use*. Cambridge: Cambridge University Press.

Bolinger, Dwight. 1968. "Entailment and the meaning of structures". *Glossa* 2: 119–27.

Bolinger, Dwight. 1977. *Meaning and Form*. London: Longman.

Booij, Geert. 2005. *The Grammar of Words*. Oxford: Oxford University Press.

Brugman, Claudia. 1988. *The Story of Over: Polysemy, Semantics and the Structure of the Lexicon*. New York: Garland Press.

Bybee, Joan. 1985. *Morphology: An Inquiry into the Relation between Meaning and Form*. Amsterdam: Benjamins.

Bybee, Joan. 1988. "Morphology as lexical organization". In M. Hammond and M. Noonan (eds) *Theoretical Morphology: Approaches in Modern Linguistics*. London: Academic Press. 119–41.

Bybee, Joan. and Carol Lynn Moder. 1983. "Morphological classes as natural categories". *Language* 59. 251–70.

Bybee, Joan and Paul Hopper (eds). 2001. "Introduction". *Frequency and the Emergence of Linguistic Structure*. Amsterdam: Benjamins. 1–24.

Carstairs-McCarthy, Andrew. 1992. *Current Morphology*. London: Routledge.

Casad, Eugene. 1995. "Seeing it in more than one way". In John Taylor & Robert Maclaury (eds) *Trends in Linguistics, Language and the cognitive construal of the World*. Berlin: Mouton de Gruyter. 23–45.

Chomsky, Noam. 1957. *Syntactic Structures*. The Hague: Mouton.

Chomsky, Noam. 1965. *Aspects of the Theory of Syntax*. Massachusetts: MIT Press.

Chomsky, Noam. 1995. *The Minimalist Program*. Cambridge: MIT Press.

Clausner, Timothy & William Croft. 1999. "Domains and image schemas". *Cognitive Linguistics* 10: 1–31.

Clear, Jeremy. 1994. "I Can't See the Sense in a Large Corpus". Papers in Computational Lexicography. *Complex* 94: 33–48.

Collins COBUILD *English Grammar*. 1992. London: William Collins and Sons & Co.

Collins COBUILD *Word Formation*. 1993. London: HarperCollins Publishers.

Collins, Peter. 1991. "The modals of obligation and necessity in Australian English". In Karin Aijmer & Bengt Altenberg (eds) *English Corpus Linguistics: Studies in Honour of Jan Svartvik*. London: Longman. 145–65.

Croft, William. 1993. "The role of domains in the interpretation of metaphors and metonymies". *Cognitive Linguistics* 4: 335–70.

Croft, William. 2003. *Typology and Universals*. Cambridge: Cambridge University Press.

Croft, William & D. Allen Cruse. 2004. *Cognitive Linguistics*. Cambridge: Cambridge University Press.

Cutler, Anne. 1980. "Productivity in word formation". Chicago Linguistic Society 16: 45–51.

Deane, Paul. 1992. *Grammar in Mind and Brain: Explorations in Cognitive Syntax*. Berlin: Mouton de Gruyter.

Dewell, Robert. 1994. "*Over* again: Image-schema transformations in semantic analysis". *Cognitive Linguistics* 5: 351–80.

Dirven, René & Marjolijn Verspoor (eds). 1998. *Cognitive Explorations of Language and Linguistics*. Amsterdam: Benjamins.

Dixon, Robert. 1991. *A New Approach to English Grammar on Semantic Principles*. Oxford: Clarendon.

Dressler, Wolfgang. 1985. *Morphology: The Dynamics of Derivation*. Ann Arbor: Kroma.

Evans, Vyvyan. 2004. *The Structure of Time: Language, Meaning and Temporal Cognition*. Amsterdam: Benjamins.

Evans, Vyvyan & Melanie Green. 2006. *Cognitive Linguistics: An Introduction*. Edinburgh: Edinburgh University Press.

Fabb, Nigel. 1988. "English suffixation is constrained only by selectional restrictions". *National Language and Linguistic Theory* 6: 527–39.

Fauconnier, Gills. 1985. *Mental Spaces: Aspects of Meaning Construction in Natural Language*. Cambridge: Cambridge University Press.

Fauconnier, Gills. 1997. *Mappings in thought and language*. Cambridge: Cambridge University Press.

Fillmore, Charles. 1977. "Scenes-and-frames". In Antonio Zampolli (ed.). *Linguistic Structures Processing*: 55–81.

Fillmore, Charles. 1982. "Frame semantics". In Linguistic Society of Korea (ed.) *Linguistics in the Morning Calm*. Seoul, Korea: Hanshin Pub. Co. 111–38.

Fowler, Henry. 1996. *Modern English Usage*. Oxford: Oxford University Press.

Givón, Talmy. 1985. "Function, structure, and language acquisition." In Dan Slobin (ed.) *The Cross-linguistic Study of Language Acquisition*. Vol. 2 Theoretical Issues: 1005–27. Hillsdale, NJ: Lawrence Erlbaum Associates.

Goldberg, Adele. 1995. *Constructions: A Construction Grammar Approach to Argument Structure*. Chicago: Chicago University Press.

Górska, Elzbieta. 1994. "Moonless nights and smoke-free cities, or what can be without the other?" A cognitive study of privative adjectives in English. *Folia Linguistica* 28: 413–35.

Górska, Elzbieta. 2001. "Recent derivatives with the suffix *-less*: A change in progress within the category of English privative adjectives". *Studia Anglica Posnaniensia* 36: 189–202.

Haiman, John. 1985. *Iconicity in Syntax*. Amsterdam: Benjamins.

Halliday, M. A. K. 1985. *An Introduction to Functional Grammar*. London: Arnold.

Hamawand, Zeki. 2002. *Atemporal Complement Clauses in English: A Cognitive Grammar Analysis*. München: Lincom.

Hamawand, Zeki. 2003a. "The construal of atemporalisation in complement clauses in English". *Annual Review of Cognitive Linguistics* 1: 61–87.

Hamawand, Zeki. 2003b. "For-to complement clauses in English: A Cognitive Grammar Analysis". *Studia Linguistica* 57: 171–92.

Hamawand, Zeki. 2005. "The construal of salience in atemporal complement clauses in English". *Language Sciences* 27: 193–213.

Hamawand, Zeki. 2007. *Suffixal Rivalry in Adjective Formation: A Cognitive-Corpus Analysis*. London: Equinox.

Haspelmath, Martin. 2002. *Understanding Morphology*. London: Arnold.

Heine, Bernd. 1997. *Cognitive Foundations of Grammar*. Oxford. Oxford University Press.

Hockett, Charles. 1954. "Two models of grammatical description". *Word* 10: 210–31.

Hopper, Paul & Elizabeth Traugott. 1993. *Grammaticalisation*. Cambridge: Cambridge University Press.

Hudson, Richard. 1984. *Word Grammar*. Oxford: Blackwell.

Jackendoff, Ray. 1983. *Semantics and Cognition*. Cambridge: MIT Press.

Jensen, John. 1990. *Morphology: Word Structure in Generative Grammar*. Current issues in linguistic theory 70. Amsterdam: Benjamins.

Jespersen, Otto. 1970. *A Modern English Grammar on Historical Principles*. Part V. London: George Allen & Unwin Ltd.

Johnson, Mark. 1987. *The Body in the Mind: The Bodily Basis of Meaning, Imagination and Reason*. Chicago: University of Chicago Press.

Katamba, Francis. 1993. *Morphology*. London: Macmillan Press Ltd.

Katz, Jerrold & Jerry Fodor. 1963. "The structure of a semantic theory". *Language* 39: 170–210.

Katz, Jerrold. & Paul Postal. 1964. *An Integrated Theory of Linguistic Descriptions.* Cambridge, MA: MIT Press.

Kemmer, Suzanne and Michael Barlow (eds). 2000. "Introduction". *Usage-based Models of Language.* vii–xxviii. Stanford, Calif.: CSLI.

Kennedy, Graeme. 1991. "Between and through: The company they keep and the functions they serve". In Karin Aijmer & Bengt Altenberg (eds) *English Corpus Linguistics: Studies in Honour of Jan Svartvik.* London: Longman. 95–110.

Kilgarriff, Adam & David Tugwell. 2001. "Word sketch: Extraction and display of Ignificant collocations for lexicography". In *Proceedings of ACL Workshop on Collocation: Computational Extraction, Analysis and Exploitation.* Toulouse, France: 32–8.

Kreitzer, Anatol. 1997. "Multiple levels of schematisation: A study in the conceptualisation of Space". *Cognitive Linguistics* 8: 291–325.

Kruisinga, E. 1931. *A Handbook of Present-Day English: English Accidence and Syntax.* Part II. Groningen: Noordhoff.

Lakoff, George. 1987. *Women, Fire and Dangerous Things: What Categories Reveal about the Mind.* Chicago: University of Chicago Press.

Lakoff, George. 1990. "The invariance hypothesis: Is abstract reason based on image schemas?" *Cognitive Linguistics* 1: 39–74.

Lakoff, George & Mark Johnson. 1980. *Metaphors We Live By.* Chicago: University of Chicago Press.

Langacker, Ronald. 1987. *Foundations of Cognitive Grammar.* Vol. 1: *Theoretical Prerequisites.* Stanford: Stanford University Press.

Langacker, Ronald. 1988. "A view of linguistic semantics". In Brygida Rudzka-Ostyn (ed.) *Topics in Cognitive Linguistics*: 49–90.

Langacker, Ronald W. 1990. *Concept, Image and Symbol: The Cognitive Basis of Grammar.* Berlin: Mouton de Gruyter.

Langacker, Ronald. 1991. *Foundations of Cognitive Grammar.* Vol. 2: *Descriptive Application.* Stanford: Stanford University Press.

Langacker, Ronald. 1994. "Cognitive grammar". In R. E.Asher (ed.) *The Encyclopedia of Language and Linguistics* 2: 590–4.

Langacker, Ronald. 1997a. "Consistency, dependency and conceptual grouping". *Cognitive Linguistics* 8: 1–32.

Langacker, Ronald. 1997b. "The contextual basis of cognitive semantics". In Jan Nuyts & Eric Pederson (eds). *Language and Conceptualisation.* Cambridge: Cambridge University Press. 229–32.

Langacker, Ronald. 2000. "A dynamic usage-based model". In Suzanne Kemmer and Michael Barlow (eds) *Usage-based Models of Language.* Stanford, Calif.: CSLI. 1–63.

Lee, David. 2001. *Cognitive Linguistics: An Introduction.* Oxford: Oxford University Press.

Lees, Robert. 1960. *The Grammar of English Nominalisations.* The Hague: Mouton.

Levin, Beth & Malka Pappaport. 1988. "Nonevent *-er* nominals: A probe into argument structure". *Linguistics* 26: 1067–83.

Lieber, Rochelle. 1992. *Deconstructing Morphology: Word Formation in Syntactic Theory.* Chicago: University of Chicago Press.

Lieber, Rochelle. 2004. *Morphology and Lexical Semantics.* Cambridge: Cambridge University Press.

Lieber, Rochelle. 2005. "English word-formation processes". In Pavol Stekauer & Rochelle Lieber. *Handbook of Word-Formation.* Dordrecht: Springer. 375–427.

Lubbers, K. 1965. "The development of *-ster* in modern British and American English". *English Studies* 46: 449–70.

Ljung, Magnus. 1974. *A Frequency Dictionary of English Morphemes*. Stockholm: AWE/Gebers.

Lyons, John. 1968. Introduction to theoretical linguistics. Cambridge: Cambridge University Press.

Malkiel, Yakov. 1977. "Why Ap-ish but Worm-y?" In Paul J. Hopper (ed.) *Studies in Descriptive and Historical Linguistics*. Amsterdam: Benjamins. 341–64.

Marchand, Hans. 1969. *The Categories and Types of Present-day English Word Formation: A Synchronic-Diachronic Approach*. Munich: Beck.

Matthews, Peter. 1972. *Inflectional Morphology*. Cambridge: Cambridge University Press.

Matthews, Peter. 1974. *Morphology*. Cambridge: Cambridge University Press.

McEnery, Tony & Andrew Wilson. 2001. *Corpus Linguistics*. Edinburgh: Edinburgh University Press.

Meyer, Charles. 2002. *English Corpus Linguistics*. Cambridge: Cambridge University Press.

Panther, Klaus-Uwe & Linda L. Thornburg. 2002. "The roles of metaphor and metonymy in English *-er* nominals". In René Dirven & Ralf Pörings (eds) *Metaphor and Metonymy in Comparison and Contrast*. Berlin: Mouton de Gruyter. 279–319.

Plag, Ingo. 1999. *Morphological Productivity: Structural Constraints in English Derivation*. Berlin: Mouton de Gruyter.

Plag, Ingo. 2003. *Word-Formation in English*. Cambridge: Cambridge University Press.

Portero Munoz, Carmen. 2003. "Derived nominalizations in *-ee*: A role and reference grammar-based semantic analysis". *English Language and Linguistics* 7: 129–59.

Riddle, Elizabeth. 1985. "A historical perspective on the productivity of the suffixes *-ness* and *-ity*". In Jacek Fisiak (ed.) *Historical Semantics Historical Word- Formation*: 435–61.

Rosch, Eleanor. 1977. "Human categorisation". In Neil Warren (ed.) *Studies in Cross-Cultural Psychology* 1: 3–49.

Rosch, Eleanor. 1978. "Principles of categorisation". In E. Rosch & B. B. Lloyd (eds) *Cognition and Categorisation*. UK: John Wiley & Sons Inc. 27–48.

Rudzka-Ostyn, Brygida (ed.). 1988. *Topics in Cognitive Linguistics*. Amsterdam: Benjamins.

Ryder, Mary Ellen. 1991. "*Mixers, Mufflers* and *Mousers*: The extending of the *-er* Suffix as a case of prototype reanalysis". *Berkeley Linguistics Society* 17: 299–311.

Ryder, Mary Ellen. 1999. "*Bankers* and *Blue-Chippers*: An Account of *-er* Formations in present-day English". *English Language and Linguistics* 3: 269–97.

Sandra, Dominiek & Sally Rice. 1995. "Network analyses of prepositional meaning: Mirroring whose mind – the linguist's or the language user's?" *Cognitive Linguistics* 6: 89–130.

Saussure, Ferdinand. 1916. *Cours de linguistique générale*. Paris: Payot.

Selkirk, Elisabeth. 1982. *The Syntax of Words*. Cambridge, MA: MIT Press.

Sinclair, John. 1991. *Corpus, Concordance and Collocation*. Oxford: Oxford University Press.

Spencer, Andrew. 1991. *Morphological Theory*. Oxford: Blackwell.

Spencer, Andrew. 2001. "Morphology". In Mark Aronoff and Rees-Miller (eds) *The Handbook of Linguistics*: 213–37.

Stageberg, Norman. 1965. *An Introductory English Grammar.* New York: Holt, Rinehart and Winston Inc.

Stekauer, Pavol. 2000. *English Word-Formation: A History of Research (1960–1995).* Tübingen: Gunter Narr Verlag.

Stubbs, Michael. 2001. *Words and Phrases: Corpus Studies of Lexical Semantics.* Oxford: Blackwell.

Stump, Gregory. 2001. *Inflectional Morphology. A Theory of Paradigm Structure.* Cambridge: Cambridge University Press.

Sweetser, Eve. 1990. *From Etymology to Pragmatics: Metaphorical and Cultural Aspects of Semantic Structure.* Cambridge: Cambridge University Press.

Szymanek, Bogdan. 1998. *Introduction to Morphological Analysis.* Warszawa: Wydawinctwo Naukowe PWN.

Talmy, Leonard. 1983. "How language structures space". In Herbert Pick and Linda Arcedolo (eds) *Spatial Orientation: Theory, Research, and Application.* Cambridge, Mass.: MIT Press. 225–82.

Talmy, Leonard. 1985. "Force dynamics in language and thought". *Chicago Linguistic Society* 21: 293–337.

Talmy, Leonard. 2000. *Toward a Cognitive Semantics.* Cambridge, MA: MIT Press.

Taylor, John. 1989. *Linguistic Categorisation: Prototypes in Linguistic Theory.* Oxford: Clarendon Press.

Taylor, John. 2002. *Cognitive Grammar.* Oxford: Oxford University Press.

Teubert, Wolfgang. 2005. "My version of corpus linguistics". *International Journal of Corpus Linguistics* 10: 1–13.

Tognini-Bonelli, Elena. 2001. *Corpus Linguistics at Work.* Amsterdam: Benjamins.

Tomasello, Michael. 2000. "First steps toward a usage-based theory of language acquisition". *Cognitive Linguistics* 11: 61–82.

Tummers, Jose, Kris Heylen, & Dirk Geeraerts. 2005. "Usage-based approaches in cognitive linguistics: A technical state of the art". *Corpus Linguistics and Linguistic Theory* 1–2: 225–61.

Tyler, Andrea. & Vyvyan Evans. 2001. "Reconsidering prepositional polysemy networks: The case of *over*". *Language* 77: 724–65.

Ungerer, Friedrich & Hans-Jörg Schmid. 1996. *An Introduction to Cognitive Linguistics.* London: Longman.

Urdang, Laurence. 1982. *Suffixes and other Word-final Elements of English.* Detroit: Gale Research Company.

Vandeloise, Claude. 1994. "Methodology and analyses of the preposition *in*". *Cognitive Linguistics* 5: 157–84.

Wierzbicka, Anna. 1988. *The Semantics of Grammar.* Amsterdam: Benjamins.

Williams, Edwin. 1981. "Argument structure and morphology". *Linguistic Review* 1: 81–114.

Williams, Geoffrey. 2002. "In search of representativity in specialised corpora: Categorisation through collocation". *International Journal of Corpus Linguistics* 7: 43–64.

Zernik, Uri. 1991. *Lexical Acquisition: Exploiting On-Line Resources to Build a Lexicon.* Hillsdale, NJ: Lawrence Erlbaum Associates.

Usage manuals

Fee, Margery & Janice McAlpine. 1997. *Guide to Canadian English Usage.* Oxford: Oxford University Press.

Fowler, Henry. 1996. *Modern English Usage*. Oxford: Oxford University Press.

Greenbaum, Sidney & Janet Whitcut. 1988. *Longman Guide to English Usage*. Essex: Longman.

Hughes, Barrie (ed.). 1993. *The Penguin Working Words: An Australian Guide to Modern English Usage*. Victoria: Viking.

Manser, Martin (ed.). 1991. *Bloomsbury Good Word Guide*. London: Bloomsbury.

MacKaskill, Stanley. 1981. *A Dictionary of Good English: A Guide to Current Usage*. London: The Macmillan Press Ltd.

Partridge, Eric. 1961. *Usage and Abusage: A Guide in Good English*. London: Hamish Hamilton.

Peters, Pam. 1995. *The Cambridge Australian English Style Guide*. Cambridge: Cambridge University Press.

Peters, Pam. 2004. *The Cambridge Guide to English Usage*. Cambridge: Cambridge University Press.

Shipman, Robert. 1991. *A Pun My Word*. Maryland: Rowman & Littlefield Publishers, Inc.

Treble, H. A. & G. H. Vallins. 1961. *An ABC of English Usage*. Oxford: Clarendon Press.

Wood, Frederick. 1962. *Current English Usage: A Concise Dictionary*. London: Macmillan & Co. Ltd.

Dictionaries and thesauruses

Benson, Morton, Evelyn Benson, & Robert Ilson. (eds) 1989. *Student's Dictionary of Collocations*. Berlin: Cornelson.

Cambridge Advanced Learner's Dictionary Online. Available at http://www.dictionary. cambridge.org

COBUILD English Dictionary. 1998. Glasgow: Harper Collins Publishers.

COBUILD English Dictionary and Thesaurus. 1993. Glasgow: Harper Collins Publishers.

COBUILD on CD-ROM. 1995. Glasgow: Harper Collins Publishers.

Kirkpatrick, Betty. (ed.). 1998. *Roget's Thesaurus of English Words and Phrases*. London: Penguin Books.

Little William, Henry Watson Fowler, & J. Coulson (eds). 1959. *The Oxford English Dictionary on Historical Principles*. London: Oxford University Press.

Longman Dictionary of Contemporary English. 1995. 3rd edition. London: Longman.

Longman Language Activator. 2002. London: Pearson Education Limited.

Merriam-Webster Dictionary Online. Available at http://www.m-w.com.

Oxford Advanced Learner's Dictionary. 1995. 5th edition. Oxford: Oxford University Press.

Oxford Collocations Dictionary for students of English. 2003. Oxford: Oxford University Press.

Oxford English Dictionary on CD-ROM. 1994. Oxford: Oxford University Press.

Oxford English Dictionary Online. Available at http://www.oed.com

Urdang, Laurence. 1991. *The Oxford Thesaurus: An A-Z Dictionary of synonyms*. Oxford: Clarendon Press.

Subject Index

Suffix Index

Noun Index